TENN AT ONE HUNDRED

TENN AT ONE HUNDRED

The Reputation of Tennessee Williams

Edited by

David Kaplan

HANSEN PUBLISHING GROUP

TABLE OF CONTENTS

ACKNOWLEDGEMENTS

Many people contributed to the successful completion of this book. The anthology was assembled in Provincetown and New York, researched in Chicago, New Orleans, and Washington, D.C.

Thank you.

In Chicago, to Jennie Moreau, Michael McGowan, Terry Abrahamson, Victor Saporta, Steve Besic, John Powell and the staff of the Newberry Library, and the staff of the Harold Washington Library.

In Provincetown, to Jef Hal-Flavin, Patrick Falco, Ed Martin, Joe Agostini, Deb Bowles, Scott Dolny, Joe Carleo, Tim McCarthy, Chris Busa, Loreal, Rory Marcus, Berta Walker, Sky Power, Choly, Nicoletta Poli, Robert Barret, and Mark Leach at Now Voyager Bookstore.

In New York City, to Brenda Currin, Olga Kogan, Stephen Holden, Jeremy Lawrence, John Uecker, David Landon, Helen Graves, Michael Surabian, and Thomas Keith, who served as a consulting editor for this volume.

In Washington, to Thomas Sullivan, and Karen McGruder—and in New Orleans, to Micki Beth Stiller, Marc Lamb, Paul J. Willis, and Tim Wolfe.

I would also like to thank all those people who helped with permissions, rights, contacts, and various communications, including Peggy Fox and Laurie Callahan of New Directions Publishing, Ralph Voss, Claire Evans at University Press of Alabama, Robert Brustein, Peggy Gough at University of Texas Press, Celeste Bateman, Tom Mitchell at the University of Illinois Champaign-Urbana, Sonja Smith, Peggy McKinnon, and Kate Johnson at Georges Borchardt, Inc.

Special thanks are due to Mitch Douglas, who was Tennessee Williams' agent from 1977 to 1982. For this anthology Mr. Douglas agreed to a formal interview and several conversations in person, which helped shape my understanding of Williams' and Audrey Wood's relationship, as well as lent backstage insight into Williams's late writing—its creation and reception within the professional theater world.

Jon Hansen had the idea for this book, and I am grateful to him for suggesting it and publishing it.

Personal thanks to Irwin and Ethel Kaplan, Jeffrey and Richard Kaplan, Edwin Schloss, and, forever, Jerry Stacy. I'm not in favor of dedication pages for anthologies, but if there was to be such a thing for *Tenn at One Hundred*, those six names would be on it.

INTRODUCTION

David Kaplan

Tennessee Williams wrote novels, essays, poems, short stories, screenplays, and a memoir. But his plays are the bedrock of his reputation. *Tenn at One Hundred* is a collection of eighteen reports by seventeen writers relaying, from chapter to chapter, the story of how Williams' reputation was constructed, earned, championed, manipulated, undermined, and renewed—from the beginning of his career until now, the year of his centennial.

The first person voices of the chapters change as the authors change, but read in order they tell a story. The beginning is auspicious: talent, drive, and opportunity align. More often than not, however, romantically dark forces gather to influence Williams' reputation: a constellation of well-meaning, ill-fated advisors, aggressive collaborators, reluctant censors, and desperate hangers-on. There are connivers of all sorts, including hypocritical bigots who go to their graves well-respected and with smiles on their faces. Many of these characters were public moralizers who wrote or broadcast ugly prejudices that echo long after their deaths, long after the evaporation of the values they defended.

So the story of Williams' changing reputation necessarily tells a story of the changes in what it means to be reputable: what it means to be a woman with a "certain" reputation, or to be a reputable man, or to have—man or woman—a disreputable sexuality. The story of Williams' reputation is also a chronicle of the changing importance of realism in art: at the start of Williams' long career, Grant Wood's *American Gothic* was a sensation, twenty-five years later Jackson Pollock redefined what a painting could be, and twenty-five years after that Pop Art was giving way to hyper-realism. Theater critics, despite the critical transformations in the values and modes of visual art, usually stuck to Grant Wood's aesthetic.

Judgments sometimes reveal as much about the judges as what's being judged. Sometimes old judgments are merely curiosities: *Oedipus Rex* won Sophocles no more than second place in the Athenian Dionysia the year it was first performed. Ibsen was berated as a pornographer for placing a venereal disease as the central image of his play *Ghosts*. Samuel Beckett's *Waiting for Godot* was belittled as the Emperor's New Clothes by its earliest American critics. Quite a bit of Shakespeare was "improved" by English poets, editors, and well-meaning theater professionals who removed inelegant language and crude characters and smoothed out structure that didn't measure up to Victorian ideas of decorum, the balanced rectitude of the Age of Enlightenment, or the overrated "Greek" unities of time, place, and action.

Why, then, revisit dated opinions, the gatehouses of long gone empires? Once a wall crumbles, any gatehouse still standing becomes little more than a relic. Those who pass through it to get somewhere are superstitious or sentimental, perhaps unaware the wall is gone, or pretending, for reasons of their own, that it grants entry. Why read about the architects of the gates, or the lives of the gatekeepers? Why visit those ruins at all?

When it comes to the reputation of Tennessee Williams, those phantom walls and gatehouses have risen again, thanks to the dragon's blood of the internet, where seven rumors slain beget forty-nine new ones. "Journalists" and "scholars" in a hurry have only to cut and paste a short snappy phrase from fifty years ago—without context—to complete an assignment about Tennessee Williams. It's certainly easier to cut and paste than to read or attend a performance of any of the more than fifty plays by

Williams published posthumously. When it comes to writing about Tennessee Williams' experimental work, from the 1950s, 1960s, 1970s, or even the early 1980s, it's certainly easier—and it seems perfectly acceptable to directors, producers, actors, professors, scholars, editors, and publishers—to pass on dated judgments and misinformation, preferably downloadable, than it is to form and pass on an original opinion.

So add laziness to the list of dark forces, in this case unromantic, that influence Williams' reputation.

Yet, as you follow the chapters along towards the late 1980s, you might begin to think that eventually Tennessee Williams' words will establish a reputation of their own. Twenty-eight years since Williams passed away he is being discovered by the audiences, theater artists, and critics he had been waiting for the last twenty-five years of his life. If his plays are, as we suspect, not only good, but great, then this will always be so, this kind of discovery, and renewal. Williams will remain forever modern, or better yet, slightly ahead of his audience and critics, a constant challenge for enlarging their vision and the reach of theater.

Reputation for America's great artists doesn't usually crest while they're alive. Some of the greatest American writers died without recognition of their achievement. Emily Dickinson won fame with little rolls of paper tied up in ribbons, unrolled after she had passed away. Edgar Allan Poe died of starvation. At the time of F. Scott Fitzgerald's death *The Great Gatsby* was out of print. The changing reputation of Herman Melville—*Moby Dick* was forgotten at the time of his death—demonstrates that the power of great writing outlasts politics, or criticism or ideas of decorum or literary trends or any executor's manipulation for better or worse. *Moby Dick* leaps up and away—grand, unique, always problematic—out of the sea of critical incomprehension (that lasted from when the book was first published in 1851 until 1920) and into the air of now—every time someone reads it. So, too, Williams' reputation, having survived a steep fall, leaps out of waves of critical dismissal, dated criticism, internet misinformation, and half-baked biography.

As with all writers one hundred years after their birth, and for hundreds of years to come, Williams' reputation will spring from his words. That he will have any reputation hundreds of years from now is certainly no fact, but it is my belief. That belief refreshes itself when I witness over and over again what Williams' words *do* when spoken and heard: they move people to tears and to laughter and to gasps of recognition. Williams wields the powers of a poet who, like his hero Orpheus, follows his visions to the underworld, and then returns to share with the rest of us what he has seen, experienced, survived, lost, and won. When he speaks to us—either in dialogue or poetry, and especially the poetry of the theater—the words Williams uses to describe his vision are a formula for us to witness that vision, too—and we do. This is incantation.

One hundred years after his birth, it is undeniable that Williams is among the greatest American writers. *Tenn at One Hundred* is recognition that Williams' reputation, while unfinished, has survived precipitous falls and rises, and still has a twisting path to climb.

TENN AT ONE HUNDRED

"
Tom Williams—our literary boy.
"

TENNESSEE WILLIAMS' ST. LOUIS BLUES

Allean Hale

I attended the same Blewett Junior High School in St. Louis as Tennessee Williams, and then Soldan High School, three years after he did. In seventh grade at Blewett we each were required to write something for the school paper. I wrote a mystery and Tom Williams, as he was then, wrote a description of an island trapped in a Mississippi River flood.

We each went on to write plays. I wrote on current American problems for the Methodist Church press—Tennessee wrote famous plays starting with *The Glass Menagerie* and *A Streetcar Named Desire*.

We met once in the sixties at a performance of *Small Craft Warnings,* but it was not until his death in 1983 that I decided to concentrate my writing on Tennessee Williams. At the age of ninety-six I have now published at least ninety articles on Williams, written a book (unpublished), and have enjoyed a correspondence with Williams fans all over the world.

Williams changed his subjects and style through the years; his changes reflect changes in American life and literature. He wrote a vast quantity of plays, some only recently discovered. More than thirty-three long plays can be named and there are more than twice that many short plays.

Williams dared to risk his reputation by experimenting. He understood the changes of subject matter and point of view and changed his subjects and style to accord with the times. His plays treat the end of romanticism and realistic theater, and he turned to Theatre of the Absurd and even anti-theater. When serious theater changed to Theatre of the Ridiculous, he wrote a farce. He ventured into Asian theater and wrote his own version of a Noh play.

When he became known as the Southern playwright, he found it useful to transfer to Southern settings plays and characters whose actual locale was St. Louis. Yet he lived in Mississippi only eight years and in St. Louis twenty-five. If the trauma of his youth in St. Louis was the condition that impelled him to write, I believe St. Louis was also the catalyst that transformed him into a writer.

He called it "that dreaded city," the City of St. Pollution. When asked what brought him to New Orleans, he would answer "St. Louis!" New Orleans is so glamorous that biographers and critics tend to pass over St. Louis, and Williams fostered this neglect.

The scenario is well known and was the germ for the future playwright's sense of loss: a sensitive seven-year-old, torn from the grandparents who had reared him and the sister who was more like a twin—Rose had been left behind for a year—transported overnight from an agrarian setting to a huge, smoky city, to be met by a father he scarcely knew, whose first gesture was to slap his hand for plucking a grape from a fruit stand in Union Station. Tom, sensing his mother's misery at the move, would always see St. Louis through her eyes. As the Episcopal rector's daughter in a town of 6,000, Edwina had enjoyed social prestige. Now, in the fifth largest city of the United States, she was nobody. With a reverse snobbery, she impressed on her children that St. Louis was a town where only status mattered. They could not hope to attend private schools: Mary Institute, where a girl was enrolled at birth, or the Country Day School, where the Bishop's grandson who was Tom's age attended. Years later Williams would still remember: "That name, public school, kept stabbing at my guts till I wanted, as old as I was, to sit down and cry." He wrote that in St. Louis he first learned that there were the rich and the poor and that they were poor. The sense of being an outsider would become a dominant theme in his writing.

To Cornelius Williams, his father, when they arrived in 1918, it was the city of opportunity. Cornelius would have a managerial job with the largest shoe company in the world. St. Louis had an outstanding school system, universities and libraries, a famed Symphony Orchestra, a splendid Art Museum. Its Forest Park, the most elaborate in the country next to Central Park in New York, had one of the earliest natural-habitat zoos and was building the largest outdoor theater in the United States, the Municipal Opera. St. Louis also had more motion picture theaters per capita than New York City.[1] Future biographers would assume that Tennessee learned his cinematic techniques from his six months at MGM, whereas he had spent twenty years going to the movies before he went to Hollywood.

Actually, they were not poor. "C. C.," as Williams' father was known, made a good salary, but as the frustrated Edwina held back affection, he held back money. Their new life together soon became a sort of warfare. Cornelius, lusty and boisterous, took his disappointment out in drinking; Edwina, aggressively puritanical, resorted to scolding. She would use Tom as her confidant; C. C. would retaliate by calling Tom "Miss Nancy." Caught between father and mother, the sensitive boy felt trapped. When he would escape to Forest Park, it was perhaps at the zoo that he first envisioned his household as a menagerie, each member caught in a separate cage.

As *Streetcar* is the New Orleans play, *The Glass Menagerie* belongs wholly to St. Louis. It is Williams' least disguised work. Most of the places he mentions are intact. The "mustard-yellow brick" flat with its dark rooms at 4633 Westminster Place is now called "*The Glass Menagerie* Apartment." This is commonly pointed out as the site of the play, but the Williams family lived there much earlier, when Tom and Rose were small. It shows something about Williams' distorted view of St. Louis that neither of the buildings related to *The Glass Menagerie* was a tenement as described. Westminster Place in 1918 was still a good residential district with some fine stone mansions in Renaissance style. Its 4300 and 4400 blocks were said to contain more residences of architectural interest than any other comparable blocks in the city. T. S. Eliot's family had lived at number 4446 only a few years before. But the Williamses lived in the only apartment building on the street, which to Edwina was déclassé, even though the fashionable Wednesday Club was only a block away.

In the published version of *The Glass Menagerie*, the opening description of the Wingfield apartment in "one of those vast hive-like conglomerations of cellular living-units" clearly situates it on Enright Avenue, where the events of *Menagerie* actually took place in 1933. The alley is still there and the several blocks of identical red brick apartments with their iron fire escapes look much as they did in the thirties, although the Williams' apartment building— ironically named "Grace"—has been torn down. The Tivoli Theatre where Tom "went to the movies" still operates on Delmar Boulevard and the Jewel Box where Laura played hooky still decorates Forest Park. The Soldan High School building still stands; anyone who attended that school, as I did, knows exactly how Laura felt on her intimidating walk from the back of the auditorium to the front. The auditorium seated 1,000 persons and that aisle seemed a block long.

He had been so miserable when transplanted from Clarksdale to the huge Eugene Field School, whose twin towers made it look like a penitentiary, that he was sent back to live with his grandparents for the 1921 school year. His pampered year in Mississippi only confirmed his vision of the South as his lost Eden, but one speculates what Tom Williams would have become had he continued his education in Clarksdale with its more lenient standards. Returning to enter Stix School, he had his first triumph when the class was assigned to write about some picture on the schoolroom wall. Tom, already in character, chose the romantic and doomed "Lady of Shalott." When the teacher selected his essay to read aloud in class, he felt himself an author. Then his mother bought him a second-hand typewriter and at twelve he was on his way.

Tom hit his stride when he entered Ben Blewett Junior High. St. Louis had pioneered the junior high school movement and Blewett Junior High, only seven years old, was a national model. Pupils were grouped on the basis of intelligence tests and allowed to go through grades seven to nine in two to three years, according to ability. Tom, just turning thirteen, tested 114 on the Terman I.Q. test, a form of the

Stanford-Binet intelligence tests, a grade well above average but not sufficiently high for the two year "stream."

Blewett occupied a city block and was run like a small city. It had perhaps more ethnic mix than the general population, and there was much emphasis on citizenship, student government, and activities. It had a congress, a good library, a large orchestra, baseball and basketball teams, and some thirty clubs, and students were expected to join at least one. Homerooms competed with intense rivalry for the bronze and silver medals given for achievement. It also had a newspaper, the *Junior Life*. Here Tom at thirteen found his medium. In his first year, 1924, the Blewett *Junior Life* published his story "Isolated"; the following November, in 1925, "Nature's Thanksgiving"; and in January 1926, "Old Things," an experiment in free verse. His reputation was made when an entire glossy page of *The Dune* 1925 yearbook was devoted to a poem, "Demon Smoke," by Thomas Williams, 9th grade. (St. Louis, whose factories were fueled by the system of coking, was one of the smokiest cities in the United States.) Tom's poem, an exhortation more ecological than lyrical, ended:

> For law alone and legislation
> Can banish from the air,
> Can make this Demon captive, and
> Consume him in his lair.

In a list of the thirty-seven students in his homeroom he was labeled "Tom Williams—our literary boy."

The influence of Ben Blewett School, which has never been noticed by biographers, was basic to Tom Williams' development as a writer. His experience there gave him confidence, endorsed his talent, and pointed to the one avenue in which he could succeed. His student-paper publications caused Tom to think of himself as a journalist, with the possibility of making money by writing. This would not only compensate for his father's stinginess but impressed C. C. with his ability to bring home a check. Going on to Soldan High School, at fifteen he took his friend Hazel Kramer to see the 1925 *Stella Dallas* and was moved to write a film review, which was published. Hazel was his companion on trips to the Art Museum and to the "Muny," where Tom was exposed to musical theater with imported artists. Here he first saw the combination of music, dance, and acting that he later used in numerous plays. Hazel was also his date at the graduation dance on the excursion steamer *J.S.* By now he had firmly decided to marry Hazel and the sexual stirrings she aroused may have accounted for his new habit of blushing constantly. It was doubtless Tom who had the experiences at Soldan he ascribed to Laura in *The Glass Menagerie*, as Rose attended only briefly in January 1924. Abnormally shy, Tom noted with envy such Soldanites as Edward Meisenbach, who was on the yearbook staff and president of the Honor Society, sang in the Glee Club, and was the tallest boy in class pictures—Tom was always the shortest. Later he would use Edward as half of a composite portrait of "the Gentleman Caller."

The move to Enright Avenue in September 1926 put him in University City High School. Here at sixteen he won a five-dollar prize for his answer to the question "Can a Good Wife Be a Good Sport?" His reply, published in *Smart Set*, May 1927, purported to be from the wronged husband, citing "my own unhappy marital experiences." At seventeen he sold a horror story to the pulp magazine *Weird Tales*. He continued the journalistic path in his last two years at University High, whose 1929 yearbook lists him as an assistant editor of publications. In his seventeenth summer his grandfather took him on an extensive European tour, which included Paris, Cologne, the battlefields of France, and the ruins of Pompeii. The nine travel articles Tom published in the *U. City Pep* are confident and well-observed. However, his classmates described him as unable to speak when called upon, and in the class picture he is again the smallest boy in the group. Graduation was the first example of his social phobia. He had bought his class ring and been fitted for the tuxedo his grandfather sent him for the prom, but when Edwina arrived proudly for her son's ceremony, he was not there. They found him at the downtown public library.

Had Tom stayed in Clarksdale he might have gone to the University of Mississippi or to the University of the South at Sewanee, his grandfather's choice. But the Depression and his Missouri residence dictated that he go to the state university at Columbia. An attraction was that Missouri had the oldest and best school of journalism in the country. So off he went to become a journalist.

Portions of this essay, revised for the present volume, were published in *The Mississippi Quarterly*, Volume 48, September 22, 1995. Reprinted by permission of Allean Hale.

" It bothers Mr. Williams to have

anyone ask him questions about
"
himself.

THE POET-PLAYWRIGHT'S MODEST BEGINNINGS

William Jay Smith

I was one of the earliest writer friends of Tennessee Williams (then Thomas Lanier Williams) at Washington University in St. Louis, where after three years at the University of Missouri, he enrolled as a special student in the fall of 1935. We were introduced by Clark Mills, widely recognized at the time as one of the country's most promising young poets. The three of us met frequently at Tom's house near the campus to read our work to one another and to plot our escape from a city we detested.

Like Tom, I was a displaced Southerner, born in 1918 in Winnfield, Louisiana, on my grandfather's farm. My father, unable to cope with farming, enlisted in the army in 1918 as a clarinet player in the band and was transferred three years later to Jefferson Barracks, Missouri, just south of St. Louis on the banks of the Mississippi. It was there with my beautiful Southern, part-Choctaw mother and my brother, a year and a half younger than I, that I grew up between the two world wars with only occasional visits back to Louisiana, where I thought I belonged. As with Cornelius, Tom's father, alcohol and poker got my father into serious trouble. Because of drinking on duty, he remained for years a Corporal, and my mother, as a seamstress who made clothes for the officer's wives, kept the wolf from the door. The children from the Barracks were transported by army trucks to St. Louis schools and because the city then had one of the finest school systems in the country, I benefited, as Tom did, from a St. Louis education and from excellent teachers who encouraged me and my writing.

WEIRD TALES

Tom had been writing constantly since the age of twelve. He had been encouraged by his teachers in St. Louis at Ben Blewett Junior High and later at Soldan High School. In the summer of 1928 he went with his grandfather, the Reverend Mr. Dakin, to shepherd a group of Episcopalians on a grand tour of Europe.

Just before embarking on his journey Tom had written a short story called "Vengeance of Nitocris," which was published in *Weird Tales,* for which he had received thirty-five dollars. Based on a paragraph of Herodotus, the piece opens thus: "Hushed were the streets of many-peopled Thebes."

On October 29, 1929, just one month after Tom registered at the University of Missouri at Columbia, then a pretty small college town midway between St. Louis and Kansas City, the stock market crashed. The word was soon all over the campus, and Tom wondered if he might have to join many other well-to-do students throughout the country who were having to drop out of universities. But to his amazement, his father Cornelius not only allowed Tom to remain, but expressed his great satisfaction on hearing that the young man had accepted the pledge to the fraternity Alpha Tau Omega, even though it would cost him more each month. Cornelius had prevailed on a pair of young cousins in the ATO at the University of Tennessee to notify the Columbia Chapter that, "the son of an executive in the International Shoe Company was hiding out in a boarding house and this would not do, since he was descended from the Williamses and the Seviers of East Tennessee, was a published writer and a traveller of the world."

Shortly after Tom's arrival on the University of Missouri campus a local paper ran an interview headed, "Shy Freshman Writes Romantic Love Tales for Many Magazines." It reported that Tom, who planned to enter the School of Journalism, had

had a "number" of stories published in *Weird Tales* and *Smart Set* magazines and had received twenty-five dollars for an article based on the shy freshman's "own unhappy marital experiences." Tom had already learned that reporters, like dramatists, tend to exaggerate. The description of him, however was precise and accurate:

> It bothers Mr. Williams to have anyone ask him questions about himself. He is little more than five feet tall. He has clean-cut features, and smooth brown hair. His eyes, which have a look that seems thousands of miles away, add to the unapproachable and reserved appearance which he presents. He is equally as reticent and shy as he appears and feels that having his stories published is nothing out of the ordinary.[1]

The article also said that he admitted that his inspiration for his stories rose not so much from actual experience as "from reading a wide variety of authors" including his favorite writer, Louis Bromfield.

What the article did not say was how much he disliked having attention called to his small stature. This was true for the rest of his life. It didn't help to have it pointed out that Keats, like many other great writers, was not very tall.

BEAUTY IS THE WORD

In April 1930 Tom entered his one-act play *Beauty is the Word* in the annual Dramatic Arts Club contest sponsored by Professor Ramsay of the English Department and it won a sixth place honorable mention. Set in the South Pacific, the play concerns a missionary and his wife with the unlikely names of Abelard and Mabel. Their beautiful niece Esther, reproaching them for their bleak theology, says: "Fear and God are the most utterly incompatible things under the sun. Fear is ugliness. God—at least *my* God—is beauty." Tom was the first freshman to win an honorable mention, but he would have preferred to win the fifty-dollar first prize and a workshop production of his play. In May 1930 Tom's short story, "The Lady's Beaded Bag," appeared in the campus literary magazine, *The Columns*. Having failed to be rewarded for fiction, he decided that only as a journalist could he hope to earn money with his writing.

At the end of the school term Tom was nineteen and his grades for the fall semester had been B-minus and C-plus for the spring and even with his eighteen absences this made him a better-than-average student. When he returned home for the hot summer, Cornelius told him that he would have to find work to help cover his expenses for the coming year. The only job he could find was selling subscriptions to the *Pictorial Review* for twenty-one dollars a week. Tom finally gave up on magazines and went downtown to enroll in the ten-week course at Rubicam's Business School. His older sister Rose would join him and he would help her with the work. His mother Edwina explained that they were both selling two shares of stock in their father's shoe factory to pay for the course. Tom soon became an excellent typist but Rose did not, and she found it impossible to cope with the workload.

The next year Tom continued his writing, but seemed to neglect plays. He was listed among the fifty contestants for the First Annual Mahan University Essay Contest. The first prize of one hundred dollars was won by Harold Vincent Boyle for "Confessions of a Well-Read Man." Boyle went on to become a syndicated columnist and journalist. Tom received Honorable Mention for his short story "Something by Tolstoy" but was disappointed because with first place he would have had both the top honor and one hundred dollars.

In his third year Tom began his courses in journalism, but continued writing plays and poetry. In October 1931 the Theatre Guild produced Eugene O'Neill's *Mourning Becomes Electra* starring the famous Russian actress Nazimova. There was renewed interest in O'Neill on the campus and a production of *The Hairy Ape* was proposed by Professor Ramsay for the workshop in the spring. The second play that Tom entered in the contest of the Dramatic Arts Club was one called *Hot Milk at Three in the Morning*. It was very similar to O'Neill's one act *Before Breakfast*. The play is a depiction of a poor depression-era "laborer and his whining sick wife." The figure of a man trapped by marriage like a caged animal was one that Tom had encountered in his own father.

The wife says, in the heat of their argument, "You know that before you married me you was just a common tramp, that's all you was!" Angered, he replies: "Yeah, you bet I was. An' I was satisfied, I was happy!"

Tom would later revise *Hot Milk* and rename it *Moony's Kid Don't Cry,* thinking perhaps of O'Neill's *The Dreamy Kid.* Along with two other one-act plays it would eventually win recognition in a contest sponsored by the Group Theatre in 1939.

In January 1932 Tom joined the Missouri Chapter of the College Poetry Society, of which there were twenty-five female members and seven male members. Anyone who knew Tom well would certainly not have made him treasurer, but they did so and he got hold of the Society's ledger. The first three pages were given over to 1931–1932 expenditures and receipts with Tom's dues of $2.50 noted and under expenditures, treasurer's "book and folder, 65 cents." The remainder of the 65-cent-book was blank and in 1936 Tom would put it to more practical use as his own personal journal.

Those who came to the Journalism School expected that they were just going to spend their time writing. They did not realize they would be expected to master a craft and a whole range of newspaper functions. Tom's first assignment was that of reporting the cost of local produce and listing the prices of light and heavy hens, sour cream, eggs, and geese, which left him little time for creative writing. The next beat was even worse because he was told to write an obituary. "Well, I went to the house where the death had occurred," he said later, "There was all this squalling going on, and it was not a pleasant place to be. Quite obviously a death had occurred. I reported that the professor had died. Actually, his wife had died, not he. But it came out in the paper that *he* was dead. So they immediately fired me, of course. I couldn't take journalism seriously."[2]

Tom was only beginning to experience the disappointments and rejections that most writers undergo. His play *Hot Milk at Three in the Morning* took only thirteenth place in the One-Act Play Contest and failed to have a workshop production. There was small solace in that his short story "Big Black: A Mississippi Idyll" won an honorable mention in fifth place. This story which was the narrative of a black man on a road gang and his imagined relationship with a white woman was noted for its dialogue and mature treatment of a controversial subject. It was his final effort to gain recognition for his work at the

University of Missouri. He had been praised in a letter from Professor Ramsay that he later quoted: "Your absence at the University has been a matter of real regret to all of us who knew the excellent work you did here in the last few years especially in creative writing."

While employed during the following summers at the International Shoe Company Tom would work on his verse at odd moments during the week and on Saturday would go downtown to the Mercantile Library where he would read voraciously all afternoon. On Sunday he would work on completing the short story that he had started during the week. He put much of himself and his distress on losing his girlfriend, Hazel Kramer, into the story "The Accent of a Coming Foot," based on a poem by Emily Dickinson.

Tom wanted very much to go somewhere away from home for the rest of the summer of 1935 where he could write all the time. His grandmother Dakin came to his rescue by inviting him to Memphis, Tennessee, and it was there that he wrote a play that was produced on July 12. One of the Dakins' neighbors in Memphis, to which they had just retired, was a young woman named Dorothy Shapiro, who was a member of a local little neighborhood theater group called The Rose Arbor Players. The play *Cairo, Shanghai, Bombay!* is a "one-act melodrama" and on the title page of the manuscript it is said to be by Dorothy Shapiro and Tom Williams. Tom wrote the principal part of the play and Dorothy Shapiro the prologue and epilogue. It is set in a seaport town and it was in four scenes, he said, "a farcical but rather touching little comedy about two sailors on a date with a couple of 'light ladies.'" Tom at the time had clearly seen a good many movies for the cast included, Millie "a coarse affable little girl of the Mae West type"; Chuck, "a sailor who has been around"; a noted author described as "a pretentious young intellectual." Tom recalled with pleasure the laughter, "genuine and loud" at the comedy he had written.

Returning in September from his summer in Memphis, to University City, Tom found himself in a handsome two-story house at 6634 Pershing Avenue that Tom's father had agreed to lease for two years. In a letter to his grandparents, Tom joyously described the new home that was a far cry from the dark cluttered apartment on Enright Avenue, which later served as the setting of *The Glass Menagerie*:

"The place seems so quiet and spacious and dignified after our sordid apartment-dwelling that it doesn't seem like we are the same people."[3]

The house became the regular meeting place of the core of our "Poetry Club" as Tom called it. I was the kid, the youngest of the group. Tom was seven years older than I, and Clark Mills five. Because he seemed to have read everything that mattered in both French and English, Clark became our mentor.

Well over six feet, Clark seemed even taller because he walked with a buoyancy that made him appear ready to leap forward at any moment to meet any challenge that life might offer. He was not handsome but had ordinary delicate though unremarkable features, a pencil-thin nose and mouth, both set in a fair-skinned face that flushed easily. It was his eyes that were extraordinary, a dull gray-blue that lit up like the underside of a crashing wave when, with a resonant voice and quick bubbling laugh, he gave vent to an unending irrepressible enthusiasm on every subject he attacked.

Tom and I followed intently every pronouncement he made on litewrature. He introduced us to Laforgue and Apollinaire and held forth at length on T. S. Eliot's *The Waste Land* and James Joyce's *Ulysses.*

From the time I knew him Tom never stopped writing poems and submitting them for publication. For "Sonnets for the Spring," Tom received first prize in a poetry contest at the Wednesday Club, an elite women's cultural organization. The award was presented to him on his birthday, March 26, 1936, in the same auditorium where his first full-length play, *Candles to the Sun,* would appear almost exactly a year later.

THE MAGIC TOWER

In October 1936 the Webster Groves Theatre Guild staged his one act play *The Magic Tower*. With Willard Holland and Clark Mills, Tom attended a rehearsal of *The Magic Tower*. "Pleasant evening," he wrote in his journal. "Met [Director David] Gibson in café. Drank a couple of beers and felt rather desperately gay— recited Ernest Dowson on the way home. Wet streets and lamps. Disappointed in the play. Too sugary. But I don't feel like doing anything better. I am in one of my defeatist moods about writing if I could only always love my work—then I would be a great artist. But I could never be vain."[4] A few nights later Tom attended the performance of his play with Rose, Edwina, and Dakin. After the curtain came down on *The Magic Tower*, the last of the three new plays to be performed, the judges met to decide the winner and it was Thomas Williams. The Webster Groves *News Times* gave Tom his first enthusiastic review. The play, it said, was "a poignant little tragedy with a touch of warm fantasy. It treats the love of a very young, not too talented, artist and his ex-actress wife, a love which their youthful idealism has translated into a thing of exquisite white beauty. They call the garret in which they live 'The Magic Tower' and are happy there until the artist's belief in his star fails, then 'The Magic Tower' becomes a drab garret once more and tragedy like a gray woman glides in to remain. The play was exquisitely written by its poet author." The writer of this review turned out to be a part-time member of our Poetry Club at the University. This was Anne Jennings, the wife of Blanford Jennings, who taught English in the Webster Groves High School.

When Clark and I arrived at the Williams home for our regular meetings—sometimes we met as often as three times a week—Tom's mother, Edwina, a busy little woman, always graciously greeted us, and never stopped talking. There wasn't much inflection or warmth in the steady flow of her speech. One topic, no matter how trivial, received the same emphasis as the next, which might be utterly tragic. I had the impression listening to her that the words she pronounced were like the red balls in a game of Chinese checkers, all suddenly released and clicking quickly and aimlessly about the board.

Tom was, in contrast, one of the shyest men I'd ever known, very, very quiet and soft-spoken. Once he got to know someone he would let himself go, but otherwise he was quite withdrawn. His stony-faced silence often put people off; he appeared uninterested in what was going on around him, never joining in the quick give-and-take of a conversation but rather listening carefully and taking it all in. He would sit quietly in a gathering for long periods of time until suddenly like a volcano erupting he would burst out with a high cackle and then with resounding and uncontrollable laughter.

We knew something about Tom's sister Rose but we rarely saw her when we came to the house. We were aware that she was undergoing treatment for her mental condition although we did not know, as even Tom himself did not then know, how very serious her condition was.

On one occasion when his parents were away on a holiday in the Ozarks, Tom invited Clark and me and another friend Willie Wharton, to share some whiskey with him. Clark had known Wharton at the university and found him amusing. I did not. He had little to say of any interest but he never stopped talking. At the time he was married to Minerva Prim, a former debutante, who stayed at home with their little baby. That evening at Tom's, after several drinks, Willie began making obscene telephone calls to people whose names he had picked at random from the phone book. I have a vision in my memory of Rose appearing suddenly on the stairs in a fluffy white dress and, outraged, threatening to tell her parents when they returned about what was happening. This she did to Tom's great distress.

"After she had tattled on my wild party," the playwright said in his *Memoirs*, "when I was told I could no longer entertain my first group of friends in the house—I went down the stairs as Rose was coming up them. We passed each other on the landing and I turned upon her like a wildcat and hissed at her: 'I hate the sight of your ugly old face!'

"Wordless, stricken, and crouching, she stood there motionless in a corner of the landing as I rushed on out of the house.

"This was the cruellest thing I have done in my life, I suspect, and one for which I can never properly atone."[5]

Rose's mental condition continued to deteriorate. The insulin treatments that she had been receiving did her little good. Her sexual fantasies, her obscene language, and her delusions about her father's sexual behavior continued. It was not until January 13, 1943, that a bilateral prefrontal lobotomy, with the consent of Edwina Williams, was performed in St. Louis. Already in 1937, however, Tom thought of Rose's eclipse as final, and he indicated it in this poem published in the literary magazine *The Eliot* at Washington University, which begins:

She went with morning on her lips
down an inscrutable dark way
and we who witnessed her eclipse
have found no word to say.

At about the time of the publication of this poem, June 1937, Tom was eagerly awaiting the announcement of the three one-act play winners in the annual contest in English 16, Professor William G. B. Carson's "Technique of Modern Drama." English 16, the only writing course offered at Washington University except for Professor Webster's in the short story, was quite popular on the campus. The students wrote one-act plays and at the end of the year three plays were chosen and given workshop productions. One of the three was selected as the best and its author was awarded fifty dollars, a considerable sum in those days, especially for students. Tom had received a B in the course for the first semester and after his play *Death of Pierrot* had failed to get even an honorable mention in the contest of the Webster Groves Theatre Guild that year he was hoping he would fare better with Professor Carson. "Horrible if I were eliminated," he wrote in his journal. And horrible indeed it was when that elimination of his play *Me, Vashya* was announced.

I remember his bitterness at the time. The decision was said to have been that of an "independent jury" but Tom thought, as others of us did, that it was solely Professor Carson's, especially when the winner chosen for a full production was a play by Wayne Arnold, a favorite student of Carson's. His play, *First Edition*, is a bright little piece, the absolute opposite of Tom's somber dramatization of the murder of a powerful munitions maker, Lord Vashya Shontine, who sold armaments to both sides in wartime. And war was much on everyone's mind. Tom was attempting to deal with a large and very dark subject. Ironically it was precisely this subject, Professor Carson later revealed, that caused him to eliminate Tom's play. *Me, Vashya* may now seem, as apparently it did when read aloud in Carson's class, laughably melodramatic, but as a youthful and fantastic treatment of a very real problem it was to us, his fellow beginning writers, serious and moving.

What was particularly hurtful to Tom about this defeat was that, while on the surface his subject appeared remote, he had put so much of himself and his own life into this play. Lady Shontine's madness is clearly a reflection of his sister Rose's mental breakdown which so haunted Tom at the time and the blunt, obsessive vulgarity of Vashya himself surely owed much to that of Tom's alcoholic father, who was making his sister's life and his own totally unbearable.

CANDLES TO THE SUN

I had the rare privilege of attending on Saturday, March 20, 1937, a performance of *Candles to the Sun*. The play had been produced by an amateur theatrical troupe, the Mummers, and directed by Willard Holland, who played one of the leading roles, and, more importantly, had almost single-handedly helped to shape the final version of the play.

The primary focus of the Mummers was drama of social concern and *Candles*, presenting as it does the travails and struggles of three generations of a family of coal miners in the Red Hills of Alabama, seemed definitely to fit the bill. It was for me not only a decided pleasure, but also an absolute revelation, all the more astonishing because I had come fully prepared, I thought, to give my heartfelt approval to any offering of my dear friend and close associate, Thomas Lanier Williams, however modest and unpolished it proved to be.

Dakin Williams, Tom's younger brother, together with his parents, had attended the Thursday, March 18 premiere (or preview as the Mummers preferred to call it). He remembers that Tom had sat at some distance from his family and from most of the others in the audience, alone in an aisle seat, which he had insisted on having. When to thunderous applause, loud cheers, and resonant foot-stomping the full cast gathered for numerous curtain calls, they suddenly burst out singing "Solidarity Forever." The celebrated union anthem, totally uncalled for in the script, gave the play an aura of propaganda, which the playwright, despite his pronounced sympathy for victims of social injustice, had clearly not intended.

I knew, of course, that Tom had written plays, any number of short ones, each of which he usually referred to as a "fantasy." But for me at the time he was first and foremost a poet, and it was as a poet that I expected him to make a national name for himself. And indeed he did just that, but not for his poems as such but rather for the poetry of his plays, which was powerfully revealed in *Candles to the Sun*.

Reed Hynds, reviewing *Candles to the Sun* for the *St. Louis Star-Times*, contended it was certainly not a propaganda play, as some "lobby critics" had thought, but rather "an earnest and searching examination of a particular social reality set out in human and dramatic terms." In a separate interview in the same paper, Tom had explained that "the candles (in the title of the play) represent the individual lives of the people. The sun represents group consciousness. The play ends as a tragedy for the individuals, for in the end they realize they cannot achieve success and happiness apart from the group but must sacrifice for the common good." I think at the same time that for Tom this had not only a social but also a personal reference. John Donne, a poet whom Tom particularly appreciated, had written, "No man is an island, entire of itself; every man is a piece of the continent, a part of the main," and these lines might well be an epigraph for *Candles to the Sun*. Tom, speaking personally, referred at the time to the "Island of Myself," and it was, he later declared, to "ward off the dread of loneliness" that he wrote. If he was an island, he knew that, in his life as in his work, he had to create a bridge to humanity, to a greater world beyond the self.

If taken literally as a chronicle of social protest, the play can never be fully understood. It must be read as a closely unified and carefully developed metaphor. It is an extended study of light and dark, both inside and outside the characters and the setting. The action moves from dark into light, with all the degrees of chiaroscuro and shadow along the way. The two principal pivotal characters are the heroines, Star, the miner Bram Pilcher's daughter, and Fern, his daughter-in-law. Note the careful choice of names, each with its own metaphorical implication. Star moves from her virginal purity that like the real star above her cuts clearly through the camp's darkness, drawn by her own sensuality to the false bright light of Birmingham, the urban dark. She loses her chance to regain that innocence when Red, the spiritual organizer she loves, is murdered. She turns then to the brothel that had always awaited her and from which she will send some of the dark money she earns to help Fern, ironically, purchase freedom from the mine and light for young Luke, her son, whose name means light. Fern, on the other hand, like the plant for which she is named, grows up out of darkness into light: her clean pure self is aware that she can move from her grief and her dark inner self into the blinding, liberating light of the sun. To obtain the greater freedom that the strike provides for the entire community, Fern sacrifices all that she has strived for. The final scene with Fern transcendent in the rocking chair and light streaming through the open door is heartbreaking in its intensity. The intensity is prepared for us by the stage directions of the final scene that are in themselves pure poetry: *Winter has broken up and it is now one of those clear, tenuous mornings in early spring. A thin, clear sunlight, pale as lemon-water comes through the windowpanes of the cabin which is now barer and cleaner-looking than usual in this strange light.* Heartbreaking also at the same time is Bram, the "Old Man of the Mines" who has preferred to remain in the dark, to go down daily into the dirt to dig his own grave, a mole who knows nothing but the dark and is blinded by sunlight. He moves finally into a deeper level of the dark, into the madness from which there is no return.

It is what Henry James calls "the madness of art" that saves Tom from the madness that he contemplated in his sister, and that he so feared would overtake him as well. The spirit of Rose hovers over this entire play, rising from the heavy morning mist that Luke sees, "thick as wood smoke down on the hollow." Fern and Star are both aspects of Tom's imaginative vision of Rose: Fern, evoking her enduring and transcendent innocence; Star, an innocence lost to a destructive sensuality of the powerful sort that he felt had brought on Rose's madness.

Clark has told that he and I attended the Saturday performance of *Candles to the Sun* with the "underground crew" of our rebellious Bohemian confrères. Among them may have been the star members of the League of Artists and Writers whom Tom had met when he attended their weekly meetings in 1936 at the old courthouse near the St. Louis riverfront: poet Orrick Johns, novelist (and Marxist) Jack Conroy, short-story writer J. S. Balch, and humorist Willie Wharton. Whether or not they were all there I am not sure, but I have the distinct recollection that we all went on, along with Tom, to the apartment of Jack Conroy, where we spent the rest of the night with some tough heavy-drinking types I had never before encountered. Clark had this memory of Tom that night:

> He was there at the beginning of the show, but at the intermission Tom was gone—nobody could find him. Finally, I found him outside. It was a cold night—he was sitting on the curbstone in front of the theater with a bottle of whiskey—and he was drunk as a skunk and in total despair. Apparently, something had gone wrong, or he imagined it. I know he was intensely concerned with the reaction of audiences, and now suddenly he saw the play as hopeless, and he was drinking himself into oblivion. He refused to go back in—he saw it as just a total disaster. That was the only time I ever saw him really drunk.

I have a feeling, now that I have examined the play carefully and know much more about its author than I did then, that it may not have been something that had gone wrong in the production but that it was simply too painful for him to watch a play in which he had put so much of himself and his sister. Of *The Glass Menagerie* he said late in his life: "It is the saddest play I have ever written. It is full of pain. It is painful for me to see it." To my mind *Candles to the Sun* is also one of Tom's saddest plays, full of pain, but one of the most beautiful.

FUGITIVE KIND

Tom's second full-length play was titled *Fugitive Kind*, produced by the Mummers in 1937, but not published until 2001. In her introduction to the New Directions edition of *Fugitive Kind*, Allean Hale wrote:

> It is a veritable index to his later work as he tries out characters, situations, and themes he will develop in plays from as early as *Battle of Angels* (1940) to as late as *The Red Devil Battery Sign* (1975)…For once we know the origin of an undiscovered Williams play. In January, 1937, Tom wrote in his journal that he had seen a "lovely" motion picture, Maxwell Anderson's *Winterset*.

Fugitive Kind is one play in which Clark and Tom may be said to have really collaborated. Clark recalled later a summer day in their "literary factory":

> Each of us on a kitchen chair, your typewriter
> fluent as automatic gunfire, as you sketched
> gestures and intonation, dialogue, behavior,
> and I with index finger, pecked and brooded,
> weighing the sound or color of a word.
> On one St. Louis summer day,
> sweat pouring down on us, we conjured up
> —snow!
>
> Once, I recall, you thus explored a drama in a flophouse
> while I wrote of a winter white with tons of snow…

Many words and phrases from Clark's moving poem "The White Winter" found their way into the final speeches of Tom's characters.[6]

Colin McPherson reviewed *Fugitive Kind* in the *St. Louis Post-Dispatch* when it opened in December 1937. He wrote that the play "describes vividly the life in a big city 'flophouse.' Even with the best of acting, *Fugitive Kind* would still be somewhat amateurish and the performance is spotty. Some extraordinary credit should go to the Mummers, however, for giving a local playwright his forum and for attempting to present the life close at hand in the theater." Reed Hynds also reviewed the play in the *St. Louis Star-Times*: "That Thomas Lanier Williams is a playwright to watch was demonstrated again by the Mummers last night when the dramatic group produced his new play, *Fugitive Kind*. While less intense than his *Candles to the Sun*, it is a consistent, vital and absorbing play.… Williams shares some of the faults as well as some of the virtues of the lions of the day (Sidney Howard, Ben Hecht, and Maxwell Anderson) he wants to say something forceful and true about the chaos of modern life. But like them he seems clearer about the way to say it than what to say. His play has theatrical substance, but its thought is confused."

It is ironic that *Fugitive Kind* is one of Tom's plays that his father appreciated, probably because it showed the triumph of the G-man over the criminal, as the Hollywood films of the time usually did. Tom was no doubt thinking of the outcasts, the poor fugitives, on the waterfront there below the building where his father worked, and who were the products of the capitalist greed which his own father represented to him.

In the summer of 1938 after Clark had left for a teaching position in the French department at Cornell, Tom turned his attention to the creation of what he called the St. Louis Poets' Workshop, which we formed together, and in which we were joined by Louise Krause and Elizabeth Fenwick Phillips, who later married Clark. We had some stationery printed and sent poems to all the leading magazines with a covering letter signed by a fictitious secretary of the workshop. In a few carefully chosen words the letter described the great poetic flowering then taking place in St. Louis. The poems enclosed, the secretary stated, were representative samples of this "remarkable Midwestern Renaissance." The editors addressed were less impressed by our flowering than we were: the poems all came back.

With Clark gone, Tom visited his basement where they had held forth with their "literary factory" in the summer of 1937 while I was employed in Michigan. "On the wall…directly before us," Tom wrote, "was tacked up a little verse of our own composition which was to serve as a grim reminder—as some writers keep skulls in their studies:

> For lack of food some writers died
> while some committed suicide,
> and all though great or small in fame
> returned to dust from which they came.

To this Tom now added a credo: "For every artist, experience is never complete until it has been reproduced in creative work. To the poet his travels, his adventures, his loves, his indignations are finally resolved in verse and this in the end becomes his permanent, indestructible life."[7]

At this important moment in his life, Tom realized that his experience would never be completed and finally reproduced in creative work until he made a final break with family and with St. Louis. This he was now prepared to do, and a play contest provided the incentive. The Group Theatre in New York was offering a five-hundred-dollar prize and though the age limit for entrants was twenty-five, Tom decided to send several of his plays for consideration giving his birth date as 1914 rather than 1911, and furthermore, on his way to New Orleans, he would mail the plays from the home of his grandparents in Memphis and he would sign the works "Tennessee Williams." Although Tom later was fond of ascribing the change to a Southern weakness for "climbing the family tree" and to his heritage as a Tennessee pioneer, he really had no idea at the time where the name had come from and where it would take the person that it would come to represent.

I knew nothing of the fantastic immediate impact that the city of New Orleans had on Tom and nothing of his February trip from New Orleans to Los Angeles with his new musician friend James Parrott, first by Ford V-8 and then by bicycle, until Tom returned to St. Louis in early September. He told me about New Orleans then and also that a week before his birthday in March he had received a special one-hundred-dollar award from the Group Theatre in New York for the plays he had submitted to their contest and that the Group had put him in touch with an agent, Audrey Wood, who was to represent him for almost the entire rest of his life. She placed the short story "The Field of Blue Children" with *Story* magazine, his first publication using the name "Tennessee."

Before Tom left St. Louis again for New York, he made this entry in his journal:

> Sunday—9/16/39—End of the St. Louis period—leave tomorrow midnight for New York. Time here has passed in a flash. Nothing happened. *Nothing at all.* Written practically nothing & so I don't feel too good. Had hoped—intended—to go to N.Y. with new play script. But I go almost empty handed because I want to go somewhere—to get away—the old flight motive—May God be merciful to me and open some door, some avenue of escape.[8]

This chapter is an excerpt from William Jay Smith's memoir *My Friend Tom: The Poet-Playwright Tennessee Williams*. Jackson, the University Press of Mississippi, 2011. Reprinted by permission of the author.

"
Good God, How many years have I
"
been trying to write?

THE YEAR 1939: BECOMING TENNESSEE WILLIAMS

Albert J. Devlin

The instinct and taste of Tom Williams for higher education were found wanting at three institutions before he graduated from the University of Iowa in 1938. Free at last from academe, he went to Chicago, where he failed to find work on the Federal Theatre or Writers Project; then briefly to "the City of St. Pollution,"[1] where he fell under the yoke of his father, Cornelius; then on to Memphis, New Orleans, and points west. Soon it was 1939, a year in which both the United States and Tennessee Williams seemed to mark time before plunging, respectively, into World War II and a career on Broadway. Nancy Tischler and I have followed this story in editing Volume 1 of *The Selected Letters of Tennessee Williams,* but I should like to elaborate upon this extraordinary year of preparation, especially upon two literary models that Williams considered in his travels. As the year progressed, he was still trying to answer the most basic questions of life, often posed in his journal with a kind of sophomoric splendor, and to deal with a new set of professional ones that came with his finally being a regarded author.

It was Williams who distinguished 1939 by signing himself "Tennessee" when he applied in the preceding December to a Group Theatre contest for young playwrights. The facts are few and sketchy, and I doubt that they solve the riddle of when Tom first became

"Tennessee." If the memory of his mother, Edwina, can be trusted, Williams mailed at least one play from St. Louis before he left on (or about) December 26 to visit his grandparents in Memphis. From there he mailed additional plays, "in plenty of time"[2] to meet the contest deadline, as he informed Edwina on January 2 from New Orleans. Contest rules limited the event to playwrights under the age of twenty-five, a bar that the twenty-seven-year-old Williams easily ducked, the Memphis postmark and the indigenous name a ruse, as he later revealed, to shield his deception from "friends"[3] in St. Louis who might otherwise expose him. Apparently no covering letter(s) exists to confirm Williams' self-description, but when Molly Day Thacher, play-reader for the Group Theatre, wrote with news of a special award on March 20, 1939, she congratulated "Mr. Tennessee Williams."[4]

"Tennessee" replaced Thomas Lanier Williams, a name that smacked of belles lettres and ruefully reminded the subject of William Lyon Phelps, a Yale Brahmin of the 1920s and 1930s. ("Tennessee," I should add, briefly gave way to "Valentine Xavier," as Williams inscribed a typescript in New Orleans in January 1939, but the allusion to the Catholic roots of his father's family was canceled in favor of "Tennessee.") Immeasurable is the gulf between the venial motives that led Williams to rename himself and the iconic intuition from which the new name must have sprung. Something of this inspiration was recorded in his journal shortly after Williams arrived in New Orleans. He was "enchanted" by the "fabulous old town" and convinced that "here surely is the place that I was *made* for if any place on this funny old world" (December 28, 1938).[5] The nagging final clause bespeaks the fear that pervades Williams' journal, beginning as it does in March 1936. His estrangement from the world is one that is general and natural in origin rather than political or economic; it is often encoded by such grim cosmological imagery as *Dead Planet, the Moon!*—a working title that he chose in January 1939 for the play *Vieux Carré*; and it is inherent, charged with the displacement of birth and realized in a lifetime that does not take place. Rose Williams modeled the pathological excess of this alienation, while her younger brother was stunted in "the active desires of loving and growing."[6]

But in New Orleans, in early 1939, a peace and promise seemed to arise, as "Tennessee" Williams felt at home in the "funny old world." He wrote with uncharacteristic poise on January 14 that "things are impending in my life—of that I feel sure—& so I am reasonably content for the nonce—willing to wait & see what's up!" This auspicious moment led Williams to isolate the lyrical "something"[7] that had survived the stupefying treadmill days of St. Louis, days that had seemed "short" because they "repeat themselves so....It was all one day over and over,"[8] he lamented in the journal. New Orleans, by contrast, promised an advancing plot, impending events, a personal equipoise. Two weeks later, an epoch in the whirling Williams psyche, he was still "sailing bravely into another week—not knowing what it may bring—wondering but not too daunted by those speculations" (January 29, 1939).[9] "Silly old Tommy," as Williams described himself in the New Orleans journal, had assumed a Whitmanesque pose of waiting and watching, of absorbing, of seeing "what's up!"

The journal and letters both confirm and complicate the familiar view of Tennessee Williams as an unstable man. Physical weakness and strength, fear and resolution, ignorance and prophecy alternate like the rhythm of a song played "over and over" in the oppressive Williams household, where a radio did indeed often blare in the background. The career itself was subject to the same oscillation. Williams routinely despaired that his work was "smashed" and that he was "artistically defunct" (November 21, 1936, September 15, 1937).[10] "Maybe I am not a poet but just a blooming idiot,"[11] he opined gloomily in June 1937, as he reflected upon his own enervation and the artist's general disadvantage in the modern world. Several months later, before leaving for the University of Iowa, he was buoyed by the near completion of *Fugitive Kind* and affirmed that "the next play is always the important play. The past, however satisfactory, is only a challenge to the future. I want to go on creating. I *will!!!*" (September 16, 1937).[12] After a wasted year at Iowa, he caught the forward march once again in New Orleans and held it for much of 1939, largely oblivious to the growing disorder in the world and finely attuned to the prompting of his own career. In August he wrote from Taos to his friend and traveling companion Jim Parrott, whose dreams of an acting career would not be realized: "The nature of progress is a repercussion from tumbles, it seems to me....It's a slow, slow, bulldog battle that we all have to fight—Good God, How many years have I been trying to write? Since I was eleven or twelve! And maybe five years from now I will begin to be known."[13] Precisely five years later, in August 1944, in another artistic enclave at Provincetown, Williams was typing a dramatic work—*The Glass Menagerie,* of course—that would soon be optioned by Broadway and that would make him "known" without a nagging "maybe."

The year 1939 was a watershed in the "bulldog battle" of apprenticeship that Tennessee Williams waged. The periodic "tumbles" occasioned by his "crazy blue devil" of fear and depression, and the times, which threatened to reduce his generation to abstractions of economic and political history, were held in abeyance as Williams began his life as a traveler-artist. In "repercussions" of identity and prophecy, he named himself and foresaw the time of his success, and by year's end he had completed a draft of his first mature work—if *Battle of Angels* may be so described. This is the outer story, and naturally the acquisition of a powerful agent, Audrey Wood, in April 1939, is a critical chapter that must be addressed, but the inner story is the more interesting and elusive and the one that I should like to consider. Now that Williams had separated himself from St. Louis (although he would return after this and many other apparent breaks), had gained recognition by the Group Theatre as a promising young playwright, and had found an agent, how did he begin to construct a literary life that was commensurate with the outward circumstances of his career? Two models came to his attention in early 1939, and not surprisingly both were roving artists: Nicholas Vachel Lindsay and Richard Halliburton.

Vachel Lindsay (1879–1931) is remembered today, if at all, for the vivid imagery and syncopated rhythms of "General William Booth Enters into Heaven" (1913) and especially "The Congo" (1914), with its simulation of a pounding African cadence. These and several other poems (including ones devoted to his political heroes Abraham Lincoln and William Jennings Bryan) were immensely popular from 1913, when "General Booth" appeared in Harriet Monroe's *Poetry* magazine, to the mid-1920s, when Lindsay's fragile hold upon fame began to loosen. At his peak, he was the "inimitably original"[14] protégé of Harriet Monroe; for the (later) poet laureate John Masefield, he sang of America "as lustily as Whitman did"; and he was praised by William Dean Howells as an inspired singer, who "fills the empyrean from the expanses of the whole great West."[15] Lindsay's evangelistic tramping and prolonged apprenticeship were redeemed, as it were, in 1914, when William Butler Yeats arrived in Chicago on a reading tour and paid tribute to the "strange beauty"[16] of "General Booth." Lindsay responded by reciting "The Congo" at a banquet given in Yeats' honor by *Poetry* magazine. He did indeed "pound the table hard,"[17] as he had warned Harriet Monroe, in a performance that was a long-delayed triumph for the thirty-four-year-old poet from Springfield, Illinois.

How Tennessee Williams first became aware of Lindsay is a matter of speculation. Perhaps as a student chanting "The Congo," as did the Williams scholar Allean Hale in 1930: "Boomlay, boomlay, boomlay, Boom." Perhaps as a literary-minded St. Louisan who knew of Lindsay's courtship of the St. Louis-born poet Sara Teasdale. Williams' later friendship with the Filsinger sisters, nieces of Lindsay's rival and the man who finally married Teasdale in 1914, may have reinforced his knowledge of this awkward lover's address to a poet whose work he admired. Before Williams' first documented reference to Lindsay in June 1939, he may have shown his attention by the adage that "imitation is the sincerest form of flattery." In February 1939, Williams and Jim Parrott found themselves out of money and gas but not wits as they paused in El Paso before making a final push for California. Williams wrote a mock-serious letter to an unnamed "Editor" in which he tried to barter poems for gas:

> The author of these poems and his friend, Jimmy, a jobless musician, have run out of money and gas in El Paso, Texas. There is a terrific dust-storm raging and a sheriff named Fox who puts undesirable transients in the house of detention for thirty days. The author and the musician…Are not quite sure of their

desirability and would like to continue westward to California where they understand that unemployed artists can make fifty cents an hour picking fruit. Their jalopy, running on kerosene or low-grade gas, could make Cal. on ten or fifteen dollars. If you like the poems an acceptance would aid materially in the author's survival.[18]

The itinerant Williams would soon remind his new agent, Audrey Wood, that Vachel Lindsay "was…for many years a tramp selling his poems for two cents—from door to door."[19] Both Lindsay and Williams were supremely restless and unsuited for any ordinary vocation or regularity in life. They tramped to keep their eccentricity intact and to stave off, as Lindsay put it, "the usual Middle West crucifixion of the artist."[20]

Williams' first documented reference to Lindsay occurs in a letter written to Audrey Wood in June 1939 from Laguna Beach, California, where he and Jim Parrott had settled for the summer in a primitive cabin named "Airy Edges." To date, Miss Wood had received letters of thanks and introduction; with the latest correspondence, she began to see, no doubt, the far reach of Williams' imagination and the dramaturgic problems that it would occasion. Williams had been reading Edgar Lee Masters' biography of Lindsay, which he thought filled with "a wealth of dramatic material." As he informed Wood, his biographical play about Vachel Lindsay:

> would concern, in large, the whole problem of the poet or creative artist in America or any other capitalistic state…Nobody with a desire to create has ever put up a braver, more pitiful struggle against the intellectual apathy and the economic tyranny of his times!…My play would center, I think, upon the closing chapter of his life—in Springfield, Illinois.…The play would terminate, of course, with Lindsay's suicide— that awful, grotesque crawling upstairs on hands and knees at midnight!—but would strike some positive, assertive note—I mean I would not want it to be just another futilitarian tragedy about a beaten-down artist.[21]

In reading Masters' biography, Williams could not have failed to notice the bold parallels between his own domestic history and Vachel Lindsay's. Both were the offspring of ill-matched parents; both were frail, bookish children, each more the mother's son than the father's. Both also had a complicated relation with nearby midwestern cities, Springfield and St. Louis, from which they derived much of their aesthetic energy and personal frustration. Lindsay dreamed of converting the cynical politicians and "climacteric women"[22] of the capital city by preaching a "gospel of beauty." Williams held no such hope for "the City of St. Pollution." All that remains (to my knowledge) of his enthusiasm for Lindsay are two undated, fragmentary typescripts in which he paid homage to "the last great poet in the troubadour tradition."[23] In the more substantial draft, entitled "Suitable Entrances to Springfield or Heaven," the scene is a Pullman car approaching Springfield, and the situation, the last homecoming of Lindsay in November 1931, a few days before his suicide. Also on the train are Luke and his wife Alice, a knife-throwing act whose sad but true story has Luke drinking heavily and Alice, his target, taking stage fright, as it were, with a transposed case of the shakes. Their presence is gratuitous unless it can be seen as Williams' attempt to echo Lindsay's theory of poetry as a "higher vaudeville" and his practice of this popular art form in the exuberant, capering stage recitals that he gave for years. Williams' script is feeble—by no means does it even approach the grandiose theme announced to Audrey Wood—but it is unerring in framing the vulnerability of the artist-performer and in suggesting the forces that work to destroy him. Of these Lindsay wrote astutely in 1929, in anticipation of Tennessee Williams' own "catastrophe of success":

> I begin to see how machinery closes in around the very topmost-seeming Americans. And how subtle is the appeal. It's a temptation and a complex of gathering forces no European ever faces, and hysterical shrieking against it keeps you right on the level with it, like Mencken, Lewis, *The Nation, The New Republic.* ... So how would I define supremacy in America? Here it is: *to be above every single piece of machinery without shrieking against it. And yet to be completely effective as a traditional American.*[24]

Williams wrote to Audrey Wood of his Lindsay play soon after he and Jim Parrott had settled for the summer in Laguna Beach, one of the many havens of artistic and sexual freedom that attracted Williams over the years. Earlier in May he corrected Edwina's "impression" that he planned to settle in Hollywood and assured her that he had not "been infected with the money-disease out here." He would keep his distance from that "putrid" atmosphere of "sham and corruption." "What I *want* to do," he continued, "is live out here this summer in a little beach colony for artists and writers which I have discovered on my bicycle tour. It is an indescribably beautiful place—Laguna Beach—lovelier than anything I saw in Europe."[25] By May 10 he and Jim Parrott had moved from Hawthorne, in south Los Angeles County, where Jim's aunt and uncle lived, and Williams wrote to his maternal grandmother—Rosina Otte Dakin, "Grand"—with further details of Santa Catalina Bay and the rugged mountains that surrounded Laguna Beach: "The water is a marvelous blue and the hills thickly wooded and covered with gorgeous wild flowers. The coast along here is very rocky but we have a beautiful sandy beach for swimming." For good measure, he added that "there are two beautiful twin girls we met in Los Angeles who entertain us frequently at their beautiful house on the beach— so we are ideally located."[26] Rarely in such dutiful correspondence did Williams violate the conventional expectations or values of his family. His allusion to girlfriends is doubly strategic, however, for in precisely a month's time his first known gay adventure would be recorded in the journal. He would also in the same letter to Grand make reference to the author-traveler Richard Halliburton, whose secret, now rendered profoundly academic, was in all probability the same as Tennessee Williams'.

Richard Halliburton (1900–1939) discovered Laguna Beach in 1930 and in 1937 completed the building of a "modernistic residence" overlooking the bay that he aptly named "Hangover House." Williams described both Halliburton and this curious edifice to his grandmother in the same letter of May 10:

> Richard Halliburton, who travelled all over the world, selected this place as his permanent home and has a big modernistic

residence on one of the peaks overlooking the sea. Incidentally he has apparently met a tragic end in crossing the Pacific—I will enclose an article I just cut from the Laguna papers. I thought the sub-head about "County turns off water" added a rather grotesquely humorous touch. People around here say that Paul Mooney, mentioned as his collaborator, actually did most of his writing for him. They both went down in the junk—unless it all turns out to be a big publicity stunt.[27]

Williams probably mentioned Halliburton to his grandmother, and not to Edwina in a concurrent letter, because Halliburton's parents lived in Memphis, where the Dakins were retired. Halliburton had sailed from Hong Kong on March 4 in a Chinese junk bound for the Golden Gate Exposition in San Francisco. His arrival was timed for the opening of the fair and designed to create publicity for a national tour that would be the subject of his ninth book of travel. On March 24 radio contact with the *Sea Dragon* was broken and the woeful junk presumed lost in a typhoon in the western Pacific. Williams' surmise that this "tragic end" might be a "publicity stunt" echoed a general knowledge of Halliburton's genius for self-promotion and especially his history of filing premature reports of his own demise. But he and his companion Paul Mooney and a crew of twelve had indeed died at sea, and Halliburton was declared legally dead in October 1939.

Richard Halliburton was a restless youth who eagerly left Princeton after his graduation in 1921 to begin a life of tramping. There was, he told his father, a worried realtor, "something in turmoil inside me all the time…. The idea of leading a monotonous confined respectable life is horrible to me."[28] Upon reaching his majority in 1921 he wistfully reflected: "I feel like Conrad in quest of his youth. Nine more years and I'll be thirty and the last vestige of youth will be gone…. I can look forward to no joy in life beyond thirty."[29] He spent a frantic 600 days of travel doing research for his first book, *The Royal Road to Romance,* which was published in 1925 and became a national best-seller. It was followed quickly by a second, *The Glorious Adventure* (1927), in which Halliburton retraced the journey of Ulysses from Troy to Ithaca. This book was also "a *true* narrative," he said, "with buckets of bright paint flung over it," an image that he had used earlier to describe his mission as a writer: to "splash a little red paint"[30] over the commonplaceness of earth. By the mid-1930s, a Halliburton legend had been extruded from his headlong prose, dramatic photographs that showed him crossing the Alps on an elephant, posing in front of the Taj Mahal, consulting the oracle at Delphi, and embarking on a vast lecture tour in which he performed like "Apollo." The heroic pretension was no accident. If the commodification of the American literary career may be said to begin with Mark Twain, then Richard Halliburton, as well as Vachel Lindsay and Tennessee Williams, is a notable contributor to the process whereby art has come to be enfolded in fashion and publicity.

To my knowledge, Tennessee Williams made no further reference to Halliburton, nor is there any proof that he ever read his frothy prose. Their affinity, however, is pronounced and bears testimony to the power of the popular culture to sustain images that are used on many different levels. Williams and Halliburton were similar in defying fathers who offered conventional careers in shoes and real estate. They were also built along the same hypertensive lines and were given to depression, morbidity, and wide swings in mood. Halliburton used the conventional avenues of the media to exert a countervailing pressure upon the routines of life. More devoted to personal success than liberation, he was no exile or traveler in the way that Paul Bowles would later expound; but his projection of youthful dreams of escape onto the national culture was pervasive and compelling and may be said to have formed a background for Tennessee Williams' own similar plots of stagnation and defeat. In 1935, in his first produced play, in Halliburton's hometown of Memphis, a naïve young sailor and his girlfriend intone "Cairo, Shanghai, Bombay!" with a reverence for the exotic and faraway that might have been learned from Halliburton. In *The Glass Menagerie*, Tom Wingfield "boils" in a hyperventilated speech that is sharply reminiscent of Halliburton's prose: "I know I seem dreamy, but inside—well, I'm boiling! Whenever I pick up a shoe, I shudder a little thinking how short life is and what I am doing!"[31] When Tom leaves his "two-by-four" life in St. Louis, he goes as a merchant seaman, precisely the same way that Halliburton began his own travel on "The Royal Road to Romance."

A second and more delicate affinity between Williams and Halliburton is their sexual nature. The letter of May 10 to Grand, with its tale of beautiful girlfriends, is double-voiced in assuming normative airs shortly before Williams recorded his first homosexual experience. If not New Orleans, then Laguna Beach began in 1939 the arduous process of revealing to Williams his own complicated sexuality. "Getting a pack of neuroses on my heels," he wrote on June 11 after spending a "rather horrible night with a picked up acquaintance Doug whose amorous advance made me sick at the stomach."

This foray quickly brought down the summer's idyll, "so marvelously calm and serene," so like one of Williams' favorite Gauguins, "'Nave Nave Mahana' The Careless Days." It was with "a feeling of spiritual nausea" (June 14, 1939),[32] he wrote, that he escaped briefly to Hawthorne, where Jim Parrott's family lived. An intuition of the spiritual dangers of Laguna Beach had also led Dick Halliburton's parents to object to the building of Hangover House and especially to the influence of Paul Mooney upon their son. They feared that the modernistic rectangle of glass and concrete, built sheer with a precipice of 600 feet, was not designed to soften their son's "unsociable nature" or to sanctify "the women situation," which seemed from afar to be one of profligacy and excess. He was not "morose" or "cynical," he answered in late 1936, and "the women situation is no cause for alarm. They play a very small part in my life, chiefly because their minds and natures bore me worse than men's." "Please," he concluded the letter, "don't be distressed because I'm the way I am. Just be grateful that I'm so much happier than most people and growing on a continually up-climbing curve."[33] Did Williams in writing to his grandmother make a similar, if still more densely hedged, plea for understanding, with the strange conjunction of beautiful girls and a misogynous writer closeted high above the exotica of Laguna Beach? It was to Grand, of course, whom Williams went in life for understanding, and it was to her "transparent figure"[34] in "The Angel in the Alcove" that he turned for benediction upon his sexual difference. After his death,

Halliburton quickly passed from view, but his rather prolonged vogue may have framed for a moment for Tennessee Williams the essential components of his own evolving career: art, celebrity, commerce, and a closeted sexuality, all grounded in the matrix of an equivocal family discourse.

Snapshots for the remaining months of 1939 show Tennessee Williams in August in Taos, New Mexico, where he met Frieda Lawrence and Dorothy Brett and began research at the Harwood Foundation for a play about D. H. Lawrence's life in America. Vachel Lindsay had given way to a much greater literary subject, whose love ethic Williams appropriated in an unpublished story written at Taos entitled "Why Did Desdemona Love the Moor?" It was also at Taos that "the foreign situation" finally broke into Williams' self-absorbed world and took, predictably, a theatrical turn. A now forgotten Cleveland artist named William Eastman passed through Taos in the company of Hedvig Kraikow, a Polish baroness who was "very distraught" by the current German-Polish crisis. "To forget her troubles," Williams reported (in early September 1939) in a letter to Grand, the baroness "gave a big dinner party" and "then went to a big casino" where she won "several hundred dollars at roulette! By the end of the evening she was quite unconcerned about the foreign situation,"[35] and so too was Tennessee Williams. A brief "neurotic period" (September, 17, 1939)[36] in St. Louis, a month in New York observing the Broadway theater and meeting Audrey Wood, a return to St. Louis, the completion of a first draft of *Battle of Angels,* and the award of a Rockefeller grant in late December brought 1939 to a conclusion that abruptly reversed Williams' growing conviction of his becoming "a decimated individual" (December 19, 1939)[37] once again. Edwina "literally wept with joy" at the glad tidings from New York, while Williams was more restrained: "I have had to insulate my spirit against shocks in order to survive—result I'm dulled even to happiness" (December 21, 1939).[38] Williams wrote these prescient lines well in advance of his own catastrophic success, but the example of Lindsay and Halliburton had left him with few vague guesses, if any, about the writer's life in America. It was, he knew, not "a peaceful profession."[39]

It is no accident that Williams' chief interest or point of intersection with Vachel Lindsay and Richard Halliburton came with their premature deaths. Lindsay drank Lysol in 1931, while the journey of the *Sea Dragon* in 1939 was foolhardy, measured even by Dick Halliburton's wide standards of adventure, and may in retrospect seem suicidal. It is fair to say, I think, that each writer enjoyed a prolonged vogue rather than a career, with its phases and depth and maturation. They were far less gifted than Williams, but their very limitations seemed to expose them more directly to the national "machinery" of which Lindsay spoke in 1929, as "clos[ing] in around the very topmost-seeming Americans" and requiring that they trim their art to a mendacious popular culture. Even the dreamy Lindsay realized, as Williams once said, that it was "as hard to get rich on poetry as fat on vinegar";[40] and so he developed a highly expressive, interactive platform style that drew admiring audiences to his "higher vaudeville." He boasted that his publisher, Macmillan, had lent him "the whole weight of their advertising and punch and prestige. You will see me rolling across the literary asphalt."

It proved, however, an exhausting and demeaning circuit that he trod before untold civic, educational, and literary groups. In 1925 a sympathetic reviewer saw not the "boyish poet who pranced across the stage" but a man "weary, worn and inexpressibly sad" and lacking "the old spirit of comradeship"[41] with his now dwindling audience. On his last tour, in 1931, he refused to recite "The Congo" and wrote in explanation to his young wife, Elizabeth: "You will have to wait till you are all of 51 before you know what it means to be doomed to sit in the attic with your dustiest poetry and feel your creative force thwarted every day....I will *not* be a *slave* to my yesterdays. I will not. I was born a *creator* not a parrot."[42] Richard Halliburton followed precisely the same arc of ambition, exuberant performance, and diminishing spiritual returns. By 1936 it was clear to him that his book sales and lecture draw were down and that "much of the joyous wonder" had gone out of his writing. "It would have gone out anyway," he wrote to his mother in October, "because I am older and less astonished and amused by what I see."[43] Still, he too was haunted by his "yesterdays" and driven to top these exploits with a final daring raid. The local news story that Williams sent to his grandmother with the subhead "County turns off water" was indeed grotesquely humorous and wholly in keeping with the cartoon persona that Halliburton had succeeded in creating.

The truest line that Williams wrote in homage to Lindsay was the poet's valediction to his wife Elizabeth: "A poet dies two deaths. He dies the death of his genius: that's the hard one, the hard one comes first."[44] Williams certainly knew this truth at the end of his own life, when the "whomped up" myth of Tennessee Williams had lost its power to protect him from the "machinery" of Broadway. But he also knew it at the outset, in 1939, when he magically wrote "Tennessee Williams" and indentured himself to a "bulldog battle" with his own "crazy blue devil" and with those of the culture. He could not have failed to see that Lindsay and Halliburton had endured a demeaning exposure in marketing their books and in holding the attention of a capricious mass audience.

No literary text, their consecutive experience seemed to say, could pretend to claim authority. Their words instead required incessant annotation, with "trick entrances and exits," and in Halliburton's case, simulations of death through deeds of mock valor. Williams endured precisely the same exposure, and although he would mildly echo Artaud in describing the "benevolent anarchy"[45] of art, he too was often a complaisant performer in the marketplace of signs. I am still intrigued by a prognostic hypothetical scene in which Tennessee Williams, "sun-drenched and serene" at Laguna Beach, and feeling himself "a perfect young animal" (May 25, 1939),[46] saw the concrete box high above the bay and intuitively adopted it as a defensive emblem of his own career. A year later he reverted to a similar constructional metaphor in a letter to his friend Joe Hazan:

> We are clutching at hard, firm things that will hold us up, the few eternal values which we are able to grasp in this welter of broken pieces, wreckage, that floats on the surface of life. Yes, it is possible, I think, to surround one's self with stone pillars that

hold the roof off your head. It takes time to build them, time and careful selection of materials, infinite patience, endurance. We must make a religion of that last thing—endurance.[47]

"On the Road: Becoming Tennessee Williams," by Albert J. Devlin, from MAGICAL MUSE: MILLENIAL ESSAYS ON TENNESSEE WILLIAMS ed. Ralph Voss (UAP 2002). Reprinted by permission of The University of Alabama Press.

Bibliographical Note: quotations from Williams' published correspondence follow the text of *The Selected Letters of Tennessee Williams, Volume I: 1920-1945*. Unpublished letters are identified parenthetically by date and provenance. Quotations from *The Notebooks of Tennessee Williams* are also dated and identified parenthetically in the text.

" <u>Battle of Angels</u> turned out badly

but who knows whether the next one

by the same author may not prove
"
a success.

BATTLE IN BOSTON: TENNESSEE WILLIAMS' FIRST PROFESSIONAL PRODUCTION

Claudia Wilsch Case

The Theatre Guild's staging of *Battle of Angels* in 1940 marked Williams' first professional production, and the process of working with the Guild played a major role in his development as a writer. The process of producing a play for the commercial theater introduced Williams to the conflict between artistic ambitions and financial considerations, an issue he would deal with for the rest of his career.

Founded shortly after World War I when melodramas, farces, and revues were the standard Broadway fare, the Theatre Guild set out to present sophisticated, intellectual plays to subscription audiences in New York and quickly expanded this effort throughout the United States. The Guild's early productions met with critical acclaim as well as commercial success, and the organization soon developed into one of America's most important theatrical producers, presenting both European and American plays and nurturing young American dramatists.

The Theatre Guild was initially directed by six people, several of whom had been part of the Washington Square Players in the prewar years: playwright and attorney Lawrence Langner; actress Helen Westley; designer Lee Simonson; director Philip Moeller; writer and critic Theresa Helburn; and banker Maurice Wertheim.

This board of directors guided the company's aesthetic for two decades, after which its leadership passed exclusively into the hands of Langner and Helburn.

During the Guild's early years, its directors were particularly drawn to European drama, which, as a result of America's isolationist stance at the time, had been neglected (or heavily adapted and Americanized) by most other New York producers. The Theatre Guild's first seasons featured Spanish, Irish, Russian, British, Hungarian, French, German, Czech, and Norwegian plays, some of them innovative in content or form, such as George Bernard Shaw's *Heartbreak House* (1920), Georg Kaiser's *From Morn to Midnight* (1922), or Karel Čapek's *R.U.R.* (1922). A production of Elmer Rice's *The Adding Machine* in 1923 was a notable exception to the company's emphasis on foreign works. Although the Theatre Guild would eventually become known as a strong advocate of American playwriting, its directors were at first hesitant to take a chance on staging American work because they supposedly felt that, with few exceptions, America had not yet produced talented playwrights whose craft could measure up to that of European dramatists. There was also a financial incentive, since the young company's limited resources dictated that all early productions had to "open cold," without benefit of the out-of-town tryouts that prepared previously unproduced works for commercially successful New York runs.[1] Thus, the Theatre Guild initially looked to European plays that had already proven their theatrical potential. Shaw's work, for instance, quickly became a staple of the Guild's early seasons.[2] As Lawrence Langner points out, by presenting "the important plays of European authors," the directors hoped "to set a standard for American writers."[3]

The Theatre Guild's initial preference for European drama drew criticism from the press, yet that phase was short-lived. As early as the mid-1920s, the organization, now more stable financially, began holding playwriting classes and competitions and started to focus on staging the work of American authors. In the mid-to-late 1920s, the Theatre Guild produced plays such as Sidney Howard's *They Knew What They Wanted* (1924), and Du Bose and Dorothy Heyward's *Porgy* (1927). By the end of the decade, the company had forged a bond with the already established Eugene O'Neill, staging his *Marco Millions* and *Strange Interlude* in 1928, and for the rest of his life producing all of his full-length New York premieres. The Guild continued to emphasize American drama in the 1930s and 1940s, staging a wide selection of works by O'Neill, Behrman, Philip Barry, Maxwell Anderson, Robert E. Sherwood, and William Saroyan, as well as single plays by such writers as Lynn Riggs, Dawn Powell, Ben Hecht, and Sophie Treadwell.[4]

In late 1939, after they had officially taken over the leadership of the Theatre Guild, Lawrence Langner and Theresa Helburn discovered Tennessee Williams through the Guild's play reader, John Gassner. Williams' agent, Audrey Wood, had sent Gassner some of her client's work and obtained a scholarship for Williams at the playwriting seminar that Gassner and Helburn were running at the New School for Social Research. Before considering *Battle of Angels* in early 1940, Gassner had seen manuscripts of *Fugitive Kind*, *Spring Storm*, and three one-act plays under the collective title *American Blues*.[5] The first two are full-length plays set, respectively, in the Mississippi Delta and in St. Louis. Williams had won a special prize in a Group Theatre playwriting contest with the latter collection of short plays, but while Harold Clurman and his collaborators liked Williams' work and were reading *Battle of Angels*, Williams suspected that his latest play, since it was "not laden with social significance," would not be right for the Group. Instead, Williams felt that *Battle of Angels* was "Commercial!" with a "Capital 'C' as in CASH!" and urged Wood to send a copy of the play to the Theatre Guild, since he deemed the company a "good producer who is not afraid of strong stuff" and was clearly drawn to its reputation for making a profit with artistically ambitious work.[6] Impressed with Williams' writing, John Gassner convinced Langner and Helburn to consider *Battle of Angels* for production. In their work with American authors, the Theatre Guild's producers often adopted the roles of dramaturgs, guiding new plays through revisions to ready them for the stage. Williams was happy but surprised when Langner and Helburn took out an option on *Battle of Angels*, since he did not consider his 1939 version of the play "a final draft."[7] The producers, however, were fully aware that the work would need "some rewriting" to "straighten out its defects."[8] Although he was resistant to some of the Guild's suggestions, Williams, hopeful of persuading such a prestigious theater to commit to a production, rewrote the script during much of 1940. In the process of revising *Battle of Angels*, he tailored the play to the Guild's requirements, drastically restructuring the plot, and his efforts resulted in a production at the end of the year.[9]

Battle of Angels tells the story of Val Xavier, a young vagabond torn between sexual and intellectual longings, who arrives in a small Southern town and finds work in a store owned by Myra Torrance, a disillusioned woman trapped in an unfortunate marriage. While working for Myra, Val befriends Vee Talbott, a religious fanatic and painter who is married to the sheriff. He also attracts the attention of Cassandra Whiteside, a wealthy drifter. A stranger who associates with social outcasts, Val soon provokes the ire of the townspeople. When Myra's husband Jabe finds out that Myra and Val have been having an affair, he shoots Myra, but blames her death on Val, who is subsequently killed by a mob.

Cassandra, who is shunned because of her eccentric behavior, public drinking, and sexual promiscuity, recognizes in the roving Val the same passionate nature and disregard for convention that have made her a social pariah. She points out to Val that they are alike: "You—savage. And me—aristocrat. Both of us things whose license has been revoked in the civilized world. Both of us equally damned and for the same good reason. Because we both want freedom."[10] She also sees Myra as part of this group of exiles, warning her, "They've passed a law against passion. Our license has been revoked. We have to give it up or else be ostracized by Memphis society. Jackson and Vicksburg, too. Whoever has too much passion, we're going to be burned like witches because we know too much."[11] Ultimately, Cassandra's prophecy that those who do not conform must suffer proves true, as these three outcasts die at the hands of the intolerant community.

Val's journey echoes that of Christ. As the action unfolds against the backdrop of Easter week, Val is persecuted, betrayed, and dies a martyr, thus reenacting the biblical passion. Reinforcing this motif, Vee experiences the suffering of Val/Jesus viscerally and physically.

On Good Friday her palms are "inflamed" and show "red marks" that signify the wounds of Christ on the cross.[12] In the past Vee has had visions of the twelve apostles and is now expecting a vision of Jesus. As Williams suggests in his script, however, the spiritual nature of Vee's revelations is questionable. Members of the community have noted that each of the apostles Vee has painted "looks like some man around Two River County," and Val has pointed out the phallic nature of the red church steeple in one of Vee's paintings.[13] When Vee experiences her vision of Christ and paints a picture of the face that has appeared to her, the townspeople, and even Vee herself, quickly recognize it not as Jesus' but as Val's.[14] Vee's claim that Jesus/Val touched her bosom when he appeared to her only feeds the ridicule to which Vee is subjected.[15] The exposure of Vee's religious experience as a manifestation of her sexual imagination points to Williams' idea that "intense religiosity and hysterical sexuality" can coexist "in one person," a view he likely adopted from D. H. Lawrence, to whom Williams dedicated *Battle of Angels*.[16]

According to Williams, the play's title implies the "struggle" between the "desires of the flesh and the spirit," a conflict he expresses in his depictions of both Vee and Val.[17] Myra, who married Jabe not out of affection, but out of necessity after her lover David "married into the Delta Planters' Bank," is involved in a struggle of her own between her thirst for life and her husband's oppression of her desires.[18] When *Battle of Angels* opens, Jabe is on his deathbed; Myra, who has been unhappy and "barren" in her marriage, revives as Val enters the scene.[19] In a symbolic revolt against Jabe, Myra redecorates her store's confectionery "to achieve a striking effect of an orchard in full bloom."[20] Another sign of Myra's regeneration is her pregnancy, which she announces by establishing a connection to nature; Myra compares herself to a fig tree she had in her garden as a child, a tree which, after many years of bearing no fruit, unexpectedly produced figs one spring. However, her resurgence comes to an abrupt end when Jabe descends from his sickbed, enters the confectionery, and discovers his wife's affair. Val's phrase, "Death's in the orchard," evokes Jabe's stifling effect on Myra's newfound vitality and foretells Jabe's eventual murder of her, a killing he will blame on Val.[21]

In Williams' initial version of the script, which he submitted to Audrey Wood as a draft in late 1939, Acts One and Two are set in Myra's store, and Myra's death marks the end of Act Two. Act Three takes place in Vee's home which is connected to the town's jail, and ends with Val's killing. In the last scene of the original script, Vee visits Val in prison after he has been arrested for Myra's murder. In hopes that she will help him escape from jail, Val uses the opportunity to charm Vee, insisting that they both have "visions" and that "fate brought us together." Drawing parallels between Vee, the artist, and himself, an aspiring writer, Val manipulates her to open his cell door.[22] After Val repeatedly demands, "Unlock—the door—Vee," she breaks down and exclaims, "Oh, Val—I want love…"[23] But by the time Vee manages to set Val free, a mob with burning torches has arrived on the scene, and Val realizes he has no way out. In a sacrificial manner, Val "retreats back into the cell and flattens himself against the back wall—arms outstretched as though pinioned or nailed to a cross."[24]

While Williams valued the spiritual and sexual connection he saw between Val and Vee, the Theatre Guild feared that *Battle of Angels*, with its two strong female protagonists, lacked dramaturgical focus. As Williams told his mother, Theresa Helburn suggested so many changes that "his original script was covered with red ink."[25] In consultation with Williams in April 1940, Helburn and Langner argued that "the play lost unity after the second act, since the emphasis shifts from Myra to Vee," and cautioned, "the play is practically over when Myra is killed."[26] To bring the third act together with the rest of the play and to shift its focus towards Myra—as well as to save money on sets—Helburn proposed that Williams cut the scene of Vee painting her vision in her living room and transfer the jailhouse scene to Myra's store. With those changes, Helburn hoped the play would "retain the presence of Myra at least in spirit to the very end."[27]

But Williams initially resisted the Guild's suggestion to assign greater importance to Myra's part in the play. For him the connection between Vee and Val was a crucial element of *Battle of Angels*, as was "the 'locked door' theme" that illustrates the relationship of these characters in his early version of the script. Williams argued that "one of most powerful things in the play is [Val's] passionate exhortation to Vee to release him by unlocking the door, which is a symbol of her own dammed-up passion," and he also saw Vee's opening of the prison door as a symbol of her "power to set Val free." Williams feared that these symbols would be diluted should he follow the Guild's advice and have Val locked up in the store instead of the jail.[28] In the end, the Guild's producers succeeded in persuading Williams to confine the action of his play to one locale. Although he had difficulty letting go of the prison setting, Williams reasoned, "I am not going to be obstinate about a thing like this with a possible production by the Theatre Guild impinging upon it," and declared, "I shall make every human effort to transfer the action to the store without sacrificing anything essential or making the whole thing implausible or false."[29]

A few weeks after Williams had agreed to adjust the setting of *Battle of Angels*, the Theatre Guild, now preparing to cast the play, made further demands for revision. Helburn and Langner, who had previously expressed their reservations about the Val/Vee plot and their desire to see Myra's part enlarged, now asked Williams to keep Myra alive until the end of the play. While the request grew out of the producers' original concern that the play lost focus after the second act, it was also strongly motivated by Langner and Helburn's hope to attract a star to the role of Myra, specifically Joan Crawford, an actress Williams did not admire. In a letter to his grandparents, he told of "many stormy sessions" at the Guild offices where Helburn and Langner asked him to make "some changes I didn't approve." Williams complained, "They want everything to be subordinated to [Crawford's] part," and acutely sensed the tension between his own concern for "[preserving] the artistic value of the play" and the profit-oriented goals of the Theatre Guild's producers, who had reportedly told him it was "possible to make a fortune touring on the road with a big movie star, and of course the film sale might be something colossal."[30] Williams, who had early on touted *Battle of Angels* for its commercial potential, now wrote to his mother, "You would think the Theatre Guild would be interested primarily in an artistic production. But no! They are really commercial at heart." He courageously asserted, "I am determined, however, not to cheapen the play, as my reputation is more important right now than making quick money."[31]

Ultimately, however, Williams did make compromises to prepare *Battle of Angels* for a Theatre Guild production. Before he went to Provincetown for the summer, Williams spent some time working on the play at Lawrence Langner's Westport, Connecticut, home where he made "many radical changes such as eliminating the whole third act and writing a new first scene."[32] By composing an introductory scene showing Val's arrival at Myra's store and by cutting the third act, Williams enlarged Myra's importance and put Myra and Val's relationship at the center of the plot. As a result of these changes, Williams abandoned his exploration of Val's relationship with Vee and relegated Vee to a secondary role. The revised version of *Battle of Angels* ends with a mob setting fire to the store and with the sacrifice of Myra, Val, and Cassandra among flames, as Vee mourns the scene of their deaths. Although Williams was initially reluctant to restructure the play as drastically as the Guild's producers had requested, he never reversed these changes in any of his later versions. Both the 1945 published text of *Battle of Angels* and the 1957 play *Orpheus Descending* primarily focus on Myra (the character of Lady in *Orpheus*) and end with her death.[33]

With the desired script changes in place by the late summer of 1940, the Theatre Guild began planning its production of *Battle of Angels*. After Joan Crawford had dismissed the part as "low and common," the Guild considered Katharine Cornell, Tallulah Bankhead, and Miriam Hopkins for the role of Myra.[34] By fall, Helburn and Langner had gotten Hopkins interested in starring in *Battle of Angels*.[35] After spending seven years in Hollywood, the actress hoped that the play would mark her return to the Broadway stage and decided to invest her own money in the production.[36] Williams was pleased with the Guild's choice; upon seeing Hopkins perform in another play, he supposedly pondered, "Now here is a woman who could take my frequently over-written speeches and match them with an emotional opulence of her own that would make them not only natural but tremendously moving as well!"[37] With Hopkins confirmed for the role of Myra, and with Margaret Webster directing the production, rehearsals began on December 3, 1940, albeit with an incomplete cast.[38] Finding actors for the other leads who, according to Williams, "seemed anything better than arbitrarily thrust into the parts," had turned out to be difficult, and the casting process became chaotic when performers were added to and fired from the show as late as mid-December.[39] In a letter to his family, Williams outlined the complications of finding a leading man, stating that Hopkins "won't have anybody not attractive to her and is very hard to please."[40] Eventually, the Guild settled on Wesley Addy for the role of Val. Miriam Hopkins not only influenced the casting, but also kept asking Williams and the Guild for changes in the script that would result in an even greater focus on the character of Myra.[41]

As the company was scrambling to get *Battle of Angels* into opening-night shape, Langner and Helburn cancelled the play's New Haven performances, scheduled to begin on December 27, and decided to open the play three days later in Boston instead.[42] Even a December 30 opening, however, meant that *Battle of Angels* would not get much more than two weeks of rehearsal with a complete cast. As produced in Boston, the play ended with an onstage fire that consumes Myra, Val, and Cassandra. Williams planted hints at Val's almost paranoid fear of fire throughout the 1939 version of the script and the promptbook, and it comes as no surprise that Val perishes amidst flames. Having been told that Val has robbed the store and killed Myra, a mob arrives with torches and throws them through the windows of the store, where Val, Myra, and Cassandra are trapped. In a ritualistic spectacle, the town's three "prodigals" die together.[43] Cassandra, clairvoyant like her Greek namesake, had prophesied that she, Val, and Myra would be killed because they understand that the "passion" of their bodies signifies the "freedom" of their spirits.[44]

As they die, a "tragic purgation" takes place which, according to Cassandra, enables them "to be free of the flesh that confused our purpose."[45] As a religious metaphor, the scene suggests the biblical image of the deaths of Jesus and the two thieves on the cross. Vee enters, and, "with her arms upraised in a gesture of grief and adoration, she stumbles and kneels at the foot of the stairs," resembling the biblical Mary who kneels before the cross. The "white brilliance" that "floods down upon her face from above" signifies a divine light that brings about the purification of Myra, Val, and Cassandra.[46] Williams intended for the deaths by fire to symbolize the liberation of his characters from the worldly obsessions of the flesh.

At the premiere, however, the desired effect of "the all-important scene," which, in the author's view, "lifted the play to katharsis," was drowned out by the elements of production.[47] After the fire effects had failed during the one-and-only Boston dress rehearsal, Margaret Webster had encouraged the stagehands to augment the pyrotechnics for the opening. As Williams reports, this proved to be a fatal mistake:

> [On] opening night when it came time for the store to burn down it was like the burning of Rome. Great sulphurous billows rolled chokingly onto the stage and coiled over the foot-lights. To an already antagonistic audience this was sufficient to excite something in the way of pandemonium. Outraged squawks, gabbling, spluttering spread through all the front rows of the theater. Nothing that happened on the stage from then on was of any importance. Indeed the scene was nearly eclipsed by the fumes. Voices were lost in the banging up of seats as the front rows were evacuated.[48]

If the audience was horrified, the Boston reviewers were not pleased with *Battle of Angels*, either. While critics praised the acting of Miriam Hopkins, the direction of Margaret Webster, and the expressionistic set design of Cleon Throckmorton, few had kind words for the play itself.[49] The reviewer for the *Boston Transcript* described *Battle of Angels* as "a stumbling pointless affair…that loses itself in deeper and deeper obscurity," and the *Boston Globe's* critic deemed the play an "embarrassment" for the actors who appeared in it, proposing that it "gives the audience a sensation of having been dunked in mire."[50] Even years later, George Jean Nathan dismissed *Battle* as "a cheap sex shocker."[51] Although the play's "symbolic implications" were lost on most reviewers, a couple of Boston critics recognized Williams' raw genius, proposing it might be harnessed as the author acquired greater technical skill.[52] "Given a few years in the theater," Elinor Hughes noted in the *Boston Herald*, "and Tennessee Williams should add craftsmanship to imagination and produce important work."[53] In a similar fashion, Elliot Norton commented in the *Boston Post*, "If he can learn to walk with the theater's craftsmen, he may find himself riding the clouds with the theater's dramatists. His talent is most interesting."[54] In retrospect, puritanical Boston was not the ideal place to open an untried play that frankly examines delicate issues of sexuality and religion, but neither Williams nor the Theatre Guild suspected at the time that *Battle of Angels* "might be attacked on grounds of morality."[55] In preparation for the Boston run and the customary scrutiny of script and production by the local censor's office, Webster had compiled a list of "Censorable Lines" and had asked Helburn and Langner to let her know "which of these lines should be cut or altered ahead of the Boston dress rehearsal, and which should remain until actual objections may be raised by the authorities."[56] The lines in question were mainly characterized by profane and sexually suggestive language, but there is no evidence that the Theatre Guild actually eliminated any of them prior to the first Boston performance. Helburn and Langner's lack of concern seemed to be justified, since the censors, so eager to ban the Guild's production of Eugene O'Neill's *Strange Interlude* a decade earlier, were conspicuously absent from Boston's Wilbur Theatre at the opening of *Battle of Angels*. That occurrence led a *New York World-Telegram* reporter to speculate whether the city might have changed its morals:

> What's all this nonsense about a "squeamish" Boston? Don't give it another thought. Days when the censors up that way and Broadway showfolk fought over censorship seem to be over. The authorities of that city had plenty of opportunity to look at the Miriam Hopkins play, *Battle of Angels*, which is a play about sex with a capital S, before permitting it to come there—and didn't even seem shocked when they read the script.[57]

Yet Boston had not changed as much as it first appeared. Once *Battle of Angels* had opened, the play attracted the attention of Boston's City Council. Based on reports from enraged spectators that "a picture of Christ was being torn up," a Council member who had himself not seen the play described *Battle of Angels* as "putrid," suggested that "the production should be closed," and recommended that "the police should arrest the persons responsible for bringing shows of that type to Boston." As a result, a week after the opening Boston's City Censor John Spencer sent Police Commissioner Timilty and a mayoral aide to the Wilbur Theatre to investigate the play.[58]

In the version that had premiered in Boston, Vee leaves her painting of Jesus at the store, and Myra, who jealously realizes that Vee's sexual interest in Val must have led her to paint him as Jesus, "smashes the canvas stretcher over her knee and stuffs the picture into the stove's red belly."[59] It was this part of the performance that upset some members of the audience, who, as a sympathetic reporter carefully framed it, did not necessarily understand that it was not actually a painting of Jesus, but "a portrait of another character in the drama," that was being destroyed.[60]

By the time the censor's office decided to examine *Battle of Angels*, Williams, Webster, Helburn, and Langner had already left Boston, and the show's stage manager, John Haggott, was left in charge of the production. In anticipation of the censors' visit, he took steps to modify the treatment of Vee's painting onstage, including having Miriam Hopkins' character put Vee's painting "in a closet" instead of tearing it up.[61] This change, however, was not enough to satisfy the censors, who were not only concerned with the complaint that had launched the investigation, but also took issue with Williams' blunt discussions of sexuality. After witnessing the performance, Timilty and his colleague classified *Battle of Angels* as "a play about cheap, white trash," finding many of its lines "indecent and improper," "lascivious and immoral," and were scandalized by the "double meaning" of some of Val's and Myra's speeches.[62]

For the production to remain on the boards, the censors ordered modifications and deletions of several lines, including Myra's comment to Val, "I can feel the weight of your body bearing me backwards," and demanded that two entire scenes be cut.[63] One of the passages in question was the "bayou scene" in act one of the promptbook in which Val tells of his first sexual experience with a Cajun girl, a part of the plot that is crucial to the understanding of Val's character as being torn between physical and spiritual pursuits.[64] The other scene to which the censors objected shows

Myra in Act Three bursting forth with resentment for her dying husband Jabe and admitting to him that she committed adultery and is carrying Val's child.[65] The latter passage is important because it conveys the symbolic difference between Jabe, who represents death, and Val, who represents life, to Myra. Additional changes made for the January 7 performance included the substitution of Vee's painting with one that clearly did not depict Jesus, as well as the cutting of "all references to [the] deity and Christ," and "to [the] stigmatae" on Vee's hands.[66] Williams "was completely taken by surprise and greatly shaken" when he learned about the censorship investigation. "It seemed to me," he declared, according to Webster, "that if *Battle of Angels* was nothing else, it was certainly clean, it was certainly idealistic."[67] Miriam Hopkins publicly defended *Battle of Angels* against the censors' accusation that it was "a dirty play," insisting, "That's an insult to the fine young man who wrote it." She argued, "The dirt is something in the minds of some of the people who have seen it. They read meanings into it according to their own suppressed feelings."[68]

Despite Williams' shocked reaction and Hopkins' defiant stance, the Theatre Guild, probably trying to avoid more negative publicity and the financial setbacks that come with a show closing before the end of its scheduled run, did not fight back. The Boston papers reported that the producers "agreed to make the changes" requested by the censors.[69] Although those changes were drastic and cut away passages that conveyed important themes of the play, John Haggott stated publicly that the censors found "nothing particularly objectionable" and announced, "We may have to alter a few lines, but there will be no important changes."[70] When Margaret Webster returned to Boston from a lecture assignment in Minnesota, she reportedly "found a castrated and largely incomprehensible edition of the play dying an inevitable death at the Wilbur Theatre."[71] In the end, however, it was not the Boston censors' investigation of the play's morally offensive content, but the Theatre Guild's own reservations about Williams' abilities as a playwright that shut down *Battle of Angels*. As early as January 2, 1941, three days after the play opened and long before the censors ever visited the Wilbur Theatre, the Guild's producers had come to the decision that *Battle of Angels* would have to close for revisions at the end of its scheduled two-week Boston engagement.[72] Still a relatively inexperienced writer, Williams, who later pondered he might have "fooled" the Theatre Guild in the beginning into believing he was "an accomplished playwright," ultimately could not meet the company's expectation to revise *Battle of Angels* while the play was running, and became defensive to save face.[73] His various tactics were avoidance, as expressed in "his routine of lying down on the nearest suitable piece of furniture, putting his feet up on the cushions and closing his eyes" whenever he was asked to make changes during rehearsals, or flat-out denial.[74] During an emergency meeting after the show's disastrous opening, Williams reportedly told the producers and cast, "I put it down this-a way, and that's the only way I know how to put it down."[75] As Webster points out, "We were deceived by the maturity of the play into misjudging the immaturity of the author," and it soon became clear that Williams would have to "get away" for a while in order to accomplish the necessary rewrites.[76]

The Theatre Guild initially postponed, then cancelled the Washington, D.C., engagement that was supposed to follow the play's Boston showing and abandoned the planned Broadway run. In a letter sent to the Guild's Boston subscribers and published in the *Boston Herald* on January 26, Langner and Helburn outlined their "reasons for producing the play" and apologized to audiences for the "disappointment" that *Battle of Angels* had been. While they considered Williams a writer with "genuine poetic gifts and an interesting insight into a particular American scene" and defended his depiction of Vee's "religious obsession" as "a sincere and honest attempt to present a true psychological picture" that did not warrant the censors' intervention, they admitted that *Battle of Angels* "did not come off successfully in dramatic terms."

True to their mission to support new American playwriting, the producers suggested that "we should be able to expect our members to be indulgent towards an occasional experimental play and even bear with its failure, since it is only by this experimentation that we can feed new authors into the American theater." And indeed, their speculation, contained in the letter's closing comments, "*The Battle of Angels* [sic] turned out badly but who knows whether the next one by the same author may not prove a success," would turn out to be an accurate prognosis.[77] With the Theatre Guild's financial support, Williams rewrote *Battle of Angels* in the spring of 1941 in Florida, creating the manuscript that would become the 1945 published version of the play. He framed his revision with a prologue and an epilogue, adjusted the characterizations of his protagonists, added a few minor characters to the plot, among them two African-Americans who lent a social and political dimension to the play, and devised an ending that omitted the problematic fire effects by having Val lynched offstage. However, when Williams submitted his revised play to the Theatre Guild in the spring of 1941, Lawrence Langner, who had contemplated a new production at his Westport Country Playhouse and had stored the Boston scenery there, expressed his dissatisfaction with the work.[78] Yet, Langner promised Williams as late as 1945 that the Guild would restage *Battle of Angels* if Williams rewrote it further, a promise that by this time only amused Williams, considering his difficulties with the Theatre Guild production, and given the success he had known in the meantime with *The Glass Menagerie*.[79] After his experience with *Battle of Angels*, Williams did not trust the Theatre Guild again with new plays. While he praised the Guild's "idealism" in staging *Battle*, he nevertheless complained, offhandedly in an interview in the *The New York Times*, that the Guild had "messed up" his first professional production.[80, 81]

A previous version of this essay was published as "Inventing Tennessee Williams: The Theatre Guild and His First Professional Production" in the *Tennessee Williams Annual Review* 8 (2006). Reprinted courtesy of the *Tennessee Williams Annual Review*.

"
The play leaves you in the air.

"

But I like this air. It is rare, rich.

RESCUING THE GLASS MENAGERIE

David Kaplan

The dedicated advocacy of two theater critics in Chicago, Claudia Cassidy and Ashton Stevens, changed the reputation of Tennessee Williams forever. At the end of 1944 and on into the spring of 1945, as the Allied forces were pressing toward Berlin to end World War II in Europe, Cassidy, who wrote for the *Chicago Tribune,* and Stevens, who wrote for the *Chicago Herald-American*, joined forces to rescue the endangered first production of *The Glass Menagerie* from collapsing at the Chicago box office. Their efforts were successful: the production did more than survive, it triumphed in Chicago and consequently made its way to Broadway. Critics are often remembered for their witty put-downs. These two, Stevens and Cassidy, should be remembered for the power of their writing to defend and champion what they recognized before others: "the courage of true poetry couched in colloquial prose" of Tennessee Williams' writing for the stage.

Claudia Cassidy, forty-four years old in 1944, red-haired, short, and with a widely-recognized mean streak, was no pushover, and no fool. She earned her nickname "Acidy Cassidy." When Cassidy retired as a critic from the *Chicago Tribune* in 1965, *Time* magazine headlined the story, "Exit of the Executioner."[1]

Miss Cassidy began writing music criticism in the 1920s for the *Chicago Journal of Commerce* when a desperate editor tapped her, the new office secretary fresh from the University of Illinois, for a review of some concert. They took music seriously in the days of Al Capone. She was immediately popular with readers and her subsequent columns of theater and music criticism helped increase subscriptions. In 1940 she accepted an offer from the department store heir Marshall Field III to move to the newspaper he was founding, the *Chicago Sun*. A year later she left the *Sun* for the better-paying *Tribune*, whose circulation, according to *Time* magazine, which ran a national story about Miss Cassidy's rising career, was 1,150,000 readers. The *Boston Globe*, for comparison's sake, had a subscription base of 353,000 for its Sunday edition, the *Chicago Sun* 310,000, the *Chicago Journal of Commerce* 21,000.[2]

By December 1944, Claudia Cassidy reigned over Chicago's music, dance, and theater in her weekly column titled "On the Aisle." She was aware of her power and used it. She could coin a memorable putdown. "What 'Sleep No More' needs is its own potion," she'd written that October. Just before Christmas she went to previews of a new play whose chief interest, for most of her *Tribune* readers, would be the return of the actress Laurette Taylor after a long absence from the Chicago stage. Taylor was beloved for playing the title role, thirty-two years before, in the long-running Broadway hit, *Peg o' My Heart*. A silent version of the play, filmed in 1922, cemented Laurette Taylor's fame as Peg, a poor Irish orphan who inherits a fortune, though she'd rather be happy than rich.

Claudia Cassidy's first review of *The Glass Menagerie* on December 27, 1944, helped set in motion the rest of Tennessee Williams' life:

FRAGILE DRAMA HOLDS THEATER IN TIGHT SPELL
"The Glass Menagerie."

Staged by Eddie Dowling and Margo Jones, with setting and lighting by Jo Mielziner, costumes by Brooks, music by Paul Bowles. Supervised by Alex Yokel and presented by Mr. Dowling and Louis J. Singer at the Civic Theater Tuesday evening, December 26, 1944

THE CAST

The Mother	Laurette Taylor
The Son	Eddie Dowling
Her Daughter	Julie Haydon
The Gentleman Caller	Anthony Ross

Too many theatrical bubbles burst in the blowing, but *The Glass Menagerie* holds in its shadowed fragility the stamina of success. This brand new play, which turned the Civic theater into a place of steadily increasing enchantment last night, is still fluid with change, but it is vividly written, and in the main superbly acted. Paradoxically, it is a dream in the dusk and a tough little play that knows people and how they tick. Etched in the shadows of a man's memory, it comes alive in theater terms of words, motion, lighting, and music. If it is your play, as it is mine, it reaches out tentacles, first tentative, then gripping, and you are caught in its spell

Tennessee Williams, who wrote it, has been unbelievably lucky. His play, which might have been smashed by the insensitive or botched by the fatuous, has fallen into expert hands. He found Eddie Dowling, who liked it enough to fight for it, Jo Mielziner, who devoted his first time out of army service to lighting it magnificently. He found other people, too, but ah, that Laurette Taylor!

****

I never saw Miss Taylor as Peg, but if that was the role of her youth, this is the role of her maturity. As a draggled southern belle who married the wrong man, living in a near-tenement, alienating her children by her nagging fight to shove them up to her pathetically remembered gentility, she gives a magnificent performance. The crest of her career in the delta was the simultaneous arrival of 17 gentlemen callers, and her pitiful quest in this play—as often funny as sad—is the acquisition of just one gentleman caller for her neurotically shy daughter, the crippled girl played by Julie Haydon. Her preparations for that creature, once she has heckled her son into inviting him, his arrival in the hilarious extrovert played by Anthony Ross, and the aftermath of frustration—these are not things quickly told in their true terms. They are theater, and they take seeing.

Fortunately, I have been able to hang around the Civic at previews and I have seen *The Glass Menagerie* twice. Mr. Dowling was good last night in the double role of the son and narrator [who says the first narrator was the angel of the annunciation?], but he is twice as good as that when he is relaxed and easy. He had strokes of brilliance last night, but the long easy stride of his earlier performance is on a plane with Miss Taylor's playing and gives the play greater strength.

Mr. Ross enters late, but leaves an impression as unforgettable as his green coat and his face, which is perilously close to being a mug. Late of *Winged Victory*, this stalwart actor does a superb job as the gentleman caller who finds his visit a little more than he had bargained for.

Which leaves only Julie Haydon and there, frankly, I'm puzzled. At times she has the frailty of the glass animals of the title which are her refuge from reality. But I couldn't quite believe her and my sympathy went to her nagging mother and her frustrated brother—because whatever the writing, acting is the final word, and they acted circles around her.

The morning after the play opened, anyone in Chicago reading this review in the *Herald* would have woken up with a temperature of seven degrees below zero outside to the front page headline: "CITY SNUGGLES AGAINST LAKE AS BLIZZARD HOWLS." The *Chicago Herald-American*, a Hearst-owned tabloid, reported eight people had frozen to death in a nearby suburb. Snow and ice continued for days, excuses for ticket buyers to stay home rather than go see a new play outside the Loop, where most plays were shown. The first week of *The Glass Menagerie*'s paid performances, gross sales were too small to keep the production running for long. It looked like the play would close without coming to New York.

Then, and not by accident, an audience started to build. Slowly the nine hundred pink velvet seats of the Civic Theater began to fill with theatergoers curious to know what all the fuss was about. Along with the *Chicago Herald-American*'s Ashton Stevens, Cassidy kept up a steady rain of articles over the next twelve weeks, sometimes mentioning the play several times in one week, in order to try and keep the production alive.

Four days after the play opened, in her overview of the entire year she wrote: "On top of 1944's basket is *The Glass Menagerie*, brand new and worth treasuring. More about this fascinating play later, but in the meantime don't neglect it. It is a beautiful piece of work, absorbing, amusing, and stimulating."

She cleverly found excuses to bring up *The Glass Menagerie* in her columns. These included her lunch with the producer, letters she'd received about the play, phone calls she'd received about the play and, four weeks after the play opened, an interview with Mr. Williams. Later published under the title "The Author Tells Why it is Called the Glass Menagerie," but in "On the Aisle":

"Alley Cats and Glass Animals"

Do you mind knowing that "The Glass Menagerie" is in part autobiographical, or did you know that all the time? Perhaps you would like to know Tennessee Williams' own explanation of the title of his play, now established as what amounts to a national success at the Civic Theater.

As others did, Cassidy described Laurette Taylor as the genius behind the success of the play, but she made a point of giving credit to the playwright. In her January 7 "On the Aisle" column:

I doubt that any one will say *The Glass Menagerie* is pretty good, or not bad, or so so, or any of the other terms of mild disparagement. If you like this play, you love it–and maybe it works the other way around, too. I wouldn't know. I saw it three times in three days, and will be going back, which is risky business in the realm of make believe. But it is an honest, tender, tough, and, to me, brilliant play. The brief prologue warns you it isn't realistic. Maybe not. But it is deeply etched as a sudden stab of memory, as poignant in detail as a dream. It knows people. Some of its dialog haunts you. Taylor at the telephone in gallant attempt to prepare for the gentleman caller by snaring magazine subscriptions from bored acquaintances in the D.A.R. That terrifying description of the genteel spinster, "a birdlike little woman without a nest." The brief, searing sentences, that like so much of tragedy, cling to the precipice of comedy, so that some of the saddest people are the most endearingly ludicrous. This man Williams can write, sharply, revealingly in the vernacular, and if what he writes sometimes soars in the dusk like Mielziner's alley lighting, you yourself have helped it take flight. Theater is a two sides of the footlights business.

Cassidy's sustained support of the play was a rare thing for her, as she herself wrote:

> Things like this remind you sharply how much of your life you spend in the dreary treadmill of inertia that is the theater's and music's second best. It's harder to accept the shoddy substitute after your eyes and ears have had such rich reminders of the real thing.

On January 8 she reported that the box office had doubled, that movie director Otto Preminger had offered to buy the property for Gary Cooper, though Dowling, as stage producer, had refused. She wrote on January 14 about writing herself "blue in the face," when the phone rang and a woman asked her about the play, saying she hadn't seen a thing about it. Cassidy did have limits: she pulled away from the use of a quote in an advertisement for the play, taken from a letter she had reprinted, attributing to her, not the letter, that the play was "the greatest to come to Chicago." On the next day, though, the *Tribune* ran two more stories mentioning *The Glass Menagerie* approvingly, including the interview, "Alley Cats and Glass Animals." Throughout February, she repeated gossip about the show's planned move to New York.

She wrote about what other critics had to say about the show, including Ashton Stevens, who claimed in his *Chicago Herald-American* column that the play could have been performed in a barn and still it would have worked.

Ashton Stevens—tall, elegant, and bespectacled—was seventy-three years old when *The Glass Menagerie* opened in Chicago. He had been writing drama criticism for Hearst newspapers since 1894, when he was twenty-two, first in San Francisco, then in New York, then for forty years in Chicago. He had interviewed Sarah Bernhardt and Ethel Barrymore—and had offered them advice. Orson Welles (whose guardian was personal friends with Ashton Stevens) is said to have taken Mr. Stevens as the model of the newspaper critic in *Citizen Kane*, who loses his job by writing a review critical of the publisher's wife.

In his column called "Excursions in Stageland," Stevens shared gossip from—and about—his show business connections, which were many. In 1944 his former assistant, with the memorable name of Alex Yokel, worked as general manager for Eddie Dowling, the star and producer of *The Glass Menagerie*. Two days before the play opened, Stevens relayed to his readers Yokel's 2:00 A.M. note written during a coffee break as *The Glass Menagerie* scenery was being brought into the Civic Theater by twenty-two stagehands. A show typically used one control panel for the lights, but Jo Mielziner, the lighting designer, was having seven panels installed. Yokel praises the actors' hard work and finishes up:

> But just like any manager with his own dough in the show, I've forgotten to tell you, Ashton, anything about the script. *The Glass Menagerie* is a fantasy working concurrently with the present and the memory of the past. It has a mood like no other piece of my experience, because that's the way that sad-looking little guy Tennessee Williams writes. His words are warm, and I think you will find that they thrill with hidden poetry.

Three days later, on December 27, 1944, Stevens' review appeared in the *Chicago Herald-American*, balancing accolades for Laurette Taylor with a prescient acknowledgement of Tennessee Williams' talent and his future.

GREAT ACTRESS PROVES IT IN FINE PLAY

It would be very easy to say that in last evening's premiere of Tennessee Williams' *The Glass Menagerie* at the Civic Theater, Laurette Taylor submitted as distinguished an achievement in acting as has been offered to American playgoers since Eleanora Duse gave them her last performances on this planet. So why not say it? As the burbling, down-at-the-heels mother of Eddie Dowling's worker and dreamer in a warehouse, and Julie Haydon's shy, lovelorn, and crippled moonbeam of a daughter, Miss Taylor, in a role which might have been named Fallen Grandeur, reached the peak of a theatrical career that, despite interruptions and indolences, has been going only upward for as much of the current century as has been crossed off the calendar.

In a beautiful and mystically vivid play, whose setting and lighting by Jo Mielziner is a new note in the poetics of the modern stagery, Laurette Taylor vouchsafes a characterization that is more than beautiful. It removed this first-nighter so far from this earth that the return to mundane desk and typewriter finds him unaccustomedly dizzy in the head, to say nothing of the heart. Fifty years of first-nighting have provided him with very few jolts so miraculously electrical as the jolt Laurette Taylor gave him last night.

Lovely, Original

Whether Mr. Williams' play is as undebatably great as Miss Taylor's performance, I have my just doubts. But it is a lovely thing, and an original thing. It has the courage of true poetry couched in colloquial prose. It is eerie and earthy in the same breath. It is never glossy and glittering and Broadwise. Its unforced wit is as pure as its understated pathos. It glows most humanly in a sustained atmosphere of other-worldliness.

How much of it is symbolism I do not know, nor seem to care to know. You might call it a series of dramatic sketches, each one prefaced, as was the Moscow Art Theater's *The Brothers Karamazov*, by an always enlightening and sometimes ironical narrator. Only here the narrator is also one of the principal characters—in fact Mr. Dowling, who not only acts the youthful, restless visionary son as no lad of half his years could hope to act him, but has directed (together with Margo Jones) the presentation with a sensitiveness and appreciation such as perhaps only the author fully realizes.

Telling Character

Sometimes hidden, sometimes revealed, is the love story of the crippled daughter, superbly played by Miss Haydon. It comes to realization when her brother brings home from the warehouse the gusty rough fellow his sister had secretly loved at school. Anthony Ross gives him lusty identity. He is—to go back a quarter of a century for the name—a budding Babbitt, but with a friendliness as contagious as his self-confidence. He cheers the girl, breaks her painful silences, dances her to the old Victrola records her deserter father left behind, even kisses her.

But his is not the kind of kiss on which romantic curtains commonly crash. He has his own girl, and they are to be June-married; and so he won't come back to this ghostly little alley flat in St. Louis.

And the brother goes, and he won't back to the little flat, either, but will follow the vagrant footsteps of his long-departed father, who is one of the most telling characters in the play, although all you see of him is a the beaming photograph he left behind.

Rare, Rich Air

That's about all there is. There isn't, as Miss Barrymore and her hundred imitators used to say, any more. The burbling mother with her gorgeous imaginotions of southern aristocracy (albeit she married a telephone wireman instead of a cotton planter) and her crippled daughter with her treasured menagerie of miniature glass animals are left there alone, as Life sometime does leave women and the Stage hardly ever.

The play leaves you in the air. But I like this air. It is rare, rich. It is the only air in which a woman so powerfully enchanting as Laurette Taylor's Mother could have her being.

P.S.—From neighboring seats I heard William Saroyan mentioned, and Paul Vincent Carroll, and Sean O'Casey, and even a playwright named Barrie. But the only author's name I could think of was Tennessee Williams, whose magic is all his own.

Stevens' postscript is meant to put Williams in some context: Paul Vincent Carroll was an Irish playwright who wrote plays set in Irish villages. He had won the 1939 Dramatist Critic's Circle Award for *The White Steed*. Barrie is Scottish playwright J. M. Barrie, best known for writing *Peter Pan*. Sean O'Casey, associated with the glory days of Dublin's Abbey Theatre, wrote about Irish tenement life. William Saroyan had won both the Dramatist Critic's Circle Award and the Pulitzer (a first) in 1939 for *The Time of Your Life*, another play with a lower class setting directed by and starring Eddie Dowling,

Stevens mentioned *The Glass Menagerie* in print more than twenty-five times in twelve weeks. Laurette Taylor was his usual hook: Miss Taylor's dinners at restaurants, her hats, how he met her husband thirty years before. Thinking she was single, he had tried to flirt with her. An invented scandal about Taylor uncovering the price of roses doubling for Valentine's Day in Chicago was good for several articles and letters to the editors from protesting florists. His wife helped Miss Taylor pack for New York, which made a story. His March 21 article was headlined "Ashton Stevens Writes Again About Laurette Taylor."

Importantly, Ashton Stevens defended Williams. On December 31, just five days after the opening, he wrote:

"No debate, no drama, and it is very encouraging for the ultimate fate of Tennessee Williams' *The Glass Menagerie* that the critics who attended its premiere at the Civic Theater Tuesday are not agreed on the artistic value of the play, although they chime as one huge uncracked bell for the acting of Laurette Taylor."

He goes on to say that acting makes its impact immediately, but original playwrights need time to be appreciated.

Sometimes authors have a hell of a time getting audiences to look at their stuff from anything like the same point of view in which it was written. There was Ibsen. The ultimate acceptance of Ibsen's point of view is, I should imagine (for there are no statistics at the moment handy) the most painful kick in the seat ever administered to the know-it-alls that nobody loves and who are called drama critics.

And then, speaking for himself, Stevens continues:

But once in a rare break comes something to the theater that is more than show business, that I reach out for with tentacles of appreciation which I had almost forgotten existed. *The Glass Menagerie* sounded little depths in me which seemed to have been sealed. I was literally enchanted....And I hope you will enjoy the same experience at this magically written...adventure in imagination.

Claudia Cassidy wrote that Stevens went so often to *The Glass Menagerie* he was "camping out in the Civic Theater." Stevens mentioned Cassidy's "evenly paced paean" and wrote an article about other critics going to see the play several times. *The New York Times* took notice of what was going on in Chicago and published an article reporting the play's success.

Meanwhile, in New York, George Jean Nathan, the theater critic who had made Eugene O'Neill's reputation twenty years before, was receiving his own private reports from the actress who was playing Laura, Julie Haydon, Nathan's then girlfriend and future wife. Mr.

Nathan was friends with Eddie Dowling, too, who had shown him *The Glass Menagerie* in manuscript. Nathan liked this kind of respectful private solicitation from those he would later write about publicly. While meeting with Dowling, Nathan nixed the idea of the film star Lillian Gish in the role of the mother, though that was the casting Williams favored. Several years before Miss Gish had turned down Mr. Nathan's offer of marriage—one of many he extended to her during the 1920s—after she learned he was secretly Jewish. Mr. Nathan had insisted that information be removed from his authorized biography.

With Julie Haydon, who had replaced Miss Gish in his affections, cast in a plum role for *The Glass Menagerie*, or so it seemed in the manuscript, Mr. Nathan took an interest in what was happening in Chicago. He went so far as to write a drunk scene for Eddie Dowling and Julie Haydon. It was inserted into a performance. Mr. Williams was not amused, and demanded it be cut. Mr. Nathan did not forget this, nor did he quite remember it accurately, either. He was ready with quite a lot to say about Williams when the time came to write about the play, and that would be soon.

On February 18, Claudia Cassidy announced in her column that the play would close in Chicago on March 24, and open in New York a week later, March 31, 1945.

When *The Glass Menagerie* reached Broadway, word on the street was that something special was about to happen. Tickets cost $50 on opening night, though the top on Broadway that year was $6. New York reviews were enthusiastic for the production. In New York, for the most part, Laurette Taylor was credited with the play's success. It was well known she had lost whatever money she had made playing Peg, and lost, too, for ten years, a battle with booze. Most people rooted for her success and sobriety.

On the day of the premiere George Jean Nathan sent Taylor a bottle of scotch.

"Thanks for your confidence in me," Laurette Taylor wrote back to Mr. Nathan—and made sure the story was repeated.

The review published April 4, 1945 in the New York *Journal-American* column, "George Jean Nathan's Theater Week," was topped with a headline in elegant and thin lettering, "Eddie

Dowling Again Proves Faith in a Play." Five out of the column's seven paragraphs discuss what a fine fellow Eddie Dowling had been in producing Tennessee Williams "freakish experiment," "a play no other producer would touch" "deficient in any touches of humor." Dowling, according to Nathan, had taken "the play, which is intrinsically rather less a play than a palette of pastels [and] brushed [it] up into a semblance of one." According to Nathan, "the role of the narrator character, originally the routine wooden compere, has similarly been rewritten into some living plausibility."

Stung, Williams responded:

> —the out and out falsity of the charge that my script has been "rewritten"…has aroused in me a feeling of ire the like of which I cannot recall since that remote day in my childhood when the bully on the block seized my red tissue-paper kite and plunged his fist through it just when I was about to give it the first time to the sky![3]

Williams was dissuaded from mailing his rebuttal, which surely would have been published. It wasn't until 2009 that his rightful anger was set in print in a revised collection of Williams' essays, aptly titled, *Where I Live.*

Ashton Stevens defended Williams against Nathan's claim that Williams had no humor. "He may not have a whit of the wit of a Nathan, but in my humble and grateful opinion he has that deep and self-conscious humor that has been the quicksilver of all true American poetry.…But I'm fighting with Nathan, not against him."[4]

Until he died in 1958 Nathan rarely lost an opportunity to denigrate Williams' writing on grounds of craft or morality. For him, *The Rose Tattoo* was Williams' "latest peep show," *Battle of Angels* "a cheap sex-shocker." The opening (and success) of *A Streetcar Named Desire* brought out this rant from Nathan in the *New York Journal-American*:

> The borderline between the unpleasant and disgusting is…a shadowy one, as inferior playwrights have at times found out to their surprise and grief. Williams has managed to keep his play wholly in hand. But there is, too, a much more shadowy

borderline between the unpleasant and the enlightening, and
Williams has tripped over it, badly. While he has succeeded
in making realistically dramatic such elements as sexual
abnormality, harlotry, perversion, seduction and lunacy, he has
scarcely contrived to distil from them any elevation and purge.
His play as a consequence remains largely a theatrical shocker,
which, while it may shock the emotions of its audience, doesn't
in the slightest shock them into any spiritual education.

For decades Nathan's disgust at "moral degenerates" revealed
a special kind of scorn for homosexuals. He called Noel Coward's
Design for Living "a pansy paraphrase of Candida."[5] He complained
about actors, saying he preferred to watch a world-class boxer rather
than "queers":

> What we need, are more actors like Jack Dempsey, who tried the
> stage a little while ago. Jack may not be much at an actor, but his
> worst enemy certainly cannot accuse him of belonging to the
> court of Titania.[6]

It is best to understand George Jean Nathan's historical importance—
because he was, at one time, important—the way whalebone was
important for making corsets. He used to be taken seriously, and
he deserved to be. He cared passionately about the theater, about its
importance in culture, about its worth as art—and like many people
with a cause they believe in, he did not scruple too much over
the means used to achieve his ends. He championed O'Neill over
melodrama and tripe, but once he had won, and the trash he fought
against vanished, thanks in, part, to his tireless passion, George Jean
Nathan, like the Model T-Ford, became a means to go somewhere
that need no longer be taken—and isn't. By the time he was writing
about Williams, his prissy hypocritical sense of public morality
was expressed in too shrill a manner to win over many readers
and left little impression, even at the time it was first published.
His repugnant adolescent name-calling about homosexuals and
lesbians, however, gave later drama critics an unfortunate idea of
what was acceptable to say on the subject.

As to the charge that *The Glass Menagerie* was composed by a committee, Williams did not need to send his rebuttal. Others, Laurette Taylor among them, took the time to refute Nathan's ludicrous and inaccurate accusation that Dowling had written any part of *The Glass Menagerie*.

Fortunately for Williams, Mr. Nathan resigned from the New York Drama Critics' Circle in 1944. In April 1945, the remaining critics, from fourteen different newspapers and magazines, voted to award *The Glass Menagerie* as the best play of the 1944–45 season. Lewis Nichols, who was chief drama critic for *The New York Times* that year,[7] voted for *I Remember Mama*. In his *Times* review two weeks before, Nichols liked the production of *The Glass Menagerie*, but considered the play little more than a vehicle for Laurette Taylor. The Pulitzer Prize that year went to Mary Chase's play *Harvey*, best known today as the basis for the 1950 movie with Jimmy Stewart as a man with an invisible rabbit for a friend.

Laurette Taylor passed away nearly two years into the Broadway run, on December 7, 1946. In a memorial to his leading lady, Williams wrote:

> The last word that I received from her was a telegram which reached me early this fall. It was immediately after the road company of our play had opened in Pittsburgh. The notices spoke warmly of Pauline Lord's performance in the part of Amanda. "I have just read the Pittsburgh notices," Laurette wired me. "What did I tell you, my boy? You don't need me."

At the time of Laurette Taylor's death, Mr. Nathan, characteristically, wrote an article in which he said Taylor's success in the role of Amanda was due to her chucking what Williams had written for her and making up fresh lines in performance. There is no way to verify this—and it's a winning bet she did improvise— but the play has lived on well past whatever improvisations it may have had in performance: Williams carefully corrected the text for publication, including the excision of a curtain line that Dowling used to slip into his performance: "Here's where my memory stops and your imagination begins." The play has lived on past

Mr. Nathan's evaluation of it, along with his dismissal of Beckett's *Waiting for Godot* as "the little play that wasn't there" and Thornton Wilder's *Our Town* as "more of a theatrical stunt than a play."

Nathan wrote well: there will always be advocates for his writing, and apologists for his ugliness, just as there will always be Charleston enthusiasts. He died in 1958, and is perhaps best known—without being known—for the satirical portrait based on him played by George Sanders in the Joseph L. Mankiewicz film *All About Eve* (1950). There, as the theater critic Addison DeWitt, he offers caustic advice, and squires a much younger Marilyn Monroe, much as Nathan is supposed to have done with Julie Haydon who was twenty-two years his junior.

Ashton Stevens died in 1951 at the age of seventy-eight, with obituaries calling him, "the Dean of the country's play reviewers," and noting he had been one of the first banjo enthusiasts "writing the Encyclopedia Britannica's article on the subject" according to *The New York Times*. His paper, the *Chicago-American,* was bought by the rival *Tribune,* renamed *Chicago's American* in 1956, and then called *Chicago Today* until it went out of business in 1974.

Claudia Cassidy lived a long time. In 1982, when she was eighty-two years old, the last play by Williams to be performed during his life, *A House Not Meant to Stand,* was playing at the Goodman Theatre in Chicago. Cassidy broadcast a radio review on WFMT:

> If we take the term in the sense of the mysterious, the grotesque, and the desolate, then *A House Not Meant to Stand* is a gothic structure, and southern Gothic at that. But it is Tennessee Williams' Southern gothic and it is shrewd as well as bitter, acidly funny as well as sad . . . a rotting house pictured in the playbill as on the edge of an abyss, a kind of metaphor for the human condition inside.
>
> It is indeed mysterious, grotesque, and desolate but whoever said that theater is none of those things? There is here the acute compassion Tennessee Williams has always had for the victims of the world we live in.

She died in 1996 at the age of ninety-seven. Her husband, to whom she had been married for fifty-seven years, passed away four years before and she had secluded herself in Chicago's aristocratic Drake Hotel, no longer going out in public. She'd seen enough.

Claudia Cassidy and Ashton Stevens' efforts were heroic. They were the first critics to champion Tennessee Williams and help him build a reputation as an unusual talent, someone and something worth paying attention to, someone exceptional. Williams began writing *A Streetcar Named Desire*, his next play for Broadway, while he was in Chicago, and toyed with setting it in Chicago, too, but eventually decided upon New Orleans. The Broadway producer of *Streetcar* also decided against an out of town tryout in the Windy City. "Until New York is satiated, Chicago starves," wrote Cassidy.

" On and on the audience applauded,

"

yelled, stomped, and cheered.

A NIGHT TO GO DOWN IN HISTORY:
THE PREMIERE OF A STREETCAR NAMED DESIRE

Sam Staggs

The night is December 3, 1947, and the final curtain has just dropped at the Ethel Barrymore Theatre on Forty-seventh Street. For a long moment Irene Selznick, seated not down front but at her impromptu command station in the last row on the side aisle, does not breathe. The silence in the theater clangs in her ears. Has she descended into the breathless darkness of a tomb, that grave of failed dramas?

Tennessee Williams, far from her in his orchestra seat, could use another drink. How many hours has it been? He does not regard his mother and his younger brother, Dakin. They are seated with him, but they bring no comfort as he faces the gallows.

Suddenly his pulse leaps. The audience has burst from its silent spell. The noise it's making is greater than applause—a chain of rolling thunderclaps. Then every person in the house stands up.

"In those days people stood only for the national anthem," said Irene Selznick. Certainly a standing ovation was not the cheap reflex it now is. The curtain rose again and the cast bowed. The roar grew louder as shouts overlapped manic clapping. On and on the audience applauded, yelled, stomped, and cheered. Jessica Tandy, Brando, Kim Hunter, and Karl Malden came on again, then the remaining cast members. All went off, expecting the house to quiet, but it did not, nor did the raucous accolades subside until the cast came back for another bow and another and—twelve curtain calls.

Then the audience began to chant, "Author! Author!" Having already made his way backstage, Tennessee Williams emerged from the wings and shambled downstage center as the cast moved aside and joined in the applause for him. He gave a few choppy bows, though not toward the audience. In his daze he bowed to the actors instead. Everyone in the theater loved him even more for his shyness and befuddlement.

Brooks Atkinson, principal drama critic for *The New York Times* and *ipso facto* Broadway's most important opinion giver, missed not only Blanche's "kindness of strangers," but also the ovation, the curtain calls, everything that stamped "bravo" onto an evening of brilliance. For he had a deadline. Sometime during the final half-hour he slipped out of his seat and back to his office a few blocks away, where he wrote a review that is still remembered.

Though not especially memorable. It reads like a quickie, which it was, for Atkinson had little more than an hour to write it. Nor is it a rave, though it's highly favorable. The review begins, "Tennessee Williams has brought us a superb drama." In the next sentence he cites Jessica Tandy's "superb performance," and from that point relies on flat reviewer words such as "limpid," "sensitive," "luminous," and "revealing."

More intriguing than Atkinson's review is his departure from the theater before play's end. When I questioned Frank Rich, a recent theater critic at *The New York Times*, he said, "This was entirely routine practice at the time. Until the late 1970s, when the extended preview system began, critics attended opening nights against tight deadlines and frequently departed en masse before the show ended. Luckily, this barbaric system was kaput when I began as *Times* theater critic."

I wondered how the playwright and others in the production tolerated the custom. "I doubt that Williams, et. al., even thought of being angry about the critics' departure to meet their deadlines," Rich said. "Strange as it seems now, plays were expected then to be covered (by newspapers anyway) as if they were breaking news stories. In all my readings of Broadway history, I never found any account of anyone protesting."

Back at the Ethel Barrymore, exhilaration and fatigue. It's not surprising, really, that no one connected with the production wrote more than scant details about opening night. For one thing, not one of them could gad about the theater observing from various points of view. Cast members, confined backstage and onstage, must concentrate only on performance. Selznick and Williams, overloaded, recalled opening night as a blur. Even Kazan, always in control, was overcome. In his autobiography, which stops just short of a thousand pages, he devoted a single paragraph to December 3, 1947: "My mother and father came to the opening night in New York, heard the cries of 'Author! Author!' and saw Tennessee hustle onstage with his campy shuffle. I was in the darkest upstage corner of the stage house and had tears in my eyes: exhaustion and relief. I listened to it all as if it were happening to other people. I was told that after many curtain calls for Williams, a few people called for me. I didn't respond, but I did wonder if my father had heard." (Kazan felt that his father undervalued him and his accomplishments.)

An assortment of other relatives also attended opening night. Mr. and Mrs. Marlon Brando Sr. were in the audience; Hume Cronyn; Mona Malden, wife of Karl; David O. Selznick. ("Did you expect me to stay away?" he asked his estranged wife. Her reply, years later in her autobiography: "I didn't want him at the opening.")

Days earlier, Mrs. Selznick decided that an opening-night party thrown by her would be "too splashy." From a businesswoman's point of view, however, she did not want to offend those who wished to attend—they had been asking her, "Should we make plans?"—but who weren't invited. She found a sly solution.

George Cukor gave the party. He was to be her escort for the evening, so she asked him to come East a few days early. She said, "I informed him that he was giving a party at '21' and all the arrangements were up to him. He'd get the credit and I'd get the bill." Thus, anyone omitted could put the blame on George.

Dakin Williams said, many years later, that he, Tennessee, and their mother were silent in the cab most of the way from the theater to "21." (The silence could not have been prolonged, however; it's a five-block ride.) Then, according to him, Tennessee said, "What do you think is going to happen?" The flamboyant younger brother, hero of his own anecdotes, says that he replied, "Well, I think we've got another hit." (Spoken like an investor in the show, which he was not.) Dakin now claims he brought along a Catholic priest who was called on to read the reviews. This bizarre detail was not confirmed by anyone else present. If it is true, however, the irony is exquisite. And execrable, considering how the Roman Catholic Church hounded Tennessee's work, causing great damage a few years later to Kazan's film version of *Streetcar*. (In the 1983 biography of Tennessee that Dakin wrote with Shepherd Mead, the playwright's brother omits the priest and has Kazan reading the reviews.)

Although the after-theater party was all that such events should be, members of the company had trouble unwinding. Having spent two tense months in rehearsals and tryouts, followed by this grueling performance, they must now relearn the lost technique of relaxation. Only when early editions of the newspapers appeared did the room fill with gaiety.

Tennessee wandered among the guests, accepting congratulations. But there came a moment later on when he found himself temporarily alone and as always his thoughts turned inward and his eyes gazed far away. Then someone appeared at his elbow and said, "Tenn, are you really happy?" It was Audrey Wood.

"Of course I am," Williams replied in surprise.

"Are you a completely fulfilled young man?" she asked sternly.

"Completely," said Williams. "Why do you ask?"

Miss Wood looked at him searchingly. "I just wanted to hear you say it," she said.

Audrey Wood knew him well. She asked that question—"Are you a completely fulfilled young man?"—as if to ward off future harm that she sensed might come to him from the world and from himself. No doubt she guessed also that it would be extremely difficult, even for Tennessee Williams, ever to surpass the art of *A Streetcar Named Desire*.

Even before the newspapers arrived at "21"—the *Times*, the *Post*, the *Herald Tribune*, the *Daily News*, the *World-Telegram*, the *Journal-American*—Irene Selznick's press agent had phoned with the good news. The predictions had come true: *Streetcar* was a hit, a smash. Finally, after so much tension, excitement, relief, Selznick began to give way. "I could scarcely read Brooks Atkinson for the tears," she said. "Oh, how I wept. I embraced everyone right and left. I wanted the evening never to end."

It ended very late, but the production went on for two years and two weeks; that is, until December 17, 1949, for a total of 855 performances, making it the longest original run of any Williams play. Although Irene Selznick didn't say it that night, she has the last word on December 3, 1947: "What I couldn't have foreseen even at that moment of glory was that the play would completely alter the lives of its four leads. Indeed, it fixed the pattern of mine and made Gadge a king. Most suitably, it gave Tennessee enduring glory."

This chapter is an excerpt from Chapter 10 of Sam Staggs' *When Blanche Met Brando: The Scandalous Story of "A Streetcar Named Desire."* New York: St. Martin's Press, 2005. Reprinted courtesy of the author.

Editor Note: [Elia Kazan] proved to be just what The Group [Theatre] had long needed—someone willing to do the scut work the rest of the company disdained. People started calling him by his Yale nickname, "Gadget," because he was such a handy little human tool to have around. It was a name he came to detest—even in its shortened form, "Gadge," by which only his oldest and closest friends dared address him in his later years. From Richard Schickel, *Elia Kazan: A Biography.* New York: HarperCollins, 2005, 21-22.

"
You are not a finished dramatist

although I do say I think you are
"
highly promising.

AUDREY WOOD AND TENNESSEE WILLIAMS: A REVEALING CORRESPONDENCE

Albert J. Devlin

One of Williams' longest and most revealing correspondences was with his agent Audrey Wood. Their productive relationship lasted for thirty-one years, beginning in 1939 when Williams was a seldom-published writer, and ending in 1971 when his career had faltered with a string of personal and artistic failures. Both have told the story of their nasty parting scene—he in 1975 in *Memoirs*, she in 1981 in an autobiography entitled *Represented by Audrey Wood* (and published shortly after her death). Their notorious and regrettable breakup is not my subject, although the letters that I shall cite give essential foreground to its peculiar dynamics. My purpose instead is to begin an inventory of the correspondence in order to understand better the role that letters may have played in forming and sustaining Tennessee Williams' far-flung literary life.

Generally, Williams' correspondence slackened after 1955, but sources reveal that author and agent corresponded well into the 1960s. While Williams' nomadic life insured that many recipient letters were not kept, Audrey Wood was a cautious businesswoman who seems to have copied every word that she wrote to the mercurial Williams, and to have filed his own letters as well. The Liebling-Wood collection of letters at the Harry Ransom Center tells a story of literary self-discovery and creation that Tennessee Williams recorded with unusual candor and entrepreneurial skill.

By the end of 1939, the astute literary agent must have realized the complexity of her recent discovery. In early April, in his first known letter to "Miss Wood" Williams confessed, "My personal affairs are in quite a muddle just now," and he went on to express an eagerness to "jump into the arms of any agent who could assure me the quick sale of anything—even my soul to the devil!" (April 10, 1939). He was frustrated in part by repeated failure to breach the "fortress" of *Story* magazine, which he knew to be a distinguished market for experimental fiction. By late April, Williams and Wood had agreed to terms of agency, and Williams' letters from Southern California continued the lifelong process of mythologizing his personal "muddle." To Audrey Wood, in New York City, these first letters may have seemed to arrive from the back of the American cultural beyond, or so Williams hoped to suggest. They spoke of his descent from "Indian-fighting Tennessee pioneers" (May 5, 1939), his relentless travel in the South and West in the preceding months, comic misadventures on a chicken ranch in California, a myriad of casual jobs, and always his poverty. "Do literary agents dispense any advice about feeding small chickens," he asked facetiously in June, after reporting that some of "the poor little bastards" under his care "had starved or foundered themselves!" (June 1939). Audrey Wood had been warned in effect that representing "Tennessee" Williams (as he had now called himself for six months) would exceed mere literary agency. His creativity, she realized no doubt, would often be self-absorbed, and she would be called upon to assist in its painful exercises and rehearsals. She then answered, setting the tone for their relationship: "One of my virtues, unfortunately, is extreme honesty and I cannot at this point promise you any kind of a quick sale on anything....You are not a finished dramatist although I do say I think you are highly promising" (April 28, 1939).

When Williams wrote to Audrey of his literary plans in 1939, they came with a pent-up rush. In closely succeeding letters, he cited "two long plays in progress" (May 5, 1939) and proposed writing others about the wandering poet Vachel Lindsay, "D. H.

Lawrence's life in New Mexico," "writers fired off the WPA" (July 16, 1939), and a "fugitive from life" (July 30, 1939) named Jonathan Melrose, who was a prototype for Val Xavier and later Chance Wayne. In addition, he was writing new sketches for the American Blues "gallery," and he had "several ideas for short novels" tucked away, never a favorite genre of Williams, as well as "a great mass" of verse (July 16, 1939). Wood tried to moderate this excess, if only by delaying judgment of new ideas and scripts—many unsalable to her practiced eye, and only of passing interest to Williams. But the profusion itself was another manifestation of "muddle" and it implicitly defined Tennessee Williams as "that most common American phenomenon, the rootless, wandering writer,"[1] peddling his vast store of experience. Tennessee Williams *was* Kilroy, the ubiquitous American wartime graffito, well before he wrote about him in *Camino Real* (1953).

There is a familiar overreaching in the scope of Williams' plan. The play about Vachel Lindsay eventuated only in an unpublished fragment of homage entitled "Suitable Entrances to Springfield or Heaven."[2] But Vachel Lindsay's "struggle" to maintain artistic purity and reserve was an inspiring model for Williams, who knew well (underlined by a father's harsh pressure) the artist's vulnerability in a "capitalist state."

In the following summer, he secluded himself at Acapulco and drafted a "serious comedy" entitled *Stairs to the Roof* that was a scathing indictment of the "economic tyranny" of the time. Tennessee Williams, a spiritual southerner, had come under the sway of a literary nationalism peculiar to the 1930s. In this early key, his was a native American voice of protest straining to be heard above the moral and economic din of the republic. Soon Williams would confirm this prophetic identity in several important letters to his friend Joe Hazan, but already its outline must have been clear to Audrey Wood, who with equal bravery took up its service.

In June 1939 Williams began a letter to Audrey by excusing her delay in answering a letter of his: "Your 'long delay in answering my long descriptive letter concerning myself' is perfectly understandable. Perhaps you have known enough writers (I have) not to be too surprised when they show an unusual propensity for talking about themselves." Williams continued then to talk about himself, and in ways that further embellished his precarious literary life. "Since I am now living in a lonely canyon with a minimum of social intercourse I see no promise of checking that tendancy [sic] in myself, as letters are just about my only means of advertising my ego at the present time." It was in this same letter, mailed from "a little cabin" in "'Bootleg Canyon,'" near Laguna Beach, that Williams had first described the Vachel Lindsay project, claiming in effect his own desolating "personal experiences" as authority for a play idea that he found "very hard to dismiss" (June 1939).

As Williams was putting the finishing touches on his lonely outpost, he was also writing to his mother in St. Louis as a dutiful son of the middle border. No isolation or anxious leisure, no febrile "advertising" of the artistic ego, no poverty occasioned by "economic tyranny" were broached to Edwina at this time. She was treated instead to a sunny tour, as should all mothers be. The cabin described to Wood as a remote and lonely "shack" (June 1939) was equipped now with a congenial roommate, Jim Parrott, and was "marvelously comfortable and attractive." Laguna Beach itself was located on a bay surrounded by beautiful wooded hills," Williams said in his best tourist style, and there were "endless places to visit and things to see!" His writing, he claimed, had prospered in this Eden, and when actually forced to work, it was with the nonchalance of a lazy southerner: "I work some nights in a bowling alley (setting up pins) and Jim plays Saturday nights in Los Angeles bands[,] so we do some toiling and spinning in return for our magnificant [sic] raiment!" (Summer 1939).

Always an avid player himself, Williams has spoken eloquently of the mystique of theater. Stage characters "do not return our looks," he wrote in 1951: "We do not have to answer their questions nor make any sign of being in company with them, nor do we have to compete with their virtues nor resist their offenses. All at once, for this reason, we are able to *see* them!" ("The Timeless World of a Play"). Letters, I think, give us the same spectatorial advantage and freedom. In the summer of 1939, we can see Williams enacting a self-scripted drama of disclosure and disguise. The interplay of parts, seeming disingenuous, does not, however, warrant a judgment, for no particular virtue or vice exists in his surpassing drama of self-display. He is by turns Tennessee and Tom, to adapt Lyle Leverich's useful typology, and they are not merely the deconstructing bits of an illusory paper author. They are complementary modes of a writer who is evolving from the sinuosities of domestic and artistic emotion. It is a structure that will crop up again and again in letters, but not with more poignance or clarity than in 1954, when Williams asked his publisher, New Directions, to censor the collection entitled *Hard Candy*. "Don't distribute the book any where that my mother would be likely to get her hands on it," he urged Robert MacGregor: "That is, around St. Louis. It must not be displayed in windows or on counters anywhere....My mother's reaction is the only one that concerns me. Isn't it awful to have conventional blood ties? You just can't break them" (May 27, 1954). Letters written to Audrey Wood and Edwina in mid-1939 and, residually, to Bob MacGregor in 1954, allow us to see Williams enacting vivid, authentic roles, rather than mere editorial fictions, in a self-revealing selection of letters. And finally, they reveal the double paradox of his later distinguished career: a personal dynamic of allegiance and resistance to domestic emotion mediated by a commercial stage whose own master discourse was governed by the canons of familial realism.

In their continuing correspondence, Williams averaged nearly twenty-five communications per year with Audrey Wood over the next sixteen years. One prominent effect of these letters (along, of course, with Wood's own letters) is that they characterize Wood almost as fully as they do Tennessee Williams. Above all, she was his primary and most trusted reader for at least the first two decades of their association. "Would you like me to send it to you scene by scene, so that you can criticize it as I go along?" he asked her in 1946, as he began revision either of *A Streetcar Named Desire* or *Summer and Smoke* (simultaneous works-in-progress that are often hard to disentangle in the correspondence). His dependence was still evident in 1950, when he anxiously sought Wood's reaction to *The Rose Tattoo*. "It is totally impossible to judge for yourself" (February 3, 1950), he wrote in defense of his usual impatience. And in 1953, after Wood had shown little enthusiasm for still another revision of *Battle of Angels*, he reassured her that her "reaction to a script means much more to me than anyone else's, including the critics" (October 14, 1953). By the late 1940s, Williams came to suspect that the firm of Liebling-Wood (he considered Wood's husband and partner, William Liebling, to be unduly self-interested) required oversight as managers of his finances. But for another decade, his confidence in Audrey Wood's literary taste and her astute knowledge of Broadway mores did not waver substantially, and thus she was admitted time and again to the most intimate recesses of his literary life.

If the early letters to Audrey Wood allowed Williams to mythologize his personal "muddle," then their ensuing correspondence often helped him to deal with the strain of writing for the commercial theater. In late 1941, in the sobering aftermath of the failure of *Battle of Angels*, Williams described his thin skin while thanking Audrey for a testimonial (from John Tebbel, managing editor of the *American Mercury*) that she had slipped into a recent letter of hers. "I don't believe anyone ever suspects how completely unsure I am of my work and myself and what tortures of self-doubting the doubt of others has always given me" (September 25, 1941). In a following letter, Williams tilted his sensitivity toward stoicism, telling Wood that "I have lived behind the mobile fortress of a deep and tranquil pessimism for so long that I feel almost impregnable" (October 1940). Torture and tranquility, exposure and protection, publicity and reserve, the regularity of the "see-saw" motion (April 3, 1950), as Williams would later describe it to Wood, was already familiar to the agent by 1941. But these and other such letters addressed to Wood were also an occasion for Williams to objectify and adjust his own "precarious balance of nerves" (September 4, 1942) as no other correspondent had allowed to date. She might not be an infallible "Court of Human Relations" (November 5, 1946), as Williams wrote in 1946, but Wood's personal and professional stability and her reserved friendship were crucial elements in Williams' prolonged maturing as a writer. Their sad break in 1971 has a long foreground in the letters, one that begins ironically with the most enduring product of their relationship; the production of *A Streetcar Named Desire* in 1947.

In April 1947 Williams wired Audrey Wood that her choice of Irene Selznick as a relatively untried producer for *Streetcar* "had better be good" (April 8, 1947). It was a warning tinged with comical bravado, but soon Williams' mood had turned serious and he complained to Audrey that his "irreducible rights as an author" were being compromised by a "high-handed" producer. There was a kind of fatality involved, or so he thought: "A play is my life's blood" (August 25, 1947), he protested. By 1947, their relationship was sufficiently weighty and secure to allow such candid exchange, but the more subtle point is the one conveyed by tone. The important letter of August 25 has the clear accent of a progress toward maturity and self-possession. Williams' criticism of "the Selznick company" does not proceed from mere carping or a familiar ease of nerves, but from a conviction that the play in question is special. "I am not going to lose this play because of poor management and I am going to see to it that it is protected in every possible and reasonable way because that is what I have a right to expect as the one who has given most and who has the most at stake." His identification of the play with his "life's blood" might have been written from a residue of Blanche DuBois' own hysteria, but it was delivered to Audrey with measure and precision and emotional reserve. The naïve, accommodating author who had been subject to the whims of producers and directors in the staging of *Battle of Angels* (1940) and *The Glass Menagerie* (1945) was now determined to give his classic work "the maximum protection" (August 25, 1947). Was there not finally an impressive trading or transfer of stability and resolve in the author-agent relationship?

It is not surprising, however, that *Streetcar* was both the vehicle of a great and apparently lasting success and the site of the first serious breach in the author-agent relationship. On December 5, 1948, Williams informed Audrey that he wished his younger brother Dakin to assume oversight of his financial affairs. Dakin had completed a law degree at Washington University in 1942 and had some additional training in business at Harvard. Eddie Colton, the present financial advisor, did not give Williams the "security or understanding" that he required in the flush times following *Streetcar*, especially when Williams contemplated his staggering tax bill for 1948. Dakin's "double check" of Eddie Colton, who had the support of Liebling-Wood, would both protect his financial interests and insulate him from "the business side of life," or so he hoped to persuade Audrey Wood.

On December 9, Williams wrote a two-part letter to Dakin, one with straightforward instructions that he might show to Audrey, the other not for her eyes. In the second, he advised Dakin to practice great "TACT!" in dealing with Audrey when he reached New York City. "I am very, very anxious to have you avoid betraying any sign of any distrust of her handling of my affairs....You must handle her with great tact and diplomacy; a breach in my relations with her would be extremely dangerous and detrimental." Read comparatively, Williams' revealing correspondence with Audrey and Dakin evokes the same feeling of vulnerability as his identification with Vachel Lindsay had produced in a time of obscurity. What has erupted paradoxically as a consequence of success is Williams' awareness of the writer's precarious existence on Broadway and his fear of being silenced. Writing and production were truly his "life's blood," as he had told Audrey, and as he would write to Brooks Atkinson in 1955, after reading his smash review of *Cat on a Hot Tin Roof*. "I love writing too much, and to love anything too much is to feel a terror of loss: it's a kind of madness" (March 25, 1955).

During his prolonged apprenticeship, Williams lived a simple set of alternatives: either succeed as a writer or accept stagnation and defeat in some such unforgiving city as St. Louis. In stories and plays, in letters and journals, and then in the midst of his great success on Broadway, he returned to these alternatives, all the while attempting to master the fear that framed his view of life. Writing and being were inseparable for him, and the urgency of their connection made the familiar Williams "sins" of prevarication, self-aggrandizement, and the breaking of friendships the survival techniques of a desperate man. He voiced precisely this fear of a conspiracy against his work in 1971 in his parting scene with Audrey Wood. "And as for you," she has recalled his shouting, "you have wished I was dead for the last ten years."[3] The neglect that he attributed to her agency in the 1960s was a matter of life and death, as were her power and prestige on Broadway two decades earlier.

Excerpted from "The Selected Letters of Tennessee Williams: Prospects for Research" originally published in *The Tennessee Williams Annual Review*, 1998 (premier issue). Reprinted courtesy of the *Tennessee Williams Annual Review.*

" ... an enormous jumble of five-

cent philosophy, $3.98 words,

ballet, music, symbolism, allegory,

pretentiousness, portentousness,

lackwit humor, existentialism and
"

overall bushwah.

THE WORST PLAY BY THE BEST PLAYWRIGHT

Michael Paller

C amino Real opened at the National Theatre on Broadway on March 19th, 1953. Its reception was divided and intense.[1] The New York Times would later report that four of the local daily critics liked it and four did not, saying, "Many patrons have called it a masterpiece; many others a monstrosity."[2] The review headlines indicated the division: "Symbols Clash in Camino Real" in the Daily News; "Williams' Play Baffling to Some" in the Journal-American; "Camino Real is Pure Emotion" in the World-Telegram; "An Enigma by Tennessee Williams" in the Post; "Camino Real Will Please Some, Anger Others," in the Daily Mirror.[3] Wolcott Gibbs' review in The New Yorker was headlined simply, "Erewhon," the title of Samuel Butler's utopian satire about a mysterious country the name of which, with the w and h reversed, spells "Nowhere" backwards.[4]

None of Williams' previous plays had provoked such violent reactions. Cheryl Crawford, the producer, responded to the negative press with a letter-writing campaign; the play's defenders included the actress Shirley Booth and the poet Dame Edith Sitwell, who wrote:

> I have long thought Mr. Williams a playwright of very great importance. I now believe him to be a very great playwright. I understand that various persons whose spiritual fare is Chu-

Chin-Chow are conspiring to deprive us of this very great play. We have never sought to deprive them of the nonsense they like. Why are people who can see a little deeper to be deprived of a work which throws a blinding light on the whole of our civilization?[5]

The Sunday *Times* ran these and other letters, pro and con, covering a full page on April 5th. Crawford excerpted some of them, positive and negative, in the *Times*' ABC theater listings, hoping that the unfavorable comments would prove as effective come-ons as the favorable ones: "An emotional strip-tease," "Appalled my aunt," and "It's too sexy" vied with, "Must see it for oneself" and "I've been four times."

It didn't help. In the end, the expensive production, with its cast of thirty, eked out sixty performances. To save money at the last few, Crawford cut the confetti the actors threw during the fiesta scene. On the last night, the cast paid for it themselves.[6]

Williams' arrival in the public consciousness in 1945 with *The Glass Menagerie* was a triumph so complete that it overshadowed the failure later that year of *You Touched Me!*, the adaptation he wrote with Donald Windham of a story by D. H. Lawrence. *A Streetcar Named Desire* followed in 1947. It was a bigger hit than *Menagerie* and won Williams his first Pulitzer Prize. *Summer and Smoke* followed in 1948 and *The Rose Tattoo* in 1950. Both received mixed reviews and lost the bulk of their investments for their producers. Still, in 1953, Williams was regarded as America's leading playwright, rivaled only by Arthur Miller. Even the relative disappointments of *Summer and Smoke* and *The Rose Tattoo* hadn't hurt him. *Camino Real* was his first significant Broadway failure. Revivals in the 1970s and 1990s have restored some of its luster, but it has never established itself among the Williams plays that are consistently revived, although its size has something to do with this. Actors, directors and audiences still argue over its merits and disagree about them with as much passion as they did in 1953. Why did the production fail to find an audience then? What damage, if any, did it do to Williams' career?

Camino Real was a point of departure for Tennessee Williams. He had rarely been a practitioner of one might call material realism, the default style of American theater in which a play and its characters look, sound and behave like the surface of everyday life, but his rejection of it in the plays that had been produced in New York was more in terms of language and stagecraft than dramaturgy. Few if any characters in American plays prior to *The Glass Menagerie* sounded like Williams' characters, whose language was poetic and heightened yet based in reality: audiences had no trouble believing in characters who spoke like that. His emphasis on "plastic theater" had been realized in large part by Jo Mielziner's set designs for *The Glass Menagerie* and *A Streetcar Named Desire* in diaphanous, dissolving drops and flats and in the use of sound effects. The worlds of these plays were rooted in specific times and locales and realistic enough for audiences to imagine themselves in them. *Camino Real* was different.

It had its origins in a solitary, hallucinatory train trip that Williams took to Mexico in 1945. Running a slight fever from a mild case of dysentery, he watched the people and landscape glide by, and images of Marguerite Gautier, Kilroy, and others presented themselves in a shifting dreamscape that was part music, part painting, all movement. He wrote in his journal,

> …a world of pawn-shops on Rampart Street, jitney dance halls …all the vivid, one-dimensional clowneries and heroisms of the nickel comic and adventure strips, celebrated in the raw colors of childhood's spectrum…Here is the new congruity of incongruities which is the root of the power in modern art, the dramatic juxtaposition of the crude and the tender, the poetic and the brutish. Yes, it could be done with paint. But with language? In some of Hart Crane, yes! But how about a play?
>
> Possibly. Yes, possibly. But not a play that is conceived just as spoken drama. It would have to be a play whose values are mainly plastic, a play that is less written than painted.[7]

The first result was a one-act called *Ten Blocks on the Camino Real*, in which a former boxer with a bad heart named Kilroy finds himself, he knows not how, in an "ostensibly…small tropical port of the Americas," from which there is no escape. [8] He meets the broke, forlorn historical figure Jacques Casanova who vainly loves the fictional Marguerite Gautier. He attempts to seduce a gypsy's daughter, appears to die, and then pawns his heart for a mass of silver and gold trinkets. Rejected by Esmeralda, he leaves with the fictional Don Quixote for a destination unknown.

Williams published the play in 1948 as part of the one-act collection, *American Blues*. The following year, Elia Kazan used it as the basis of some exercises at the Actors Studio, and invited Williams to see the result. Inspired by what he saw and urged on by Kazan, Williams agreed to expand the one-act into a full-length play while at the same time plans were made to produce *Ten Blocks* on a bill with another one-act, *27 Wagons Full of Cotton*. The double bill wasn't realized, and for the next three years, the full-length version of *Camino Real* was Williams' major project.

It has become something of a commonplace to say that *Camino Real* was a play ahead of its time. Its mixture of time periods and mingling of historical figures, original characters and those borrowed from literature in an indeterminate time and place was something the Broadway audience hadn't seen before.[9] Revivals in the 1970s and '90s were more successful, and the play deemed more worthy, after two decades of post-modern experimentalism in the theater and other arts had made the play comprehensible. This most "plastic" of plays, however, also might have been better received earlier in the twentieth century, in the 1920s or '30s, when the American theater had its first serious affair with various forms of non-material realism: O'Neill's experiments in a variety of plays from *The Emperor Jones* through *Strange Interlude*, the expressionism of *The Adding Machine* and *Machinal*, and the Elizabethan- and Greek-inspired *Our Town* all created an environment in which such styles of writing and production could be understood and appreciated alongside typical Broadway comedies, musicals, and melodramas.

When *Camino* opened in 1953, however, material realism was at one of its high-water marks and commercial theater at its most conservative. The audiences who came to its out-of-town tryouts in New Haven and Philadelphia likely would have felt more at home at the competition: the more traditional *I am a Camera* and *My 3 Angels*, which were also trying out, or *The Fourposter* which was touring in the midst of a successful Broadway run. However, even had audiences been more accustomed to the thorough-going experimentation of *Camino Real*, the play's critical and financial success—and Williams' own success in presenting so personal a vision in such an idiosyncratic language—would have been far from guaranteed.

II.

From the start, Williams and his collaborators had difficulty agreeing on what the play was about. Early in February 1952, Williams had written Crawford that the play was "essentially a plastic poem on the romantic attitude toward life."[10] In June after much courting, Kazan signed on to direct, and began a series of letters to Williams asking for guidance on the play's themes. In July, Williams responded that the play was "a poetic search for a way to live romantically, with 'honor', in our times, royally under real conditions."[11] He was hesitant to be any more specific about its meaning: "There is very deeply and earnestly an affirmative sort of mysticism in this work and I want that to stand," as opposed, he wrote, to the kind of "hot light" clarity that Crawford, he said, preferred in her productions.[12]

Kazan, though, was in need of some sort of clarity, hot or otherwise, to stage the play in such a way that Williams' themes could be understood or at least intuited by an audience. By the end of July he suggested that perhaps the play asked, "How to die with dignity and honor and gallantry?"[13] In mid-November, he was still uncertain of what Williams wanted to say, and was concerned that the play had dueling themes. It began, he wrote, with a "social" theme having to do with the exploitation of the queer and powerless by the powerful. As the play went on, however, that theme faded, replaced by another, "universal" one asking, "How do we die?" How, he wondered, did these ideas fit together?[14] Years later, he wrote that Williams told him that the play was "the story of everyone's life after he has gone through the razzle-dazzle of his youth. Time is short, baby, it betrays us as we betray each other. Work! That's all there is!… There is terror and mystery on one side, honor and tenderness on the other." Williams also told him that the play was "an encomium, despite all else, to the enduring gallantry of the human spirit."[15]

While it was in its Philadelphia tryout, Williams told the *Saturday Review* that *Camino* was "a prayer for the wild of heart kept in cages…it is merely a picture of the state of the romantic nonconformist in modern society. It stresses honor and man's own sense of inner dignity which the Bohemian must reachieve after every period of degradation he is bound to run into. The romantic should have the spirit of anarchy and not let the world drag him down to its level." He added to this rephrased version of a romantic attitude toward life a contemporary political theme: "Each time I return [to America] I sense a further reduction in human liberties, which I guess is reflected in revisions to the play." Seeing, however, that audiences were finding the play confusing, he also hedged: "Now if *Camino Real* purported to deliver a message, I would have to be clearer, but it doesn't, and I don't think the people who find it confusing in its present form would like it any better if it were clarified."[16]

Kazan's second concern was that the play's themes, whatever they were, be expressed through action, not just words. Throughout their pre-rehearsal correspondence, Kazan worried that the play had two separate lines of action that ran parallel rather than intersecting and affecting each other. First, there was the Kilroy plotline, second, that of the Romantic characters, Marguerite Gautier, Jacques Casanova and Lord Byron. Their story interrupted Kilroy's for long stretches, while he disappeared from the play for most of its middle third. In July, he wrote Williams that Williams' agent Audrey Wood, Crawford and Jo Meilziner, their first choice to design the show, were confused by the lack of the plots' integration.

In a long letter on November 17, Kazan repeated his request for clarity and a single, unified theme by integrating Kilroy, who was still absent through most of the middle of the play, thoroughly into the action. He suggested, for example, that Kilroy say the forbidden word *Hermano* rather than give it to the Dreamer, a character who struck Kazan as too symbolic, and he urged Williams to express his themes through characters who acted on what they desired in the face of the obstacles put in their paths. Otherwise, he warned, the play risked bewildering, annoying, and frustrating the audience. On an ominous note, he asked again who were the play's many characters and what were they doing on the Camino Real?[17] A similar appeal followed on December 10, in which he warned Williams about the need for a "coherent" first act and the danger of "A thousand-odd people leaving their seats for the intermission not knowing what the hell we brought them to the theater for in the first place."[18] Williams worked hard over the summer and fall of 1952 to answer these questions and to respond to Kazan's numerous suggestions for resolving them, but it wasn't always easy. He alternated between expressions of gratitude and trust and, in the privacy of his journal, annoyance at Kazan's "dictating my work to me." [19] Asking him questions was one thing, providing the answers was another.

As rehearsals neared, Williams himself was feeling uncertain about how audiences would receive the play. On December 3rd he wrote his friend Maria St. Just that he was worried about an upcoming reading for a group of potential backers: "Not many people seem to understand what it's about, and just reading it does very little good as most of its values are so plastic, pictorial and dynamic, that just listening to it or reading it is almost useless unless the listener or reader has a trained theatrical mind."[20]

Rewrites continued through rehearsal, but by the time the company reached New Haven Kazan was still concerned about clarity. He had an assistant circulate during the two intermissions to overhear audience reactions, and his worries were confirmed: they were asking three basic questions about the world of the play and its rules: "Where is this? When is this? How did they get there and where do they want to go even if they don't know where they are?"[21] The audiences were given little help when they read in the program, "The Time And Place: Not Specified." At this point, however, Williams was making no wholesale changes to the script. His revisions were on the rhetorical level: speeches were shortened to point up meaning and eliminate repetition.[22]

The New Haven reviews reflected the audiences' puzzlement. "Williams Play Leaves Audience in a Confused Mood" was the headline over the unsigned review in the *New Haven Register*. Williams, the reviewer wrote, "has leaped whole-hog into unreality," and stressed the play's symbolism, which seemed unmediated by a recognizable reality through which symbols usually worked in the American theater. Kazan had harped on this point: symbols communicate best when they arise out of a reality that the audience can recognize and with which they can identify. Without a mediating reality, the *Register* critic wrote, the result was,

> When [the performance] was over, [the audience] gave willing applause to a series of clever and colorful charades. But few observers seemed actually very certain about what had been spelled out during a long and tense evening on the stage—and Author Williams himself had given them only a few thin clues.[23]

The *Register* and *Variety* critics described a production composed of several impressive disparate elements that were difficult to discuss or describe as a whole, and the latter predicted possibly tough times ahead for the production:

> The fact that it is a severe mental challenge to an audience, in order to wring from its overall content the full import of the substance placed there by its author, indicates that the ultimate reception will be governed by the ratio of playgoers who look for stimulation rather than straight entertainment in their theatrical fare....
>
> Just as certain playgoers enjoyed the brutal overtones of Williams' *Streetcar Named Desire*, and missed the main thread of Blanche's mental deterioration, so will certain onlookers of *Real* enjoy various highlights without full appreciation of the underlying content. [24]

Reactions were only slightly better when the production opened at the Forrest Theatre in Philadelphia on March 3. Confusion and complaints about the "murkiness of the plot"[25] and "unrelated incident"[26] were mixed with admiration for the play's ambition and risk. Unfortunately for Williams and Kazan, it was the confusion that dominated the opening paragraphs of most of the reviews. "Playgoers found themselves more baffled and bewildered than they have been by any stage show seen in this city since the premiere of *The Skin of Our Teeth*," wrote Linton Martin in the *Inquirer*.[27] Wilder's play, however, overcame audiences' initial confusion, ran for ten months and won the Pulitzer Prize. So Williams and Kazan might have gained some hope from a later passage in Martin's review:

> What gives this play its universal appeal is the overall impression that Williams may mean it to say that we are all caught in a cosmic rattrap in an age of violence, and there is no way out, except by the back door of death. However, whatever moral or message may be meant, *Camino Real* is easily the most provocative and controversial play of the season thus far, to be classified technically, perhaps, as a surrealistic fantasy, but stark and disturbing, even terrifying in its performance of haunting power.[28]

Audiences, however, were unwilling to give the play that chance. The young director José Quintero was with Williams at the Forrest Theatre as they watched audiences walk out at the intermissions. "Well," he remembered Williams saying, "I don't think they are really taking the play to their hearts, would you say?"[29] By the time the play closed in New York months later, it would be clear that Williams and Kazan had failed to communicate the play's meanings—and also that they'd succeeded too well.

III.

By the time the production reached New York, Williams was nervous about the play's reception and struck a defensive note about its meaning in his pre-opening piece in the Sunday *New York Times*. He was at a loss, he wrote, to explain why so many people fled the theater in New Haven and Philadelphia "as if the building had caught on fire," and had never intended for the play to confuse anyone willing to meet it halfway. "My attitude is intransigent," he wrote. "I still don't agree that it needs any explanation."And he reiterated the play's meaning for audiences of 1953: "It is nothing more or less than my conception of the time and world that I live in." He also tried to explain how he conceived of that time and place in this particular play. It wasn't like the worlds of *Menagerie, Streetcar, Summer and Smoke* or *The Rose Tattoo*. He admitted that it existed in no specific locality or time. More important was the sense of freedom he had felt while writing it, and that he hoped that the play's unusual conventions would allow the audience to share:

> When it began to get underway I felt a new sensation of release, as if I could "ride out" like a tenor sax taking the breaks in a Dixieland combo or a piano in a bop session....
>
> My desire was to give...audiences my own sense of something wild and unrestricted that ran like water in the mountains, or clouds changing shape in a gale, or the continually dissolving and transforming images of a dream.[30]

In the best of circumstances, it might have been difficult for a 1950s Broadway audience to appreciate so plastic and painted a play. Adding to the uncertainty about the words' meanings, however, Kazan complicated the production's chances for success with his choices of what and who audiences saw: the set and the cast.

The designer Lemuel Ayers produced a plaza that was dominated by a large, crumbling wall. Its effect was to add heaviness to a play that required lightness and fluidity, a play about which Williams wrote, "I know that we have kept saying the word 'flight' to each other as if the play were merely an abstraction of the impulse to fly."[31] Its realistic appearance contributed to the audience's confusion: if an audience of 1953 saw a world that looked like everyday reality, they would expect to see action that made sense within it, that conformed to the outward ways in which the world seems to operate. Instead of creating an environment in which the audience could understand the action, the set, as Kazan admitted later, merely made it look silly.[32]

Ayers had not been anyone's first choice. Williams, Kazan and Crawford all wanted Jo Mielziner, who had designed *The Glass Menagerie* and *Streetcar*. Mielziner was an early adherent to the tenets of the New Stagecraft, which rejected American material realism for the metaphor and poetry of early twentieth century European design. He understood that Williams' plastic, poetic theater required an approach that provided the sorts of metaphor and suggestion that would allow *Camino Real* to *be* an abstraction of flight and that gave an audience permission to exercise its own imagination on what it was seeing. Mielziner had been intrigued by the script and produced a series of drawings representing a bull ring in which all the action would occur: not the metaphor that Williams had in mind, but it *was* a metaphor and not meant to be understood as a literal place. In the end, however, his schedule made him unavailable, and Ayers, who was a friend of Williams from their days at the University of Iowa and who'd had considerable success as a designer of musicals, was chosen.

Because the full-length version of *Camino Real* had its origins at the Actors Studio, and because Kazan wanted to work with actors he'd helped train and with whom he shared a mutual trust, he formed the majority of the cast from its roster. Their technique was based on Stanislavski's system, and while the Russian's approach wasn't limited to one style of writing or acting (Stanislavski had equal success across various styles from material realism to Symbolism), at the Studio, this training was wedded to American material realism. The result was a style that emphasized a moment-to-moment, cause-and-effect material and psychological realism that, for better or worse, came to define American acting for decades. Were these actors, through training and temperament, able to embrace a painted, plastic style that required acting that was as physically expressive as it was emotionally true? Was Kazan?

The problem was that there was no acting technique in America equivalent to the New Stagecraft ideals of design: a technique that was emphasized the body as much as the emotions, that believed in transformation and physical and mental suppleness as ways of getting to psychological truth. Even with his Actors Studio cast and Ayres' realistic design, Kazan understood on some level that the play needed an approach to movement and psychology that was as plastic as Williams' conception. He hired the choreographer Anna Sokolow to stage the large group scenes. She had studied with Martha Graham and had also worked on Broadway, and later influenced theater-minded choreographers such as Pina Bausch and Martha Clarke. However, it was the Studio's approach that dominated the production. Later, Kazan realized that this had been a mistake.[33]

In his next collaboration with Williams, the film *Baby Doll* Kazan faced a different clash of styles: Williams' heightened language together with a plot that combined extended sexual tension, a Sicilian thirst for revenge and outsized gothic humor, required acting that was larger and more intense than film usually could allow without collapsing into risibility. On its own terms, however, the acting in *Baby Doll* worked, even on very large movie screens: the oversized nature of the performances was contained by the strong envelope of realism provided by the stark on-location sets and the more natural performances of the many local people of Benoit, Mississippi, whom Kazan hired to play small roles and extras. On the other hand, in *Camino Real*, the acting style and design were too limited and narrow to adequately convey the painted world Williams envisioned.

IV.

Nonetheless, from the first performances in New Haven through its run in New York, the design, the acting and Kazan's direction got all the good reviews, perhaps because they represented what the audience was used to seeing. That the production was confusing and, to many, depressing was blamed entirely on Williams. After *The Glass Menagerie* the critics had been divided over Williams' work, and their reviews of *Camino* indicate that they hadn't changed their minds: those who didn't care for Williams before didn't like him now, and those who had admired him were disappointed but willing to forgive. The negative reviews were, however, the harshest that Williams had received.

John McClain in the *Journal-American* had been no fan of *The Rose Tattoo*, and he didn't like *Camino* any better. Confusion and impatience dominated his response. The play, he wrote, "will divide any audience that sees it into two sharp categories: Those who understand it, and those who don't. I'm afraid I must identify with the latter." He unwittingly identified a problem that the play faced from the day that Williams conceived it as painted rather than written: the narrow range of experience that Broadway critics and audiences had of any form other than material realism excepting musicals. "The theater," McClain wrote, "is a medium for poetry and symbolism, for freedom of thought and expression, but it should also adhere to some reasonably orthodox method of transmission." Williams had "knocked himself out being oblique," he continued, and then hit on something that Kazan had worried about all along: "One is obliged to wonder whether the utter confusion doesn't result from the fact that the original idea was itself somewhat muddled." As for what the play meant, he could only guess. The Camino Real is "Life" and what happens to the "strange people" who find themselves there, "is, I guess, the author's conception of what happens to most people—and it ain't good."[34] That was the most he could muster and, along with the other critics, could only list the various characters and episodes without comprehending what idea made them cohere.

In the *Daily News*, John Chapman got right to the point:

> *Sixteen Blocks on the Camino Real* is the full title of this work, upon which the author is reported to have spent two years expanding it from a one-acter to a three-acter. It is an enormous jumble of five-cent philosophy, $3.98 words, ballet, music, symbolism, allegory, pretentiousness, portentousness, lackwit humor, existentialism and overall bushwah.
>
> A play so irritating to one observer must have some value, though, for it arouses some kind of emotion, however unpleasant. *Camino Real* may, indeed, become the darling of self-conscious intellectuals. If you are an intellectual the piece is at the National for you to see and to make a fad of. But don't count on any help from me, because I am not the brainy type.[35]

It was not surprising that in the first flower of the Cold War, the critic for the populist *Daily News* would strike so anti-intellectual a tone. He was echoed by Robert Coleman in the *Daily Mirror* who concluded his mixed review on a note guaranteed to slow ticket sales: "One first-nighter at the National sagely observed, '*Camino Real* is burlesque for Ph.D.'s.'" He wanted to admire the play, but like his colleagues he was unable to make a whole out of its fast and furious and quiet and lyrical episodes. "There are magnificent and trivial moments, tender and tawdry ones. Somehow, they jar. They never blend into the rewarding whole that one eagerly awaits. Often there is quality, and too often a lack of it." He gave credit to the producers for their courage, to Kazan for his direction and Ayers for his "stunning" design.[36]

And so it went, with the exception of William Hawkins in the *New York World-Telegram*, who wrote a rave for which Williams, Kazan and the producers could be grateful. "*Camino Real* is a brilliant and riotous adventure," he began. "It succeeds in making tangible for all your senses the delirious pains and ecstasies of a wild dream." Neither the play's quicksilver change of moods nor its bifurcated structure disturbed him:

> The first thing evident about this brave and stimulating new play of Tennessee Williams is that explanations of it that suit you may not suit anybody else. The playwright has composed his work in terms of pure emotions. They are abstract, without excuse or motivation. What you see and hear is the effect on the heart, of human nature when it is greedy or hilarious or sorry for itself.

Nor did the meaning of the play pose a problem for him. "I believe the play says in the end that there is a special kind of endlessness for romantics who live with gallantry or who have the capacity to simply dream far beyond their material wherewithal or their evident spiritual capacity." Williams might have received some solace from Hawkins' assertion, "There is no space to do faint justice to the many thrilling aspects of this production. Its conception is so inspired, and its execution so exciting, that there is no question of not liking it, but only of just how you, personally, will happen to enjoy and find yourself stirred by it."[37] For Williams and Kazan, the biggest disappointment was Brooks Atkinson in the *Times*. Atkinson was the guardian of middlebrow playgoers, a great many of whom read the *Times*, making him the city's (and thus arguably the country's) most powerful critic. He was also one of Williams' most consistent admirers, and so the review was more damaging to the play's chances than the others. He was certainly not confused by the play; for him the play's meaning was all too clear. He was shocked by what he considered Williams' alarmingly bleak, pessimistic outlook and the types of human behavior with which he chose to express it, but leavened his response with respect for a playwright he admired:

> Since *Camino Real* is a kind of cosmic fantasy, one must not interpret it literally. But to one theatergoer it seems to be the mirror of Mr. Williams' concept of life—a dark mirror, full of black and appalling images....*Camino Real* goes beyond melancholy into melancholia. For the fantasies that boil through the central plaza of the play have a psychopathic bitterness in them.
>
> Still, this is what Mr. Williams thinks, and it has to be reckoned with. In the first place, he is honest about it. He does not hide behind any of the usual formalities. Some of it is explicit enough to be revolting.

He had praise, however, for Kazan's production:

> Although Mr. Kazan is known best for hard-headed perfor-mances, he has directed *Camino Real* with poetic ingenuity. In a massive symbolic set by Lemuel Ayers that encloses the play and blocks off the turbulent world outside, the performance moves lightly through a miasma of hopelessness, cruelty and deca-dence—never literal, never dull or diffuse.[38]

In the ensuing years' debate over the play and its reception, Walter Kerr's review in the *Herald Tribune* has held a special, controversial place thanks to its first two lines: "It is this reviewer's opinion that Tennessee Williams is the best playwright of his generation. It is also this reviewer's opinion that *Camino Real*, which opened at the National Thursday, is the worst play yet written by the best playwright of his generation."

Unlike Atkinson, he was not at all appalled by Williams' alleged dark, revolting vision. What disturbed him was what he considered its flight from reality:

> Obviously, Mr. Williams is attempting to apply the methods
> of lyric poetry—the images made of illogical and unexpected
> combinations, the processes of free association, the emphasis
> on mythology—to the spoken stage. But the poetic imagination
> must have something realistic to exercise its imagination on,
> some actuality to serve as a point of departure. *Camino Real* is
> all departure and no point. The author is here preoccupied with
> techniques for getting at the truth without having any particular
> truth he wants to get at. The play is all method—studiously
> applied—and method applied to a vacuum.[39]

For Kerr, a play that was all symbols unattached to a specific reality
was "as cold as the corpse on the imaginary operating table."[40] What
disturbed him was what had concerned Kazan as well: whatever
meanings Williams was getting at were unclear, obscured by the
divided plot and characters which struck an audience as symbolic
rather than real.

The reviews in the national news magazines, where thousands
of non-New Yorkers got their impressions of American theater,
were as harsh as the local ones. *Newsweek* was confused:

> It is reasonable to suppose that Tennessee Williams thought he had
> something to say in his latest play, and that he thought he was saying
> it. It isn't possible that he was deliberately playing an elaborate,
> depressing joke under a cloak of murky symbolism. Judging from
> the out-of-town reports, and from a limited reaction on opening
> night at New York's National Theater, there are people who know
> precisely what the playwright had in mind. But for the theatergoer
> of only normal intelligence and tolerance, the end result is a grand
> slam of bafflement and boredom, and a defeating sense of watching
> something that should be happening and never does.[41]

There was no confusion about the play in *Time*, whose critic found
it decadent and full of pessimism:

Williams has created a phantasmagoria of brutality, treachery, corruption, has doused it with sex, punctuated it with farce, dyed it in melodrama. Doubtless the play is at times revolting because it sets out to convey the author's own revulsion; and *Camino Real* is perhaps excessively pessimistic in reaction against Williams' previous *Rose Tattoo*, with its factitious "affirmation." But very excessive it is—and not only excessively black, but excessively purple. *Camino Real* lacks philosophic or dramatic progression (on that score, it might claim the dead-endness of a wasteland), but it also lacks all discipline and measure, so that the wasteland becomes a swamp.[42]

Walter Kerr had experience in the theater as a writer and director, possessed genuine ideas about what theater should be and wrote about them with force and clarity. Atkinson, although limited by a timidity of taste, knew more than others what he was looking at. The rest of the newspaper and national critics were not men of exceptional discernment, taste or sensibility. They were first and foremost newspapermen with no training in any aspect of the theater or great gifts of perception or analysis, who identified no criteria or standards by which they judged what they saw. If they didn't have, by virtue of their positions, the ability to sway opinion away from one play and toward another, their opinions wouldn't matter, especially about a play as challenging as *Camino Real*.

There were, however, critics who did possess discernment, taste, sensibility and talent. They wrote for magazines with readerships that were small but influential, comprising teachers, writers, journalists and theater-goers who looked away from the newspapers for thoughtful writing on plays. Some of these critics were sympathetic to Williams, some not; as a group they were more informed and more understanding of the fact that no one sets out to produce a failure, yet none of them felt very differently than their less-qualified colleagues did about *Camino*.

Despite Kazan's fears to the contrary they found the play's meanings all too obvious. Like Kerr, they believed that Williams had put the symbols first and characters in whom they could invest their interest and emotions second. It was not realism that they were asking for, but a world in which they could believe the actions and speech of the characters.

Eric Bentley, who began writing for the *New Republic* the year before and was emerging as among the most insightful and rigorous of American theater critics and a brilliant writer, identified the play's most significant challenge to finding an audience in the commercial theater: it was exactly Williams' rejection of material realism and devotion to a more plastic theater. "The genuine element in Tennessee Williams had always seemed to me to reside in his realism," he wrote, "his ability to make eloquent and expressive dialogue out of the real speech of men and his gift for portraiture, especially the portraiture of unhappy women." *Streetcar* was basically a realistic play, he argued, because no matter how theatrical its presentation it was rooted in a reality recognizable to an audience. *Camino*, however,

> doesn't even pretend to realism. The unreal which crept up on us [in *Streetcar*] here meets us head on. Whether New York will prefer this I do not know. Possibly the escape into unreality was welcome in the former play only because it was disguised as its opposite; and now that it is overt the public will either reject it or declare it unintelligible; in which case the play is done for.[43]

Bentley didn't hazard to say what the play meant, but suggested that an audience was likely to find it unintelligible, as perhaps he himself did. The absence of material realism didn't bother him per se; that Williams indulged in a "luscious and high falutin'" style on behalf of vague ideas instead of grappling with characters who first and foremost represented human beings did.

There was probably no American critic more knowledgeable about making theater than Harold Clurman. A co-founder of the Group Theatre, he was also a successful director and a man of deep and broad culture, possessed of a perspicacious sensibility. He was also a life long partisan of Williams' work. He had been one of the three judges of the Group Theatre play contest that awarded Williams $100 for the collection of one-acts he had submitted to them under the name of *American Blues* in 1939, the event that jump–started Williams' career. He directed the first national road company of *A Streetcar Named Desire* and later the Broadway premiere of *Orpheus Descending*. Nonetheless, writing in *The Nation,* he found serious flaws in *Camino Real.* The play's alleged pessimism didn't bother him; nor did he find the play confusing or vague. The problem was just the opposite. Referring to its origins in *Ten Blocks*, he wrote:

> Being essentially a youthful work, *Camino Real* is immature. But like the youthful and immature works of most artists, *Camino Real* is significant of its author's seed thoughts, impulses, and ambitions. Far from being obscure, the play reiterates its intentions and meaning at every point. In fact, it is too nakedly clear to be a sound work of art.
>
> [The] play, instead of being the surrealist phantasmagoria it intends to be, is far too literal—in almost every respect far less poetic than *The Glass Menagerie* or *A Streetcar Named Desire*. To say, "We're all of us guinea pigs in the laboratory of God," or to have streetcleaners represent death or an airplane named Fugitiva [sic] stand for escape, is far less imaginative than to have the hapless Blanche DuBois of *Streetcar* go off to an insane asylum depending on the kindness of strangers....In other words, Williams, like Sean O'Casey and many others, is less suggestive and poignant when he aims point-blank at his aesthetic, poetic or symbolic target than when he employs the concrete means of a real situation.[44]

The faults Clurman found were little different than those of the newspaper critics, though unlike them, he had little praise for Kazan's production. "It is too punchy, forthright and 'realistic,'" he wrote. "It stampedes where it should float; it clamors and declaims where it should insinuate. It has much less humor than the text."[45] He alone saw that the house style of the Group Theatre and Actors' Studio weighed the play down rather than set it free, however good individual performances were.

The critics writing for other small publications, including John Gassner (another early Williams champion) in *Educational*

Theatre Journal and George Jean Nathan (in earlier years a major critical voice in *The American Mercury* and *Smart Set*, now at *Theatre Arts* magazine, never a Williams enthusiast) said much the same things. Meanings that were obscure to the daily critics were all too clear to them.

V.

At the end of the season, the awards were handed out. *Camino Real* won no awards. It received two votes for the best new American play from the New York Drama Critics Circle; the winner, *Picnic* by William Inge, received thirteen. Still, *Camino* was third in the voting; the second-place play was *The Crucible*, which got four. Indeed, Arthur Miller's play didn't fare significantly better overall than *Camino*. Its reviews were as mixed and while it played three times as many performances (197), its run was brief compared with *Picnic*'s 477—not to mention that year's other hits, *My 3 Angels*' 344, *Wish You Were Here*'s 598, and *The Seven Year Itch*'s 1141. Although *The Crucible* was not considered to be nearly the equal of *All My Sons* or *Death of a Salesman*, it enhanced Miller's reputation as a politically engaged truth-teller, a standing that the subsequent withholding of his passport and trial for contempt of Congress only increased. Perhaps this had to do with the play's forthright declaration of what it stood for, as opposed to the indirect, and to very many, indecipherable political statement in *Camino Real*. *The Crucible* has had frequent major revivals and sits near the top of what are considered Miller's significant achievements, yet it has never attracted the sort of fierce loyalty that seems to accrue to *Camino Real*. Despite comments like Walter Kerr's that it, like *Camino*, was populated by symbols rather than people, that "it is the intellect which goes out [to the characters], not the heart,"[46] *The Crucible* burnished Miller's reputation. What did *Camino Real* do for Williams'?

In the 1950s, the existence of so many daily newspapers meant that a conversation could take place among the audience and the critics, several of whom reviewed a play twice—once during the week and again at more length on the weekend. That conversation might not always have been the most enlightened, but unless the reviews were unanimously negative, so many voices tended to insulate a playwright from the lasting damage that can occur when conversation is limited to a handful of participants. The fact that fifty-four plays opened that season (a relatively low figure in that decade) also added richness to the conversation—as well as the opportunity for any individual play to thrive. In the years of affordable tickets, a good night at the theater encouraged an audience member to see other plays, and so the chance of a larger audience existed for every show. In this environment, one flop was not going to do significant damage to a playwright as highly regarded as Williams. His reputation when *Camino* opened was as Walter Kerr said: the best playwright of his generation, with Miller as his only rival. It remained so the morning after *Camino* closed. Those critics who to this day remain exercised over Kerr's review forget that he wrote that phrase about Williams' position in the present tense, not the past.

Being such a personal play, *Camino*'s failure was a great blow to Williams. However, despite his many protestations of physical and emotional fragility, Williams possessed great intestinal fortitude, and his response to the play's rejection was to go back to work. The years between 1953 and 1961 saw more artistic and commercial successes than failures. In 1955 he won his second Pulitzer Prize and third Tony and Donaldson Awards for *Cat on a Hot Tin Roof*. *Suddenly Last Summer* was a *succès du scandale* in 1959 and helped to establish Off-Broadway as a viable venue for new work by major playwrights. *Sweet Bird of Youth* ran for ten months in 1959 and *The Night of the Iguana* won the Critics Circle Award in 1961. All were made into major films with mass-market paperback tie-ins. Only later in life, with the plays he wrote after *Iguana*, did his reputation truly suffer, due to serial critical failures. In 1953, damage had been done to the reputation of *Camino Real*, but not to that of its playwright.

In the short run, of course, the play's failure didn't help Williams, either. However, its fate has endeared it to later critics and audiences who see it as a play ahead of its time, a victim of commercial and artistic narrow-mindedness. Nor did its failure long interfere with

Williams' experimental bent. In 1957, he embraced expressionism in *Orpheus Descending* more fully than he had in *Streetcar* (even if it was largely erased in production), and the 1960s brought forth one theatrical experiment after another, beginning with *The Milk Train Doesn't Stop Here Anymore*, a play heavily inflected by his own interpretation of Noh theater. More than half a century later, *Camino* heralds Williams' more radical experiments in form and expression, and thus for many it has retrospectively enhanced his reputation.

In the years ahead, Williams did his reputation no favors by insisting that those post-*Iguana* plays be produced on Broadway. In his *Nation* review of *Camino*, Harold Clurman, who had learned first hand at the Group Theatre the perils of producing in an atmosphere where every play needed to be a hit, criticized the limited horizons of an American commercial theater that provided no outlet for it other than Broadway.

> The sad fact of our theater is that a play like *Camino Real* with all its faults ought to be produced, listened to, criticized with measure and affection, but that this is difficult when production costs a fortune, when it is forced to become part of the grand machinery of investment, real estate, Broadway brokerage and competition for reputation. A play like *Camino Real* should be produced—as it might be in France, for example—with modest means in a small theater where it would be quietly seen, enjoyed, and judged for what it is—a fallible, minor work of a young artist of important talent.[47]

Indeed, one such theater already existed in New York. The young Circle in the Square had made its reputation a year earlier with a revival of *Summer and Smoke*. In the small Greenwich Village theater under José Quintero's direction, the play revealed itself as a minor gem rather than the misbegotten, schematic bore it appeared to many in its Broadway production of 1948. Williams hadn't been involved in the production and was unaware of it until it opened to rave reviews. However grateful he was to Quintero, he took to heart neither the lesson of its intimate production nor

Clurman's advice. If he had, he might have suffered less heartbreak and failure, and his career less damage in the years after 1961 when he was writing plays better suited to a less formal, less pressurized commercial atmosphere than the Broadway productions he continued to demand.

" The subject matter of this film

is morally repellent both in theme

and treatment . . . . Its unmitigated

emphasis on lust and the various

scenes of cruelty are degrading and
"
corruptive.

COURTING CONTROVERSY: THE MAKING AND SELLING OF BABY DOLL AND THE DEMISE OF THE PRODUCTION CODE

Vincent Brook

In December 1956, Francis Joseph Spellman, Roman Catholic Cardinal of New York, strode to the pulpit at St. Patrick's Cathedral and delivered a scathing sermon. The source of his ire: a motion picture just released by Warner Brothers Studios, directed by Elia Kazan, written by Tennessee Williams, and featuring a relative unknown, Carroll Baker, in the eponymous role of Baby Doll. Cardinal Spellman, just back from Korea where he had conducted Christmas mass for U.S. troops, denounced *Baby Doll* as both unpatriotic and immoral.[1] "The revolting theme of this picture is a contemptuous defiance of the natural law," he intoned, and forbade Catholics from seeing it "under pain of sin."[2]

In fact, the cardinal hadn't seen the film himself: "Must you have a disease to know what it is?" he would later admit.[3] Spellman was essentially echoing the sentiments of American Catholics' official film rating board, the National Legion of Decency. The Legion had placed *Baby Doll*—the story of a child bride, her 40-year-old husband, and a smarmy Sicilian-immigrant business rival bent on using both of them—its "C" classification (Condemned), the lowest of its four rating categories. As the Legion explained in a news release:

> The subject matter of this film is morally repellent both in theme and treatment. It dwells almost without variation or relief upon carnal suggestiveness in action, dialogue and costuming. Its unmitigated emphasis on lust and the various scenes of cruelty are degrading and corruptive. As such it is grievously offensive to Christian and traditional standards of morality and Decency.[4]

The Legion's condemnation didn't stop with the film. Another broadside was leveled at the movie industry's self-censorship board, the Production Code Administration (PCA), which had approved *Baby Doll* for wide release: "Although this film is an obvious violation of the spirit and purposes of the Motion Picture Code, it, nevertheless, bears a Seal of Approval of this Code Authority. The subject matter of the film indicates an open disregard of the Code by its administrators."[5]

Such a public rift between the Legion and the PCA was unprecedented, as was Warner Brothers' counterattack.[6] In a news release issued the same day as the Legion's, Warners touted *Baby Doll*'s artistic qualities and referred to advance press comments that acclaimed the film as "superior adult entertainment." Kazan was quoted as having cut the film in his own way. "I have no intention of being pressured," he stated. "As for the judgment of the Legion of Decency, I think in our country all people finally judge for themselves."[7]

The battle over *Baby Doll* had begun. But what are we to make of this bellicose exchange between Hollywood and a prominent religious body? Did the controversy erupt spontaneously or was it deliberately provoked? What broader institutional and societal forces were involved? Did the incident mark an historic moment in the struggle for creative expression, or was it yet another example of the collusion between art and commerce that has characterized the movie industry from its inception? In order to gauge this particular conflict's significance and to contextualize it in relation to the larger Hollywood censorship wars, it is useful to begin with an examination of the first Warners/Kazan/Williams collaboration, *A Streetcar Named Desire*.

"PRE-CURSERS": A CASE FOR SEPARATION OF CHURCH AND STUDIO

"Whatever has been creeping in on us in the form of widening censorship pressures began with *A Streetcar Named Desire.*" So declared Geoffrey Shurlock, assistant director of the PCA at the time the *Streetcar* project was proposed by Warner Brothers in the early 1950s. "For the first time," Shurlock added, "we were confronted with a picture that was obviously not family entertainment."[8]

The PCA's problems with "adult" fare in general were articulated by PCA chief Joseph Breen: "The provisions of the Production Code are quite patently set down in the knowledge that motion pictures, unlike stage plays, appeal to mass audiences; to the mature and immature; the young and the not-so-young…. Material which may be perfectly valid for dramatization and treatment on the stage may be questionable, or even completely unacceptable, when presented in a motion picture."[9]

Breen's specific objections to the film adaptation of Williams' Pulitzer Prize-winning play centered on two scenes: one dealing with homosexuality, the other with rape. Director Kazan was surprisingly conciliatory on the first point, averring that the story was actually strengthened by eliminating the homosexual element: "I prefer debility and weakness over any kind of suggestion of perversion."[10] On the issue of rape, however, Kazan held firm, threatening to withdraw from the project if the rape scene was removed. Williams explained the scene's importance: "The rape of Blanche is a pivotal, integral truth in the play, without which the play loses its meaning, which is the ravishment of the tender, the sensitive, the delicate, by the savage and brutal forces of modern society. It is a poetic plea for comprehension."[11]

Ultimately, Breen permitted an allusion to rape if it was "done by suggestion and delicacy," but he still demanded that the ending be changed. In order to satisfy the Code's fundamental tenet of "compensating moral values," the perpetrator of the rape, Stanley Kowalski, played by Marlon Brando, had to be punished.[12] Here Williams devised a compromise, having Stanley's wife Stella, played by Kim Hunter, tell her child at the end of the film: "We're never going back. Never, never back, never back again."[13] The PCA had thus been pacified, but not the Legion of Decency. Kazan and Williams met with the Legion to discuss the matter. The two sides failed to reach a resolution, according to Kazan, but he and Williams left the meeting convinced "we were not going to do what they wanted."[14]

Why American filmmakers even had to be concerned with the wishes of an outside religious body was predicated on a long, incestuous relationship between the Legion and the Breen office (as the PCA, an arm of the Motion Picture Producers and Distributors of America [MPPDA], later Motion Picture Association of America [MPAA], was known during Breen's twenty-year reign and beyond). The Production Code had been written in 1930 by two prominent Catholics: Father Daniel Lord, a Jesuit priest, and Martin Quigley, publisher of a prominent industry trade paper, *The Motion Picture Herald*. Emboldened by a box-office boom during the first few years of the Depression, however, Hollywood initially resisted the Code's guidelines, launching instead "one of the most remarkable challenges to traditional values in the history of mass commercial entertainment."[15] Largely in response to this brief period of comparative permissiveness, Quigley and Breen— the latter then the head of the MPPDA's Studio Relations Board—teamed to form the Legion in mid-1934. Only months later, under pressure from the Legion and other religious film-reform groups, the studios—ever sensitive to charges of industry domination by Jews and fearful of government censorship and nationwide boycotts at a time of sagging box office returns—established the PCA as a means of ensuring Code compliance.[16] When Joe Breen was appointed the PCA's first director, the "pact" between Hollywood and the Legion was sealed.

That this alliance was more than tacit and less than a passing fancy is indicated by the trade paper *Variety*'s contention, in a review of *Baby Doll* in late 1956, that some movie contracts were still conditioned on both PCA and Legion approval. At the time of *Streetcar*, the Legion was powerful enough to arrange for last-minute cuts of the film, behind Kazan and Williams' backs. Besides underestimating the religious group's clout, Kazan had failed to take into account his own vulnerability as director—specifically, his lack of right to "final cut" (control of the finished state of the picture). This authority resided contractually with Warners, which in the end accepted twelve cuts suggested by the Legion.[17] Besides sexually suggestive dialogue deletions, these consisted of editing and music changes, most infamously in the climactic "Stella!"-bellowing scene, whose raw power was diluted by replacing Kazan's complex montage with a "bland long shot and a Muzak-y underscore."[18]

Kazan's reaction was understandably bitter: "Warners just wanted a [Code] seal. They didn't give a damn about the beauty or artistic value of the picture. To them it was just a piece of entertainment. It was business, not art. They wanted to get the entire family to see the picture. They didn't want anything that might keep anyone away. At the same time they wanted it to be dirty enough to pull people in. The whole business was rather an outrage."[19]

As for Williams, whatever outrage he may have felt was apparently assuaged by the film's success: *Streetcar* went on to be nominated for an unprecedented twelve Academy Awards, including Best Picture, Director and Writer. In any event, according to Warner Brothers files, in February 1952 Williams submitted to Warners a new screenplay based on four one-act plays, titled *Hide and Seek*, which would grow over four years (and five title changes) into *Baby Doll*. In his autobiography, *Elia Kazan: A Life*, Kazan writes: "*Baby Doll* was a lark from beginning to end. I even enjoyed Joseph Cardinal Spellman's attack on it."[20] Why the sudden shift from outrage to levity? Had success spoiled Elia Kazan? Had the Hollywood blacklist, and Kazan's controversial role in it, contributed to his abrupt change of attitude? A full examination of the effects of the blacklist on Kazan and Hollywood in general is, of course, beyond the purview of this chapter (indeed, it would require a book of its own to do justice). Suffice to say that Kazan was a major "player" in the second phase of the House Un-American Activities Committee (HUAC) hearings of the early 1950s. An admitted member of the Communist Party from 1934–1936, Kazan was called before HUAC in 1952.

Although he claims that he found HUAC's ritualistic practice of forcing witnesses to "name names" repugnant—and refused to do so in his first, executive session, with the committee—he did believe "it was the duty of the government to investigate the Communist movement in this country."[21] At his second, public hearing, Kazan not only named names but also took the extraordinary and highly controversial step of defending his actions in an open letter to *The New York Times*. Although it would tarnish his standing in the film industry in the post-blacklist period, up to and including his 1999 receipt of the Motion Picture Academy's Lifetime Achievement Award, Kazan's cooperation with HUAC is generally regarded to have saved, if not to have bolstered, his directorial career at the time. It certainly appears that by the post-*Streetcar* period, Kazan had learned to play the Hollywood game—a game whose rules, at least in the censorship arena, were being increasingly challenged.

THE MAKING OF BABY DOLL

The transformation of movie censorship (as documented in PCA and Warner Brothers files) is starkly reflected in the five-year struggle to bring *Baby Doll* to the screen. The studio's initial response to the project was highly skeptical. In March 1952, one month after Williams' submission of the first *Hide and Seek* script, Finlay McDermid, a Warners executive, wrote in a letter to production chief Steve Trilling, that he didn't see how the film could be made. McDermid definitely recommended keeping the script from the Breen office until significant changes had taken place.[22] By May 1952, Kazan was confident enough to write Trilling that all Breen office problems had been solved. Yet in July the same year, McDermid complained again to Trilling that the latest script version had "only one less Breen office objection."[23]

Breen's initial response to the project confirmed McDermid's apprehension. In August 1952, Breen wrote studio head Jack Warner that the script for *27 Wagonloads of Cotton* (nee *Hide and Seek*) gave him cause for "deep concern." Breen took no direct issue with the theme of "degradation of an outcast from society" (referring to the Sicilian immigrant, Silva Vacarro, eventually played by Eli Wallach). His problem rather was with "the low and sordid tone of the story, [which] was interested mainly in crime, sex, murder, and revenge," and provided "very little relief of normal, healthy decency and sanity." Breen's single greatest aversion was to the seduction scene between Vacarro and Baby Doll, which was not only too long and "distastefully lustful," but also made "deliberate use of adultery as a weapon."[24]

Still smarting from their experience on *Streetcar*, and undoubtedly emboldened by the recent anti-censorship triumphs of Otto Preminger's *The Moon is Blue* (1953) and *The Man with the Golden Arm* (1955) and perhaps also by Kazan's HUAC involvement—Kazan and Williams were in no mood to compromise. David Weisbart, the editor who had carried out the backroom cuts on *Streetcar* (and was now part of Warners' production team), wrote Williams in mid-1953 imploring him to relent to the PCA-requested changes.[25] In January 1954, however, McDermid indicated to Trilling that Williams still had made "only one concession" to the Breen office on the newly titled *Whipmaster*.[26] By March 1955, Kazan's "bargaining position" certainly should have been bolstered by his considerable success on Oscar night. This time the film he had directed, the anti-Communist/pro-HUAC allegory *On the Waterfront*, won eight awards including Best Picture, Director, Actor (Marlon Brando), Supporting Actress (Eve Marie Saint) and Writer (Budd Schulberg). Yet in September 1955, McDermid wrote Kazan that while he felt some progress had been made on *Mississippi Woman* (*Baby Doll*'s penultimate title), "I'd be derelict with my Breen office crystal ball if I didn't warn you that a lot of problems still remain."[27]

In October 1955, the first script titled *Baby Doll* was submitted to new PCA president Shurlock. Nearly four years after its inception, Shurlock opined in a letter to Jack Warner that the screenplay still contained "serious [Code] violations." There was the usual quibbling over epithets—"damns," "hells," "Oh Gods"—and overuse of a derogatory term for Negro. Shurlock's main objections dealt with the script's allusions to adultery, the unconsummated marriage between Baby Doll and Archie Lee (to be played by Karl Malden), and a doctor's visit in which Archie's impotence is implied. These and other pieces of business and lines of dialogue, Shurlock complained, pointed much too explicitly to Archie's "sex frustration." Shurlock also feared that reference to Baby Doll's "growing up" at the end of the story might be taken as an indication of her newfound sexual fulfillment.[28] In November

1955, from location in Greenville, Mississippi, Kazan responded. Writing Jack Warner, he stated:

> I will do everything the Shurlock office wants, except one thing. ...I cannot reduce the element of Archie Lee's sex frustration.... This film is about one thing and only one thing. It's about a middle-aged man who is held at arm's length by his young wife....I cannot change the doctor scene and furthermore assert unequivocally that it has nothing to do with sex frustration, since every middle-aged man is familiar with the sudden slump in ALL his powers that comes dismayingly in his late forties.... Furthermore, Baby Doll does grow up in the story, but I will make clear her growing up has nothing to do with her having had her first vaginal orgasm.[29]

Kazan's letter concludes with remarks that provide rare insight into the schizoid nature of mainstream Hollywood, its systemic melding of creativity and commerce—while also foregrounding the industry's financial troubles in the mid-1950s, particularly in regard to competition from television:

> In general, Jack, it seems to me that with fewer and fewer people leaving their TV sets and their homes after supper, we must, we MUST strike out for exceptional subject matter and really unusual treatments of these subject matters. In one sentence, we are now obliged, AS A MATTER OF PRESERVATION, to put on the screen of Motion Picture Theaters ONLY what they cannot and will never see on their screens at home. Our industry is now in a desperate situation, and we must be bold and fight for our lives. TV is improving fast, and getting bolder every day. The wide screen gimmick cannot keep our head above the water much longer. We've got to break our own taboos and strike out for increasingly unusual material. Either that or just quit and sign up with the TV guys.[30]

Of course, "signing up with TV" is exactly what Warner Brothers, and the other major Hollywood studios, were already doing. Following the lead of Columbia and Disney, Warners had just contracted with ABC to produce TV programming for the 1955–1956 season.[31] The perceived need to differentiate theatrical movies from TV persisted, however, and fueled a debate over a new rating system that would indicate which films were not acceptable for minors. Exhibitors, however, remained opposed to any system that might further stratify their rapidly decreasing audience. According to the trade paper *Show Business*: "The competition from television [has] forced studios to make better films. This inevitably involved the use of controversial themes….Classification may be a long way off, nevertheless, because Hollywood trembles at the thought of cutting into the teenage audience, which represents nearly 50% of those going to the movies."[32]

Shurlock and the all-or-nothing PCA were thus placed in "a marketing quagmire of moral obligation on the one hand and economic stability on the other." As Shurlock observed: "We have a code that is intended to provide movies for an entire family. Obviously, some pictures are not for the entire family. So the code bends and twists." It would go through contortions on *Baby Doll*.[33]

In May 1956, McDermid wrote Kazan about the latest meeting with the PCA. He praised Trilling's "masterful handling of the Breen office representatives," which had led to "highly satisfactory results."[34]

In July 1956, the PCA viewed the first rough cut of *Baby Doll*. Although the film passed muster in general, there were still significant sticking points, particularly the seduction scene between Vacarro and Baby Doll. "Everyone on the staff," PCA vice president Jack Vizzard reported, "thinks this clearly indicates that Vacarro was agitating Baby Doll," causing her to have "physical reactions which are orgiastic [sic]." Vizzard lodged numerous smaller complaints, such as over use of the word "wop," and a "gesture which, as far as we know, has an extremely vulgar meaning." All of this, he added, "will have to be removed."[35] In September 1956, after examination of the completed picture, Certificate of Approval No. 18129 was issued to Warner Brother's, by the Motion Picture Association.[36] The film was released in December.

Viewing *Baby Doll* these days (in video, non-director's cut format), it appears that the PCA's bark had been bigger than its bite.

In the end, despite the censorship bureau's manifold protestations, Kazan and Co. won out on almost all counts. Archie's "sex frustration" remains the anchor of the film. The doctor scene is intact. Not only does Vacarro announce, by no means subtly, that Baby Doll has "grown up suddenly," but the mature viewer can hardly fail to notice the change or to connect it with a sexual awakening. The swing scene, while not "orgiastic" by today's standards, does feature close-ups of a panting and cooing Baby Doll as Vacarro's hand slides suggestively downward and out of frame (a Code-bending ploy perhaps picked up from Joseph Lewis' *The Big Combo*, released the year before). In addition, Archie Lee's climactic shooting spree is clearly motivated partly by his drunkenness, despite the PCA report's declarations that "no drunkenness" is shown in the picture.[37] Viewing the film also bears out Kazan's contention, in the November 1955 letter to Jack Warner, that *Baby Doll* "has grotesque and even tragic elements, but essentially the point of view is comic and affectionate."[38]

THE MARKETING OF BABY DOLL

Promotion of the picture got off to a rocky start when, as reported in Warner Brothers' censorship report, the Censorship Committee of the Outdoor Advertising Association of America urged against posting ads for the film. Chicago's censorship board gave the film its "pink permit" (or "adults only") rating, thereby limiting box office potential in a major urban market. All state and other city censorship offices passed the film "for general patronage without eliminations." A few cities—Atlanta, Memphis, Jackson, as well as Toronto and the Canadian provinces of Alberta and Nova Scotia—banned the film in lieu of certain cuts, which Warner Brothers supplied.[39] The studio was thus forced to wage an ad war on two fronts: one to pitch the film, the second to fend off the censors. Warners' anti-censorship campaign featured a seventeen-page booklet titled "Mr. Exhibitor: Do You Know This About '*Baby Doll*'...." It included favorable comments about the film from newspaper editors, columnists, critics, religious and civic leaders, and "the man on the street." This "positive" publicity thrust showed Hollywood at its most schizoid.

One angle focused on the film's artistic merits, spotlighting Kazan, Williams, and Baker—in terms of her acting talents. The other exploited Baker's other talents; namely, her nymphet-like sexuality. "The Biggest Sign in the World"—a 15,600 square-foot billboard— was erected on Broadway in New York City; another, in Chicago. Both signs displayed a scantily-clad Baker lying in a baby crib, thumb in mouth, staring provocatively at the viewer under the heading: "This is…*Baby Doll.*"[40]

Variations on Baker's alluring pose were featured in "The Most Spectacular 24–Sheet Posting in Warner History!" Here the copy was even more explicit, and was paraphrased in voice-overs for the film's trailer: "This is the 19-year-old 'Baby Doll.' She wouldn't let her husband near 'er. She wouldn't let the stranger go away."[41] The intimately titled "Your '*Baby Doll*'…Ad-Pub Campaign" encouraged exhibitors to hang "full-color action displays" of the *Baby Doll* poster in their lobbies ("the slightest breeze makes them spin!"). "Promotion tie-ups" included bathing beauty contests to select Miss Baby Doll; a "street stunt" featuring a model in a shortie nightgown (like Baby Doll's in the film) wheeled around in a baby carriage with a sign touting the picture; and local kids writing on sidewalks and fences ("if local ordinances permit") lines like: "Oh you Baby Doll!…What a Baby Doll!…Be My Baby Doll!" Other items available: window streamers, bumper strips, lapel buttons, badges, banners, books and records, and a "Baby Doll hat" designed by Mr. John.[42] As indicated in studio advertising memos, the media was saturated with newspaper and magazine articles, radio spots and interviews. A sign that television/movie-industry synergy was well underway, TV guest appearances were slated for the film's stars and questions about Tennessee Williams were to be siphoned into the big TV quiz shows such as *The $64,000 Question* and *Twenty-One*. Gossip columnists were urged to make romantic use of the film's title, such as in "Sidney Carter's current 'Baby Doll' is Jane Haliday"— the express purpose being "to make 'Baby Doll' part of the current language."[43]

Such gross commercial exploitation of a purportedly "artistic" film wasn't limited to the domestic market, nor were its invidious implications lost on the French daily *Le Monde*, which commented,

"What can be condemned [about *Baby Doll*] is the publicity for the picture."[44] Overall, the judgment of the American press (Warner Brothers' "advance notices" notwithstanding) was decidedly mixed. "Electrifying drama!" trumpeted the *Independent Film Journal*. "A new sensation, especially Carroll Baker," effused one Los Angeles *Times* reviewer.[45] "Gloomy and obscure, with lurid trimmings," complained another, "but no need to take time to officially condemn it, it will fall from its own weight."[46] "A story of today with explosive action," proclaimed the Los Angeles *Herald Express*, but which then added that it was "a strange release for the holiday season" and wondered why the industry "has to lower itself to such tawdry themes."[47] "A step downward for the entire industry…trash," lamented the Los Angeles *Examiner*.[48]

As for audience reception, the *Citizen News* wrote that the film "proved a ban or condemnation immediately causes a rush to the box office."[49] Indeed, The Warner Brothers Story claims that "outraged moralists assured the film of box office success"[50] and there were reports early in its release of *Baby Doll*'s "breaking box-office records."[51] Receipts dropped off rapidly and sharply, however, and by the close of its initial run, the film had barely broken even.[52] In the end, Kazan—who by his contract was promised 25% of net profits in addition to his $50,000 director's fee[53]—alleges, "I never made a profit."[54]

Kazan blames Cardinal Spellman's injunction against *Baby Doll* and the resulting boycott for whatever commercial losses the film may have suffered. In some theaters, Kazan reports, "priests, stationed in the lobbies, notebooks in hand, wrote the names of parishioners who defied their spiritual leader."[55] Kazan's reaction must be taken as more than slightly disingenuous, however.

First, it is contradicted by his above-related statement regarding the positive nature of the project and his actually "enjoying" Spellman's (over)reaction. Second, the cardinal's actions could have been predicted. He had ordered a similar boycott in 1950 of the Italian import *The Miracle* that the Legion 'Condemned' as sacrilegious. Priests had policed theater lobbies then, also, and Catholic war veterans had picketed the theater where the film was premiering. New York City officials joined the opposition, and there were even two bomb threats. Leff and Simmons suggest that the virulent reaction to *The Miracle* was a major factor in Warner Bros.' decision to buckle under to the Legion on *Streetcar*.[56] Five years later, by the mid-1950s, courting rather than eschewing controversy had clearly become the studio's modus operandi. Just as the contention surrounding *The Moon is Blue* and *The Man with the Golden Arm* had contributed to these films' success, Warners hoped the Legion's condemnation would help *Baby Doll* at the box office—and despite some adverse effects, they were probably right. As Frank Miller suggests, "Without that condemnation to draw the curious, this difficult, if extremely well-made film might not have broken even."[57]

Not all organized religious responses to *Baby Doll* were critical, however. An unexpected boost to the film's fortunes came from the Protestant side of the aisle. Motivated at least partly by denominational rivalry, Bishop James Pike, dean of New York's Episcopal Cathedral of St. James the Divine, devoted his entire Advent sermon to a denunciation of Cardinal Spellman's attacks on *Baby Doll*. Pike, who a few years later would join other religious leaders in decrying Hollywood's "pathological preoccupation with sex and violence,"[58] found Kazan's film not only unsinful but cautionary and instructive, according to the Los Angeles Times.[59] He deemed its portrayal of sexuality tame compared to Cecil B. De Mille's *The Ten Commandments* (released the same year), which had been labeled "excellent" by leading New York prelates and a must-see for every parochial child. The bishop was particularly disparaging of "the efforts of a minority group to impose its views on the city."[60] Not surprisingly, the Protestant Council gave *Baby Doll* an "A" rating (for Adult), calling it a "slice of life" drama with tragic implications and lauding its "masterful directing and acting."[61]

Even in official Catholic circles, criticism of the film was far from monolithic. In England, Father John Burke, director of the Catholic Film Institute (British equivalent of the Legion) termed *Baby Doll* a "powerful denunciation of social and racial intolerance and something for thoughtful people to see," according to *The New York Times*.[62] In a strong defense of the film that would ultimately cost him his job,[63] Burke added in the *Times* article that the "X" certificate given the film by his institute assured that children would be prevented from seeing it.[64] The French Catholic film board responded similarly; as reported in a Los Angeles *Times* "*Baby Doll* Update," the French board gave *Baby Doll* a "4-A" rating: "strictly for adults, with some reservations."[65] The Joint Estimate of Current Entertainment Films, or Green Sheet, a secular American classification service for parents, also gave the film an "A" (for Adult) rating, explaining with a mixture of revulsion and titillation that "the seven deadly sins are ever present" and the seduction scene "is prolonged beyond anything the domestic screen has so far shown."[66]

THE DEMISE OF THE PRODUCTION CODE

Jewish moguls may have "invented Hollywood," in Neal Gabler's provocative allusion to the preponderance of immigrant Jews among the major studio heads,[67] but their Code-bound system, as Thomas Dougherty points out, was also in the business of "selling Roman Catholic theology to Protestant America."[68] From the mid-1930s through the mid-1950s, it was the Legion of Decency rather than studio bosses, producers or directors who "wielded virtual final cut over morality on the screen."[69] The making and selling of *Baby Doll* signaled a radical shift in Hollywood's relations with the Catholic Church. The fact that Cardinal Spellman's condemnation of *Baby Doll* not only failed to kill the film at the box office but may even have helped it turn a slight profit showed that while defiance of the Church was no guarantee for success, neither did it necessarily spell financial ruin nor public relations disaster.

The major lesson the Legion learned from the *Baby Doll* incident was that "inflammatory rhetoric and demonstrating pickets would not stem the flow of problematic films."[70] The question even began to be debated among Catholics whether the Church should interfere in the affairs of an independent enterprise such as the film industry.[71] Instead of censorship, the Legion decided to preach film classification to Hollywood. In 1961, a Catholic bishops' committee predicted "an understandable popular demand for mandatory classification should the industry refuse to regulate itself."[72]

Meanwhile, the Legion not only considered dropping its "Condemned" rating, but began promoting films on the basis of their appeal to "Youth," "General," and "Mature Audiences." In 1962, the Legion gave a modified "Separate Classification" label (for viewers over 18 years of age only) to Stanley Kubrick's *Lolita*, and Code co-author Martin Quigley actually assisted the film's producers in gaining PCA approval.

That the Production Code itself had become a dinosaur was increasingly apparent. From the late 1950s through the mid-1960s the Shurlock office was bombarded by ever-bolder *Baby Doll*s, each new challenge forcing the PCA to push its guidelines to the breaking point. As did the continuing financial crisis wrought by the rise of television, which had only worsened since Kazan's letter to Jack Warner urged "to put on the screen of Motion Picture Theaters ONLY what they cannot and will never see on their screens at home." In the pre-premium cable era, Williams' sexually charged material, especially, filled Kazan's call "to break our own taboos" to a tee. Indeed, the period from the mid-1950s to the mid-1960s can veritably be deemed the Tennessee Williams era, with five other of his plays, besides the reworked *Hide and Seek*, being adapted to the big screen: *The Rose Tattoo* (1955), *Cat on a Hot Tin Roof* (1958), *Suddenly Last Summer* (1959), *Sweet Bird of Youth* (1962), and *Night of the Iguana* (1964).

With the rating system's opening of the censorship floodgates in the mid-to-late 1960s, and with the film business still in the throes of a prolonged box-office tailspin, Hollywood henceforth would rely, in Robert Sklar's words, "more and more on elements moviemakers had known from the first would draw a crowd when everything else failed: sex and violence."[73] By the time the box office turned around in the mid-to-late1970s, the die had been cast. Courting controversy had become, for better or worse, Hollywood's favorite love story.

Portions of this essay, revised for the present volume, were previously published. Brook, Vincent. "Courting Controversy: The Making and Selling of *Baby Doll* and the Demise of the Production Code." *Quarterly Review of Film and Video*, 18. 4 (2001): 347-360. Reprinted by permission of the publisher (Taylor & Francis Group, http://www.informaworld.com).

"
Mr. Williams' idea of the

'humanity' of his characters involves

their absorption in questions of
"
sex and lust.

BENDING THE CODE: FILMING THE ROSE TATTOO

Robert Bray and Barton Palmer

BEATEN, UNKEMPT, DEPRESSING PEOPLE

Studio executives could see clearly that a Hollywood version of *The Rose Tattoo* might encounter some serious problems with the Production Code Administration. But producer Hal B. Wallis was very interested in acquiring the film rights, especially after the critical and box-office success of *A Streetcar Named Desire* and other pictures of the early 1950s that pushed the limits of the code and seemed, for that very reason, to attract filmgoers; *Tattoo*, Wallis calculated, would do much the same. The play would also suit Wallis' long-standing interest in stories that had evident literary quality (a profitable area to work in during the early 1950s in Hollywood). Perhaps most importantly, the Williams play would offer a suitable role (in the part of Alvaro) for Burt Lancaster, then signed to do a number of pictures for the producer.

Wallis had just achieved substantial success, both popular and critical, with the film version of William Inge's Broadway sensation *Come Back, Little Sheba* (Daniel Mann, 1952), in which Lancaster had starred with Shirley Booth, and the producer was especially eager to secure the rights to another play that offered a strong female lead to serve as an appropriate foil to Lancaster's dynamic style. Serafina Delle Rose was such a role, making the film an ideal Lancaster vehicle with which to follow up the success of *Sheba* (which had included an Academy Award for Booth). A significant bonus was the play's connection to international superstar Anna Magnani, who was perhaps the most sensational actress of the era, rivaled only by Marilyn Monroe. Magnani had been solicited strongly for the Broadway production, but had declined because, among other reasons, she felt her English was not strong enough for continuous stage performance, even though she was immensely flattered when learning that Williams had written the role with her in mind. Wallis rightly thought that she could be secured for the film version because her acting could be done in short bursts, and retakes were always possible.

When Wallis saw the stage version during its Chicago tryouts, he went backstage personally to open immediate negotiations with Williams, evidently fearing that some other enterprising producer might secure the rights if he waited until the Broadway run and inevitable popular success. With such a strong show of interest, Wallis was able to persuade Williams to work informally on roughing out a screenplay and even writing some additional scenes. In the event, a final agreement was quickly forthcoming. Wallis would produce the film for Paramount, with Daniel Mann, who had directed the stage version, reprising his role. Williams was uncomfortable that Mann would be directing, writing Wood: "I did so hope that it could be offered to Gadge [Kazan] for whom it was written along with Magnani, and who told me that he would like to make a film of it…if he could fit it into his schedule." Williams was wary of, as he called him, "the intellectual Mr. Mann" and thought that "with a fine director, *Tattoo* and Magnani would out-shine *Streetcar*."[1]

Williams would prepare the screenplay, with significant help from Hal Kanter, who received screen credit for the adaptation. Mann (born 1912) was no novice and by no means an insignificant figure on Broadway or in Hollywood, where his maiden directorial effort, which was to bring *Sheba* to the screen in 1952, had met with considerable acclaim. He would go on to direct such other notable films as *I'll Cry Tomorrow* (1955), *Teahouse of the August Moon* (1956),

The Last Angry Man (1959), and *Butterfield 8* (1960). But Mann was no Kazan, and no one on the set was ever in any doubt about the man actually in charge of the production being Wallis, all of whose films bear his strong personal stamp. In addition to *Sheba*, Wallis had just produced (with Daniel Mann directing) one of the most noted women's pictures of the early 1950s (though it was a box-office disappointment). *About Mrs. Leslie* (1954) features Shirley Booth as a landlady who reminisces with poignant bittersweetness about her lifelong "backstreet" affair with a rich and powerful man.

Along with *Sheba* and *Mrs. Leslie*, *Tattoo* would constitute an impressive triptych of powerfully realistic dramas with strong female leads, each of whom, in the tradition of screen melodrama, suffers from a profound sexual discontent that results from an unbreakable attachment to an unattainable man (married, alcoholically disaffected, or dead and cremated). Aware that he was departing from tradition, Wallis encountered considerable opposition from studio executives when he determined to make films of this kind. He recalled that those at Paramount were "appalled by the idea of filming *Come Back, Little Sheba* and "shocked at the thought of making a picture with beaten, unkempt, depressing people." *Tattoo* would offer more of the same; here also were no "glamorous men and women in melodramas of the seamy side of life," as had hitherto been industry practice.[2]

LA MAGNANI

As shooting progressed it became obvious that Magnani would be no ordinary "widow lady," and this film would be no *Marty* (Delbert Mann, 1955), the famous "small film" of the era in which the romantic couple, in a complete rejection of industry wisdom, is played by performers (Ernest Borgnine, Betsy Blair) who are not especially appealing. And yet *Tattoo* is likewise no *From Here to Eternity*, whose notorious beach-rendezvous scene shocked and titillated audiences, with a scantily clad Lancaster and Deborah Kerr embracing on the shore as the surf washes over their entwined bodies. Truer to a kind of Americanized neorealist style, Mann's film avoids the glamorizing escapism of *Eternity's* more conventional melodrama, including such set-piece romantic scenes. And yet it is nonetheless sensational.[3]

The reason was Anna Magnani. A unique film personality, her appeal did not depend on fine clothes and flattering setups; in fact, it might have been ruined by such an approach. Dressed in a slip or bathrobe with her hair hanging in uncombed strings, Magnani spends much of *Tattoo* in a state of profound dishabille, as had Shirley Booth in *Sheba* (though to very different effect). Emerging to prominence late in life (she was already well past forty when she made *Tattoo*, and had been playing minor film roles since the 1930s), Magnani established an international reputation for her earthiness, energy, and obvious delight in her increasingly substantial body. These unconventional qualities were displayed in a series of virtuoso performances in some of the most renowned Italian neorealist films of the late 1940s and early 1950s, beginning with a small part in Roberto Rossellini's *Open City* (1945), in which her impassioned death scene quickly made her an international sensation.

Williams confessed to being "overwhelmed" by Magnani's ungrantable demands to secure her participation in the stage play, but rightly felt that "it would be very easy to get her to do the *picture*."[4] Wallis agreed; as he remembers it: "I told Tennessee it would have to be Magnani."[5] When the two went to her apartment in Rome to finalize the deal, the encounter was certainly memorable, as Wallis recounts: "She plied us with large quantities of Johnnie Walker Red Label, the only thing she liked to drink, apart from wine. The sum total of her outburst was that the play was 'beautiful' and 'wonderful,' she would die to play Serafina, and she would master the English language in one night if necessary. She was prone to monumental exaggeration."[6]

A HAL B. WALLIS PRODUCTION

Because the same creative team was involved in producing *Sheba*, *Mrs. Leslie*, and *Tattoo* (Wallis, Mann, and James Wong Howe as cinematographer), this series is marked by a palpable thematic unity: a flat, deglamorized, and largely unsentimental approach to life's "ordinary" problems (in which regard, Vina Delmar's midcult novel about womanly suffering and self-denial strangely complements the more highbrow dramas of Inge and Williams). In

1958, Wallis would try to repeat the success of these three films with *Hot Spell*, based on yet another Broadway play (by Lonnie Coleman), in which Mann would direct Shirley Booth again, this time starring as the long-suffering wife of a middle-aged man (Anthony Quinn) eager to leave his family for a twenty-year-old mistress. Even though set in that steamy South that Williams had almost single-handedly made into a cinematic cliché, *Hot Spell* failed to equal the artistic and financial success of both *Sheba* and *Tattoo*. Within the context of Wallis' extensive work in the woman's picture during the 1950s, *Tattoo* stands out for its casting of Magnani. The thematic daring of the other three productions—all of which focus on the discontents of desire and illicit sexual connections of one kind or another—is somewhat muted by the presence of the decidedly plain, though charming and talented, Shirley Booth.

Tattoo would also break new ground for Wallis in its pagan celebration of life, a quality certainly present in the stage version, which he would emphasize, if not in the highly expressionistic manner that the playwright desired. A clear sign of Wallis' approach to the adaptation was his decision that experienced comic writer Hal Kanter should help Williams devise the dialogue (Kanter did not work on any of the other films in this Wallis series). Williams may have thought of *Tattoo* as what he called a "slapstick tragedy" (the carnivalesque treatment of Serafina's plight not fully recuperating from the deep pain of her experience with an unfaithful husband). Wallis, by contrast, evidently saw the story as more gently comic, and therefore in need of the lighter touch that an experienced humorist would bring to the project. Incidentally, the changes demanded by the PCA and eventually made by the filmmakers contributed strongly to a perceptible shift away from the semitragic tone of the stage production toward an even happier ending for Serafina, Alvaro, Rosa, and Jack.

In fact, as was the case with many of Williams' plays, there seemed to be a particular problem with the finale. In one proposed Broadway conclusion, Serafina and one of her neighbors morbidly gather up Rosario's scattered ashes, but Kazan argued that since up to this point, the play "seemed to be in praise of life, and its undying sensual base," the ending, in keeping with this tone, should be

"COMIC (in the biggest sense of that word, optimistic and healthy and uncontrollable)." [7] Once Williams embraced Kazan's idea of balancing the tragic with the comic, however, he found it difficult to decide how the play should end, going through at least twenty alternatives. As already mentioned, Williams eventually decided on a fairly positive conclusion: Serafina discovers that the mystic rose on her breast, the image of her love for Rosario that disappeared with his death, has come to life again, suggesting that her future with Alvaro will be happy and fertile.

The film, however, emphasized even more strongly the comic aspects of life, undercutting the pathos of Serafina's prolonged mourning period. In a gesture with obvious, bawdy implications, Alvaro climbs the mast of a beached sailboat to proclaim his intentions to the shocked neighborhood. Both amused and embarrassed by her lover's antics (but obviously impressed by his physicality), Serafina makes Alvaro a present of Rosario's rose-colored shirt and turns on the player piano, whose celebratory honky-tonk she had hitherto found distressing. The film then ends with a scene, though it is brief, of their boisterous laughter and conversation, suggesting that her self-imposed isolation is at an end. As with all of his film adaptations, Williams was dissatisfied with this conclusion, which, in its original form, had too obviously reflected the adaptor's humorous touch. He had observed of the earlier version that "the ending must be rewritten," confessing to being "sorry that Kanter re-wrote the scene that I gave him. Bits like this can only be written by the original author."[8] And with Wallis's agreement, he penned the final rewrite, which, still comic, was not entirely to his taste.

QUESTIONS OF LOVE AND GROSS SEX

It may have surprised the project team that the treatment initially submitted to the PCA met with even stronger disapproval than that of *Streetcar* had received. Wallis and company, perhaps, had considered only the ways in which *Tattoo* might be thought to violate specific code provisions. After all, this property had no dramatized rape, no reference to a homosexual husband, and no heroine with a desperate yen for rather young men. And yet, in a personal conference with Breen, Wallis discovered that he would be asked to surmount a rather formidable obstacle if *Tattoo* were to be brought to the screen. Breen advised him of "the basic unacceptability of the story," the most important reason being that it "seems absorbed from beginning to end with questions of love and gross sex," an undeniably accurate judgment that (could it be an accident?) closely echoed the Legion's damning evaluation of *Streetcar*. Recalling that embarrassing and damaging earlier experience, Breen must have been wary about being hoodwinked a second time by a Williams property. Specific objections to the play's sexual themes included the fact that "Serafina's problem of 'fulfillment' is solved by a sex affair with Alvaro" and that "Rosa is clearly begging Jack for a sex affair before she gives the indication she wants to go off and marry him."[9]

Tattoo, however, also posed problems of a different kind. The PCA judged that "Serafina's primitive confusion between religion and superstition seems calculated to put religion in a rather ridiculous light," once again an accurate evaluation of the way in which *Tattoo* invokes, but refuses to take seriously, Catholic antisexualism, indirectly associating it with that faith's somewhat populist, even superstitious practices. In the spirit of comedy and that genre's fundamental opposition to authoritarianism of any kind, Williams prefers a gentle debunking of unsophisticated lay-Catholic culture to a serious intellectual engagement with the religion's underlying values, for whose undermining or overthrow he certainly did not intend to push. Perhaps in the eyes of PCA officials, however, that comic approach made his treatment of religion even more offensive because it could be viewed as dismissive.

Interesting evidence of the yawning cultural divide between Williams and PCA officials is to be found in a memo, "Notes on the Filming of *Rose Tattoo*," that the playwright penned as plans for the production went forward. The purpose of this document is unclear, but it seems likely to have been an attempt to forestall PCA objections to the submitted treatment by not only suggesting that comedy should be given more latitude in subject matter, but also by offering to remedy what, based on his experience with the adaptation of *Streetcar*, Williams thought the censors would identify as *Tattoo's* main problem. Alvaro's coupling with Serafina was technically "fornication," and hence unacceptable in the absence of some punishment being visited on the "malefactors." Somewhat mysteriously, however, "Notes on the Filming of *Rose Tattoo*" was not mailed initially to the PCA office, but rather to Audrey Wood, who may have in fact commissioned its composition, perhaps in consultation either with Wallis (who was a sophisticated Hollywood old hand) or his assistants at Paramount.

It is hard to believe that Williams himself, very busy with a number of projects at the time, would have conceived of composing a lengthy memo that was not a response to already-expressed PCA objections. Whatever the circumstances of its origin, Wood forwarded the carefully written and somewhat lengthy document to Wallis's assistant Paul Nathan, who sent it on not to Breen, but to his junior assistant Jack Vizzard. Within the industry, the younger man was more culturally liberal and broad-minded than his boss and was perhaps thought to be more sympathetic toward the project.[10] "Notes" arrived at the PCA offices only three days after Wallis's discouraging meeting with Breen. Facing substantial opposition, Wallis and company, it seems, had immediately played their trump card: having the noted author himself reply to Breen and his assistants, perhaps in the hope of gently intimidating them. It seems likely, therefore, that the filmmakers had prepared their defense in advance, expecting ongoing negotiations in which questions of artistic value, as well as conformity to the code, might profitably be raised.

HUMANITY ITSELF?

Williams' comments address both these issues. As an opening gambit, he advanced the premise that "in a heavy drama the censorship problem is much more serious than in a play that is primarily a comedy such as *Tattoo*."[11] Translation: This play is funny, and thus no *Streetcar*. But such a transparent plea to the censors to take it easy this time was certainly debatable, since comedies can play fast and loose with consensus values, especially sexual mores. And those in charge at both the PCA and the Legion needed little reminding that this could be the case. Otto Preminger's light sex comedy *The Moon*

Is Blue (1953) had recently given both organizations a good deal of trouble. Tellingly, Preminger's film was also based on a Broadway smash (by F. Hugh Herbert), and the playwright had to struggle mightily to have his play transferred to the screen. Preminger and Herbert were unwilling to make all the requested changes, and so released—quite successfully—the film uncertified. After this trying experience, the PCA and the Legion were both suitably warned about the moral and, consequently, institutional dangers to be found in comedies.[12] After begging mercy, the playwright pleaded the mainstream, unobjectionable nature of his play. Williams may have believed that "the basic values of *Tattoo* are its warm humanity and its humor and its touching portrayal of a woman's devotion to her husband and daughter." And yet this summary is obviously inadequate. Breen would not be so easily persuaded that this sensational and shocking play was nothing more than a companion piece of sorts to John Van Druten's famous Broadway tear-jerker *I Remember Mama*. Even more provocative, perhaps, was the playwright's summary judgment of the ease with which he thought that PCA approval should be forthcoming: "Unless humanity itself has begun to fall under the censor's ban, there should be no serious difficulty in making a film out of this play that will not in any way violate either the story of essential truth of the characters *or* the code." Williams' proposed solution was for Mangiacavallo to return to Serafina's house drunk, lunge toward her eager embrace, fall in a faint, and be unreceptive thereafter to her attempts to revive him. In other words, the spirit would be willing but the flesh weak. Williams also thought that there would be little rewriting necessary to make the relationship of Rosa and Jack conform to the code: "As neither's chastity is violated, there will be no serious censorship problem in that scene." Notoriously unwilling to compromise on aspects of *Streetcar,* Williams now presented himself to Breen as a cooperative partner in the necessary reshaping of the material, demonstrating that he recognized in advance what might cause offense. Williams undoubtedly approached the writing of the first part of "Notes" as a somewhat unpleasant chore. It was necessary (or so he must have been advised) to ease the passage of the play from stage to screen, but disagreeable because he felt forced to recast his drama in terms he felt Hollywood censors might approve (the bathetic phrase "touching portrayal" would not have come naturally to him).

PLASTIC-POETIC ELEMENTS?

The concluding section of the memo, however, overflows with his genuine enthusiasm for the project; here he maintains that "the great problem is an artistic one," not one of censorship. At this point, the playwright's intended audience seems to be Wallis and Mann rather than Jack Vizzard. Williams argues that *Streetcar* was more successfully adapted than *Menagerie* because the Kazan film was "more faithful to the artistic concept of the original," and thus in a profound sense its equal. With *Tattoo*, however, the change in medium ought to result in substantial improvement because "the stage imposed merciless limitations on what was really the most valuable new aspects of *Tattoo*," those "plastic-poetic elements," of which only "the barest glimpse...was provided in the Broadway production." As Williams saw it, what was crucial to the play's intended effect (and what he regarded as his "plastic" elements) was what filmmakers call mise-en-scene: the visual and aural background that should provide meaning and depth to Serafina's resurrection, including such motifs as, in the playwright's colorful enumeration: "the wild play of the children, the Dionysian antics of the goat's escape and capture, the crazy Strega, the volatile life of the primitive neighborhood, the church, the chanted Mass, the organ music, the simple mysteries of the faith of a simple people, the surrounding earth, and sea, and sky, the great trucks thundering along the highway, the scarlet kite."

Vizzard quickly forwarded Williams' long memo to Breen, but the PCA head was unimpressed with Williams' argument and his proposed solutions. To his mind, these fell "far short of the basic requirements for making *Tattoo* acceptable under the Code" because "the only point with which Mr. Williams feels it is necessary to deal is the sex affair between Serafina and Alvaro." Unlike the playwright, Breen had been schooled in Thomist notions of sinfulness as primarily a matter of intentionality (the mental assent to wrongdoing being determinative of, and consequently more serious than, the resulting act). Williams' suggested rewriting, therefore, would not work, "since it will be quite evident that Alvaro returns to Serafina's house with the obvious intention of indulging in a sex affair with her, and only fails because he falls asleep in a drunken stupor." Breen makes the same point about the relationship between Rose and Jack, remarking that, even though the chastity of both young people is preserved, "a scene of a young girl begging a boy to take her sexually, would be thoroughly unacceptable under the Code." The PCA head was especially dismissive about Williams' plea that his characters were true to life (in essence, "humanity itself") and that such authenticity precludes moral objections; he snapped: "We do not know what Mr. Williams means by such statements." Breen concluded that the property would continue to be unacceptable as long as "Mr. Williams' idea of the 'humanity' of his characters involves their absorption in questions of sex and lust, as it does in the stageplay."[13]

This argument appears to be a strong stand against a by-then conventional thematic emphasis of a modernist text, but the PCA was no longer in a position to prevent such "carnality" from reaching the screen, as Breen quite evidently realized. For he ended his memo with an invitation to negotiate further after a screenplay was written: "We shall be very happy to read a script prepared from this material, if you see fit to develop one." As he had done in other cases, Breen could have simply reiterated his view of the "basic unacceptability of the story," effectively discouraging further work on the production unless major changes were made. Wallis, it seems, was supposed to read the message between the lines: compromises are possible in this case. Changes would thus be requested, made, and endorsed, but probably, on the part of Breen and his colleagues, with the somewhat dispiriting knowledge that there was no way Rosa, Alvaro, Serafina, and Jack could be freed from "their absorption in questions of sex and lust."

ROMANCE RATHER THAN LUST?

But before shooting could start, Breen's objections had in some sense to be accommodated, even if in an essentially cosmetic fashion. A year passed, and the PCA, having received a revised script, commented on the acceptability of the changes that had been made. One was easily effected: the replacement of the statue of the Madonna (to whom Serafina prays for assistance and guidance and with whom she becomes furious at one point) with "some personal memento of Serafina's dead husband."

But if this change diminished the presence of religion in the story, and hence the possibility of its seeming in some sense mocked, it ironically increased the sense of Serafina's preoccupation with the very carnality that Breen otherwise found objectionable. All jokes at the expense of religion were excised. As for the play's central scene, Breen advised that "the emphasis will not be put on [Alvaro's] desire to sleep with [Serafina], but upon romance rather than lust," a vague and difficult-to-evaluate reformulation that was, of course, entirely in line with mainstream Hollywood practice (and perfectly in keeping as well with the other pictures in the Wallis "drab melodrama" series). In fact, the general thrust of Breen's comments would have been to turn *Tattoo* more completely into a rather formulaic woman's picture: "Fundamentally this will be a story of a woman, Serafina, who is inordinately devoted to the memory of her dead husband, and who, as a result, exercises an unjust sway over her daughter's life."

Instead of centering on an ironic and mystical form of sexual healing, the proposed plot, according to this agreement between the producers and the censors, would turn on a time-honored melodramatic transformation: "The resolution of this problem will consist in Serafina growing up as a person, abandoning her fixation about her dead husband, releasing her daughter, and finally taking her proper place in the community."[14] The elements necessary for this character development are more or less present in Williams' original conception, of course, but the "growing up as a person" that Serafina does in the play and film depends entirely on the erotic renewal effected by Alvaro, who is essentially (and, of course, ironically) conceived of as a replacement for Rosario's body, thereby providing an interesting twist on the standard melodramatic theme of restoration.

There was no disguising that central element of the drama, however much Wallis and Breen might talk about the plot as if it were the stuff of a standard woman's picture. No matter that Alvaro should somehow drunkenly pass out so that the bedroom scene between him and Serafina could be avoided, as Breen advised. Perhaps sensing the intractability of the problem, Breen thought he might be deceived by Wallis and company even after both parties agreed to this explicit memorandum of understanding. And so he politely insisted on an important proviso: "May we suggest that, because of the difficult nature of the original material from which this basic story is to be derived, you might find it to your advantage to send along even the earliest draft treatments which you might prepare, on the way to developing a finished script."[15]

More negotiations followed, but by April 1954, Breen was more or less satisfied with the shape of the film, though he quibbled about minor "indiscretions" such as Alvaro discovering Rosa asleep on the couch.[16] Tellingly, that very funny scene, like most of the bawdiness of Williams' original conception, remained in the film despite the censor's disapproval. Breen was certainly dreaming when he advised the filmmakers that "the ending would be altered somewhat to emphasize the impression that Alvaro was going back to Serafina's house with marriage alone on his mind."[17] Wallis, Williams, and Mann may have humored Breen by agreeing to this demand, but, at least to judge from the finished film, they had no intention of keeping such a commitment.

Williams was less than pleased by the results of his collaboration with Hal Kanter. Concerned that the poetry was being stripped out of his work, he complained to Audrey Wood about the direction that the script was taking. Williams thought that the material was "admirably suited to the screen," but he was determined to retain "the lyrical values, the plastic values" that he described in his "Notes," lest the thrust of the material be destroyed.

In a piece entitled "A Playwright's Prayer," Williams elaborates on the complex relationship he had with his collaborators, striking a humble pose while at the same time holding his own ground.[18] In his petition, Williams asks his "Dear Father in Heaven" to "help me receive with interest and advice, whether solicited by myself or offered to me gratuitously, to read and consider all notes no matter who makes them." He also asks to be reminded "if I ever seem to forget it, that I am working with other creative artists whose dedication…may equal or exceed my own." In both the theater and the cinema, of course, artistic collaboration is not only desirable; it is obligatory.[19]

Williams asked Wood to discuss this issue with Wallis and to arrive at a solution involving "a collaborator who will be willing to work *under my direction*, since I think it is reasonable to assume that I, who created the play and the characters in it, am best able to judge whether or not they arc being re-created for the screen."[20] Kanter, he thought, "couldn't write 'I see the cat.'" The playwright worried: "Perhaps Wallis does not want *Tattoo* but another film loosely related to it." In particular, he was concerned that *Tattoo* "would be another *Menagerie* or worse, for the episodes in *Tattoo* will be grotesque and Serafina a ridiculous slob *unless* it exists in the poetic atmosphere of the original." The only thing he seemed satisfied with was the manner in which "all censorable material" had been eliminated.

Shortly after Williams sent Mann a new ending to *Tattoo* from Rome (presumably the ship's mast scene that appears in the finished film), he learned that Kanter had been removed from working on the picture, then wrote Wood that "if I am allowed to replace Kanter's stuff with my own, I think we will be in good shape."[21] The writing chores would thenceforth be his alone, and the finished film certainly bears the strong impress of his talent and interests. Wallis recalled that collaborating with Williams on the script was indeed a "happy experience," free from the producer-writer conflicts that can fatally compromise a project.[22]

Though he was initially pleased with the film fashioned from his play, Williams quickly became more ambivalent about both the picture and the work of the director, even though he managed to create more of a sensation with the Hollywood than the Broadway version. Later in 1955, the playwright declared, "It was inaccurate and unkind, equally both, to suggest that I blamed *Rose Tattoo's* relative lack of success [on Broadway] on its direction. Daniel Mann did a beautiful job on the stage version of *Tattoo* and a still more beautiful job on the film. Gadge would have demanded a stronger, tighter script from me: Danny was willing to take a chance on the script submitted."[23]

This last observation is right on target. Mann did not ask for the extensive changes that Kazan, had he directed the film, would surely have requested. The result is that the film belongs more to Williams than to Mann, Kanter, or Wallis. But this is surely very much to the good. The textures of play and film are amazingly similar, despite Williams' often fussy misgivings. Much of the original bawdy dialogue was retained, including such memorable double entendres as the heavy cargo that both Rosario and Alvaro are said to haul. Could it be anything besides king-sized bananas? And did Breen even get the joke?

This steamy (for the era) adult fare found itself that year in great favor with the viewing public. *Tattoo* proved to be, after *Streetcar*, one of the playwright's most substantial screen successes; and Wallis, despite his prominence in the industry, produced no better film in the decade. Anna Magnani's performance was hailed as one of the international screen's greatest, while Burt Lancaster, following up his well-received performance in *Sheba*, solidified his reputation as a talented actor (rather than just another pretty torso). He would go on to appear in a number of similarly "serious" roles, including tour de force character performances in two of the era's most acclaimed films, *Sweet Smell of Success* (1957) and *Judgment at Nuremberg* (1960). *Tattoo* would be well received by the members of the Academy of Motion Picture Arts and Sciences, nominated for best picture, music (Alex North), supporting actress (Marisa Pavan), and supporting actor (Ben Cooper), and receiving awards that year for best actress (Magnani), cinematography (James Wong Howe), and art direction (Hal Pereira).

THE SMELL OF ROSE OIL IN HIS HAIR

After reading the treatment submitted by Wallis, Joseph Breen had objected to *Tattoo* being absorbed with "questions of lust and gross sex." The PCA gave the production a green light only when Wallis assured him that the characters' obsession with carnality would be given a more traditional melodramatic turn, with Serafina transformed from a jealous, bitter, and sex-starved woman into a mother who, recognizing her need to "grow up," eventually becomes a proper parent to her adult daughter and assumes her proper place in the community. Breen, of course, must have been aware that such a reshaping would have ruined the value of Williams' play, which was appealing to Wallis and Paramount precisely because it was naughty and unconventional, not just another entry in the time-worn tradition of long-suffering-mother-centered melodramas, such as *Stella Dallas* (1937), *Imitation of Life* (1934, 1959), and *Madame X* (1929, 1937, 1965).

Tattoo, instead, would follow the controversial path that *Streetcar* had recently blazed. Legion of Decency raters had been struck by *Streetcar's* improper thematizing of *marital* sexuality, which, in the case of Stella and Stanley, was found to be less *caritas* and more *cupiditas,* the kind of lust rather than love that church doctrine held was an occasion for sin, even within the otherwise sacramental bonds of matrimony. At the time, the threat to rate the film a "C" was taken very seriously by Warner Brothers, which risked alienating one of Hollywood's hottest directors in order to accede to Legion demands, though they amounted to, as Kazan would point out, a tiny pointless finger in a dyke whose walls had already been irrevocably breached. If both the Legion and the PCA were in any doubt that their opinion of Williams' characters and themes was out of date, the public and the critics provided the proof, since *Streetcar* won not only four Academy Awards, but raked in huge profits at the box office as well.

The Legion had objected to a scene in *Streetcar* in which a man and his wife embraced with too much ardor and unguilty pleasure. Just a few years later, *Tattoo* would offer much more daring and more obviously carnal caresses. At the beginning of the film, Rosario is napping before the midnight smuggling run whose unexpected tragic conclusion will soon make Serafina a widow. She comes into the bedroom, where he is glimpsed posed horizontally in the foreground of the frame, naked from the waist up and wrapped in shadows that do not reveal his face but allow the rose tattoo to be seen glowing on his chest. Serafina sits down beside this sleeping form, softly strokes the muscles of his arm and chest, nuzzles his neck and back, and, with obvious delight and barely concealed ardor, smells the rose oil in his hair.

This striking tableau adumbrates the future state of Serafina's unsatisfied, mournful longing. Rosario never sits up to face her but rather remains recumbent and entirely available to her hands and eyes. The only dialogue in the scene is Serafina's ungranted plea that he not go away that night. Rosario briefly and prophetically responds that this will indeed be his last trip. More importantly, this scene also makes palpable and affecting the depth of her desire for her husband, who, in the tradition of pornographic representation, is artfully depersonalized. Reduced to near muteness, his fragmented body posed aesthetically, Rosario becomes flesh itself, the lovely *thing* for which Serafina aches. Here is no embrace of a couple whose mutual lust has been fed by violence and bitter words, but the very image of *cupiditas:* the purely carnal urge to possess and enjoy through worshipful objectification. Never moving (and avoiding close-ups), the camera clinically analyzes Serafina's psychological state from a respectful distance as Magnani gives a deeply convincing performance as a woman in barely restrained heat for a male body. Hollywood cinema had never before produced anything like this. In fact, such depictions of empowered female desire and a thoroughly objectified male body remain rare even in the post-PCA era.

It was a sign of the rapidly changing times that the PCA said not a word about this scene and that the Legion passed *Tattoo* with only the barest of demurrals and a "B" rating, signifying that the film was objectionable only in part. Just what part, we might well ask, would that be?

From *Hollywood's Tennessee: The Williams Films and Postwar America* by R. Barton Palmer and William Robert Bray, copyright © 2009. Courtesy of the authors and the University of Texas Press.

"
The expert evaluation fully

reveals that the nominated belongs

to modern drama's most promising

forces, but also that none of his

works so far correspond to the

exceptional demands that must be
"
placed here.

TENNESSEE WILLIAMS AND THE SWEDISH ACADEMY: WHY HE NEVER WON THE NOBEL PRIZE

Dirk Gindt

There are long-standing assumptions as to why Tennessee Williams never received the Nobel Prize, most of them stemming from an ill-fated visit he made to Sweden in the fall of 1955. As it turns out none of them are true. Williams went to Sweden in September 1955 at the invitation of Lilla van Saher-Riwkin and to attend the European premiere of *Cat on a Hot Tin Roof*, staged at Gothenburg City Theatre under the direction of Åke Falck. He initially spent a few days in Stockholm where he gave a press conference that created a minor stir among the assembled journalists. Not only did Saher-Riwkin's arrogant attempts to appear as Williams' agent alienate the members of the press, but the playwright himself indulged in diva-like behavior by dismissing a number of questions and dropping the ashes from his cigarette onto the carpet. As a result the papers were very unsympathetic to the author and portrayed him as an eccentric and alcoholic Southern playboy—with several homophobic allusions and descriptions barely hidden between the lines.[1] Williams was convinced that the hostility of the Swedish press cost him his chances of ever winning the Nobel Prize for Literature, a suspicion he pointed out in an interview as late as 1981.[2] After mining the archives of the Swedish Academy, I discovered that Williams was in fact nominated for the prestigious award three years later in 1958. Since the lists of nominations as well as the protocols of the Academy's internal discussions are kept secret for fifty years, Williams was understandably ignorant of this fact.[3]

IN THE NOBLE COMPANY OF STRINDBERG, IBSEN, SHAW, CHEKHOV AND O'NEILL

In order to be able to win the Nobel Prize for Literature, an author needs to be nominated. The nomination of a candidate can be put forward by previous laureates, members of the Swedish Academy or other academies, as well as by specially invited experts such as professors of languages and literature from around the world. One of these external experts was Napier Wilt (1895–1975), professor in the English Department and Dean of the Humanities at the University of Chicago. Wilt was an authority on American literature and drama and extensively studied the history of Chicago theaters. After his retirement in 1962, he lectured in Hong Kong, India, Italy and Finland. Further connections to the Nordic countries included his writings on early Norwegian dramatic societies in Chicago. He was also a personal friend of Bror Danielsson who put together a Swedish/English dictionary in 1964. When approached with a request to submit a suggestion for the 1958 Nobel Prize, Wilt proposed Williams. In a letter dated January 23, 1958, he motivated his choice by pointing to the playwright's domestic and international success as well as the universal appeal of *The Glass Menagerie*, *A Streetcar Named Desire* and *Cat on a Hot Tin Roof*: "The significance of his work lies in the fact that he has elevated the local to the universal. His dramas are not merely pictures of American life, but of well recognized aspects of human life." Wilt further called Williams "a serious, conscientious artist" who "has never tried for easy success" and concluded his recommendation stating that the playwright "belongs to…that noble company which includes Strindberg, Ibsen, Shaw, Chekhov, and O'Neill."[4]

As a next step, the Academy recruited competent advisers to write longer assessments on the literary output of the forty-one candidates that had been put forward that year. To receive a detailed overview of Williams, they approached Ebbe Linde (1897–1991), who was one of Sweden's leading theater critics. He started his career at the influential *Bonniers Litterära Magasin* [*Bonnier's Literary Magazine*] in 1941, and between 1948 and 1964 he was the main critic of Sweden's largest newspaper, *Dagens Nyheter* [*The Daily News*]. In addition to his position as reviewer, he published essays and poetry and translated both classical and contemporary drama, including Brecht's *Threepenny Opera*, as well as Latin and modernist French poetry. Linde was thus well equipped to analyze both the literary and the theatrical qualities of Williams' *oeuvre* and he submitted a fourteen-page, typewritten essay.

After a short biography and discussion of some earlier plays from Williams' period as an apprentice (including the collection *American Blues* which was unpublished in Sweden at that time), Linde started his summary of the more important works with the selection of one-act plays *27 Wagons Full of Cotton*. He praised Williams' ability to create atmospheric and dramatically charged scenes, his "lyrical sensibility"[5] and power to evoke the Southern landscapes of New Orleans and the Mississippi Delta, places with which the playwright was quite familiar. The main characters of the one-act plays were identified as mostly women whom life had treated badly and who tried to preserve some form of dignity through illusions that were often crushed by surroundings that showed little compassion for the frail and the weak: "Compassion with the eccentrics, with the trampled on and the misfits can generally be said to be the dominant motif in the author's approach, and not just in this work." Linde concluded that, "this early work already reveals its author in a nutshell. In the field of one-act plays it is probably the most significant work of this century." This enthusiastic assessment was even more striking since, at that point, none of the plays in *27 Wagons* had been performed in Sweden. Linde had obviously done his homework and made himself familiar with all of Williams' artistic output up to that point.

The critic then touched upon Williams' first full-length drama of importance, *Battle of Angels*, and even referred to the infamous smoke effects that caused a disastrous U.S. premiere in 1940. Surprisingly, he only briefly mentioned the big breakthrough with *The Glass Menagerie* and erroneously claimed that it had been directed by Elia Kazan. This disinterest in the play was an oddity because by 1958 the critical consensus in Sweden was that *The Glass Menagerie* was one of Williams' stronger plays against which every new stage work was inevitably compared.[6] Instead, Linde devoted more attention to *A Streetcar Named Desire* and its conflict between "the sensual, robust, vital, but insensitive and spiritually inexperienced human being on the one side, and the hypersensitive, divided and heavily exposed to life's thorns, spiritually striving and spiritually pretentious human being on the other hand." He stressed that Williams in this drama achieved a careful balance between these two types, although it was clear that his sympathies lay with the tragic character of Blanche and concluded: "That *A Streetcar Named Desire* is a dramatic masterpiece cannot be doubted." *Summer and Smoke* and *The Rose Tattoo* received favorable words and Linde sympathetically noted the experimental nature of *Camino Real*, never performed in Sweden, and even drew a parallel to Strindberg's last drama, *The Great Highway*. The final judgment about *Camino Real* however remained skeptical: "The idea can be called interesting, but does it succeed?"

Not surprisingly, Williams' latest hit play, *Cat on a Hot Tin Roof,* and especially its second act—"the play's tour de force" —received much praise.[7] The play's enormous international success was highlighted as well as the fact that it includes several rewarding parts for actors and a large number of strong scenes. Most strikingly, the open secret of Williams' homosexuality was raised in an ambiguous comment regarding the content of *Cat*: "The play is a piece of psychoanalytical demonstration that…is only distinguished by the fact that it is Tennessee Williams' first, if hesitant, grapple to stage the secondary issue of homosexuality, a problem that as far as is known has played some part in his personal way of life." Taking the erotic ambiguity of the character of Brick Pollitt as an excuse, Linde drew attention to how in 1958 Williams was a closeted homosexual playwright.

After a few comments on *Orpheus Descending*, Linde also discussed Williams' prose work and poetry, which he associated with Franz Werfel, the Austrian novelist and poet who left his mark on expressionism, and a young T. S. Eliot. Linde highlighted the short stories, in particular those in the collection *One Arm,* which he likened to "pearls" of literary art that deserved "to be given a high grade." He was particularly impressed by Williams' assured powers to evoke the social environment in these stories and also pointed out how both the characters and the themes were reminiscent of the one-act plays. While nothing was said of the explicitly homosexual content of the short stories, the paragraph on *The Roman Spring of Mrs. Stone* was distinguished by another ambiguous and gossipy comment, alleging that the novel "is built on erotic adventures that the author has experienced himself in the foreign environment, amongst its rootless post-war types." Once again, Williams' artistic output and his sexual lifestyle were muddled together by Linde.

In the concluding part of the essay, Linde debated the pros and cons of Williams' nomination and pointed out that the Academy had already rewarded modern American drama when it gave the Nobel Prize to Eugene O'Neill. He further mentioned that it was a close call between Williams and his contemporary Arthur Miller, briefly suggested a joint award for the two of them (even though he admitted that he would rather see Williams win the award on his own) and stated that less worthy authors had in fact won the prize. The summarizing part is worth quoting in its entirety:

> Tennessee Williams is one of the most solid and most noticed dramatic authors of our time. He can hardly be called a great formal pioneer or technical innovator, like Strindberg, Ibsen or Pirandello in their time, or like Brecht, Ionesco and even Anouilh in our days. On the other hand he is also, even if on a more modest scale, experimenting and driven by a conscious artistic will; and concerning human content, warmth and the seriousness of intention, he does not stand behind any of the above named and probably surpasses most of them.

Even though Linde's assessment was generally very favorable, it was not enough for the Swedish Academy. When its members reassembled after the summer break, they did not shortlist Williams among the five candidates for the final decision. Nevertheless, the Academy's internal attitude was far from negative and they agreed on the following statement for the protocol: "The expert evaluation fully reveals that the nominated belongs to modern drama's most promising forces, but also that none of his works so far correspond to the exceptional demands that must be placed here."[8] The suggestion of the board was to wait and see how Williams would develop as an author. The eventual recipient of the Nobel Prize for Literature in 1958 was Boris Pasternak "for his important achievement both in contemporary lyrical poetry and in the field of the great Russian epic tradition."[9] Pasternak, after severe pressure from the Soviet regime, declined to accept the award.

THE NOMINATION IN CONTEXT

Since 1901, the Nobel Prize for Literature has been awarded annually to an author who has, as stated in Alfred Nobel's will, "produced in the field of literature the most outstanding work in an ideal direction."[10] When scrutinizing the list of laureates one is struck by the amount of great playwrights that were never given the prestigious prize. Key authors such as Ibsen, Strindberg, Chekhov and Brecht are notably absent; the unsuccessful Williams can thus be said to be in good company.

In the following sections I offer a number of suggestions as to why Williams was not an interesting enough candidate for the Swedish Academy in 1958. These explanations are far from being exhaustive. Contextualizing Williams' unsuccessful nomination in 1958 in relation to the general perception of the man and his work, my objective is to give the reader a concise understanding of the cultural climate that reigned at the time as well as to illuminate Williams' critical reputation. Throughout the essay, I concentrate on *Cat on a Hot Tin Roof* to make my point, because this play in particular highlighted the contradictory status and reception of Williams in Sweden.

A HOMOPHOBIC CLIMATE

Linde's two comments alluding to Williams' homosexuality and lifestyle invite more attention. In a dubious way, the critic established a link between the subject matter of the play *Cat on a Hot Tin*

Roof, the novel *The Roman Spring of Mrs. Stone,* and their creator's personal life and sexuality. On the one hand, the comments were allusions that were never clearly elaborated. What was the exact nature of the "erotic adventures that the author has experienced" in Rome? And who were the "rootless post-war types" with whom he seemed to be very familiar? On the other hand, one could hardly misunderstand the claim that, in *Cat,* Williams attempted to represent "the secondary issue of homosexuality," a theme which was described as a "problem" and said to have "played some part" in Williams' life. This last statement illustrated to what extent by the late 1950s Williams was living in a glass closet—transparent enough for anyone to see through it. Although he had yet to come out in public, among theater artists, critics and audiences it was by then a well-established open secret that he was a homosexual.

So why would this piece of personal information be of interest or relevant to the members of the Nobel Committee? In her groundbreaking book *Epistemology of the Closet,* Eve Kosofsky Sedgwick celebrates "the precious, devalued art of gossip, immemorially associated in European thought with servants, with effeminate and gay men, with all women,"[11] because it helps to identify and create bonds with other gays, lesbians, bisexuals and transgendered people. Gossiping, "the great Gay Soap Opera quandary of wondering *Is-he-or-isn't-he?* and *Is-she-or-isn't-she?*"[12] has always been an important strategy for GLBT people to disrupt heterosexuality's claims to be a universal norm. On the other side of the same coin, as seen in Linde's assessment, gossip also plays an important part for mainstream culture to identify social and sexual deviants. Neither Williams' homosexuality nor his erotic adventures in Rome contribute to a better understanding of *Cat* and *Mrs. Stone.* I suggest, rather, that the main point of Linde's gossipy comments was simply to make Williams suspicious in the eyes of the Academy. Had its members awarded the Nobel Prize to Williams at that point, they would have recognized an author who not only frequently dealt with the subject of homosexuality, but who, moreover, was rumored to be sexually deviant. Linde certainly hammered the message home and no member of the Academy could have missed that Williams was identified as a homosexual and that he had personal experiences with the underworld of Mediterranean gigolos.

Because of these direct accusations, it is a striking oddity that the reviewer did not make a single comment about the gallery of characters in the short story collections *One Arm* and *Hard Candy*, which were explicit in their depiction of male hustlers, erotic massages and a lonely old man who seeks carnal embraces in a dark movie theater that specializes in cowboy films. The plays and the novel, two genres that reached a broader audience, are filled with allusions, codes, and hints about homosexuality without ever becoming as explicit as the short stories. They are distinguished by the aesthetics of the closet, that is, they are trying to articulate a homosexual life and experience in a world that denies, suppresses or tries to erase homosexuality.[13] The short stories however, with significantly lower distribution numbers at the time, offered a forum whereby Williams could write without being constrained by the pressures of the closet.[14] In Linde's assessment, these stories received a favorable review, but their content was never elaborated upon.

This contradiction is consistent with the general Swedish reception of Williams' closet aesthetics at the time. After *Cat* premiered in Sweden, reviewers openly debated the homoerotic friendship between Brick and Skipper. However, the play's homosexual content was constantly deferred and explained away as a matter of interest for an American audience which, unlike Swedish spectators, was said to enjoy such psycho-sexual content. The objective of this process of exoticization was to keep Swedish stages "clean" of the representation and embodiment of homosexuality.[15] As a rule, reviewers never did venture to debate the implications of mentioning, let alone staging, homosexual characters in the 1950s. Williams' closet aesthetics were thus never related to the intensively homophobic climate.[16] Officially, homosexuality in Sweden was classified as a mental disease between 1944 and 1979. Just as in many western countries, the general paranoia of the immediate post-war period conflated homophobia and the fear of communism, marking homosexuals as constituting a possible threat to national security and the corruption of the nation's youth. A number of highly publicized political scandals involved suspicions of homosexual blackmail and the tabloids sold issues with outrageous headlines about secret networks of homosexual men and their criminal activities.[17]

Based on Linde's two comments about *Cat* and *Mrs. Stone*, it is tempting to conclude that the Academy overlooking Williams was an act motivated by homophobia. However, large parts of the assessment were very enthusiastic and, as a theater critic, Linde was generally positively inclined when reviewing Williams' plays. Moreover, nothing in the Academy's internal protocol from their meeting in September 1958 corroborates that open homophobia factored into the decision. According to that statement, the members were waiting for Williams to write a work that would "correspond to the exceptional demands" of the Nobel Committee. Rather than accusing the Swedish Academy of homophobia, I suggest that the requested evaluation should be seen in context with the general homophobic discourse of the period. Homophobia certainly played an important part in the reception of Williams' plays in post-war Sweden, but there are further explanations which need to be taken into consideration when trying to understand Williams' reputation among the critical establishment and why he was not awarded the Nobel Prize.

A LACK OF FORMAL INNOVATION?

A major reason that Williams did not win the Nobel Prize when nominated in 1958 is to be found in Linde's opinion that Williams was not a "formal pioneer or technical innovator." It seems to me that the Academy was giving priority to form over content and did not deem Williams' writings to be formally innovative in the dramatic genre. A quick view at the motivations of why playwrights won the Nobel Prize reveals that the Academy traditionally welcomed and rewarded formal innovation. Maurice Maeterlinck[18] (1911) won it "in appreciation of his many-sided literary activities, and especially of his dramatic works, which are distinguished by a wealth of imagination and by a poetic fancy"; Gerhart Hauptmann[19] (1912) "primarily in recognition of his fruitful, varied and outstanding production in the realm of dramatic art"; George Bernard Shaw (1925) "for his work which is marked by both idealism and humanity, its stimulating satire often being infused with a singular poetic beauty"; Luigi Pirandello (1934) "for his bold and ingenious revival of dramatic and scenic art"; Eugene O'Neill (1936) "for the power, honesty and deep-felt emotions of his dramatic works, which embody an original concept of tragedy"; and, later, Samuel Beckett (1969) "for his writing, which—in new forms for the novel and drama—in the destitution of modern man acquires its elevation."[20]

Even though Williams scholars have convincingly argued that many of the playwright's classical dramas from the 1940s and 1950s unfold in a creative tension between realism and surrealism, most of his successful works were originally staged in a conventional realist mode, which made them appear more traditional than in fact they are.[21] The one exception is the experimental *Camino Real*, which was never staged in Sweden. In the foreword to *The Glass Menagerie*, Williams himself famously advocated a "plastic theatre which must take the place of the exhausted theatre of realistic conventions,"[22] but it was not until after *The Night of the Iguana* that he ventured into more experimental territory and more purposefully abandoned dramatic realism. Williams scholarship has made a convincing argument that many of the later plays, which stretch over a period of twenty years, should be regarded as a definitive break with realist conventions and a conscious artistic attempt to explore avant-garde forms.[23] However, given that contemporary audiences, critics, and academics were disinterested at best and downright hostile at worst in their reception of these later plays, coupled with the fact that virtually none of them were ever performed in Sweden, it is highly doubtful whether any of Williams' more formally challenging plays would have raised the Nobel Committee's interest. At this point, this is of course impossible to know and only future research will show if Williams was ever nominated again after 1958.

IN THE SHADOW OF A REVERED FATHER

Apart from the general homophobic climate of the period and the perceived lack of formal innovation in his dramas, it is useful to examine the relationship of Swedish theater to Eugene O'Neill as another explanation for why Williams was not attractive enough to be

awarded one of the most prestigous literary awards. In his overview
and assessment of Williams' *oeuvre*, Linde wondered whether the
Swedish Academy had already sufficiently recognized the qualities
of American drama by awarding the Nobel Prize to O'Neill in
1936. With this distinction, O'Neill's position as the founding
father of modern American drama was strengthened even further.
Although his career was virtually non-existent after he received
the Nobel Prize, by the late 1950s it had been successfully revived
thanks to the worldwide posthumous productions that heralded
his "second canonization."[24] The initial canonization had already
happened in the 1920s, when a new generation of critics elevated
O'Neill in a fast and consistent way to a position of worship and
declared him the key representative of legitimate American drama.
Moreover, European stages quickly accepted and embraced his
plays and perceived him as the quintessential American dramatist.[25]
Nowhere was this reverence more pronounced than in Sweden,
where the respect for and admiration of O'Neill had granted him
such a hegemonic position that a younger generation of American
playwrights would inevitably be compared to the grand master. In
fact, one of the first Swedish articles on Williams ever to appear
reported on the success of *The Glass Menagerie* and referred to the
rumors that identified him as "O'Neill's heir" on Broadway.[26] Over
the next decade and a half, Williams would frequently be judged
and evaluated against the older playwright. Not only had O'Neill
won the Nobel Prize, but the national stage, the Royal Dramatic
Theater in Stockholm (the Dramaten), which is sponsored by
government funding and whose mandate it is to preserve the
national heritage and present international works of high artistic
value, frequently produced his plays. By 1962, the Dramaten had
presented no fewer than fourteen of O'Neill's works and, as a result,
scholars and critics often speak of an "O'Neill-tradition," highlights
of which include director Olof Molander's acclaimed productions of
Mourning Becomes Electra in 1933 and *A Moon for the Misbegotten*
in 1953.[27] The biggest coup however came when UN Secretary
General Dag Hammarskjöld helped to establish a direct contact
between the Dramaten's managing director Karl Ragnar Gierow
and O'Neill's widow Carlotta, to whom the playwright had left the

rights to his dramatic work. Ignoring her late husband's wish not to stage the then unpublished play *Long Day's Journey into Night* for another twenty-five years, Carlotta entrusted the Dramaten with the world premiere in 1956. Bengt Ekerot's psychological realist production of the play became a milestone in Swedish theater history and, as a result, further posthumous premieres took place at the Dramaten—*A Touch of the Poet* (1957), *Hughie* (1958) and *More Stately Mansions* (1962)—cementing even further the house's reputation as a leading O'Neill stage.[28]

Interestingly, Gierow's attitude towards Williams was much less enthusiastic and during his time as managing director (1951–1963), not a single play penned by Williams was to be produced at the Dramaten, which had previously staged the Swedish premiere of *The Glass Menagerie* in 1946 and presented a production of *A Streetcar Named Desire* in 1949. While Gierow was busy negotiating with Carlotta O'Neill and further enhancing his theater's "O'Neill-tradition," he seemed indifferent to securing the rights for *The Rose Tattoo*, *Cat on a Hot Tin Roof*, *Suddenly Last Summer*, *Sweet Bird of Youth* or *The Night of the Iguana*.[29] Instead, Williams found a welcoming harbor in the City Theaters in Gothenburg and Malmö as well as some private theaters in Stockholm. These must not be construed as second-rate stages—on the contrary. The recently established City Theaters, especially, challenged the hegemonic position of the Dramaten, not least by trying to be the first Scandinavian (and in some cases, European) stages to present contemporary foreign dramas. The 1950s are correctly identified as the "golden age of the City Theaters"[30] and some of the country's finest actors and directors, of whom Ingmar Bergman was the most famous, frequently presented new Williams plays. Nevertheless, the national stage was highly esteemed by both theater artists and the critics. It was thus a question of cultural capital and, as long as Williams was not played at the Dramaten, this was a clear signal that important parts of the cultural establishment did not deem him worthy of being included in the noble company of O'Neill and other sophisticated playwrights. This skepticism could not have eluded the members of the Swedish Academy, an institution that, just like the Dramaten, is based in Stockholm.

The Dramaten's indifference to Williams, who, along with Jean Anouilh, was the period's most popular foreign playwright, provoked considerable disapproval from the critics. The decision not to present *Cat on a Hot Tin Roof*, for instance, was met with regret by a reviewer who stated that "one shivers when thinking of the impact this [play] could make at the Dramaten" because of the distinguished ensemble that included some of the country's finest actors.[31] Another reviewer simply called this disinterest "a scandal"[32] and a third one wondered whether the current management "wants the national stage to stick with O'Neill and dismiss later American theater as a cheap imitation."[33]

With or without the blessing of the national stage, *Cat* was a major success and, within fifteen months, five different Swedish productions were staged, all of them big successes with audiences. After the premiere, critics made very favorable comparisons to O'Neill. *Svenska Dagbladet* stated that the play established Williams as "O'Neill's obvious heir" and compared its dramatic effect, its structure and motifs to *A Moon for the Misbegotten*.[34] *Vecko-Journalen* enthusiastically proclaimed Williams to be an equal to Chekhov and O'Neill, not least because of his talents to evoke a distinct landscape and capture its atmosphere.[35] Finally, *Dagens Nyheter* claimed that the dramatic power of the long confrontation between Brick and Big Daddy in *Cat's* second act was comparable to Strindberg and O'Neill.[36] While the management of the Royal Dramatic Theater obviously did not seem to agree with such an appraisal, the Swedish critics were certainly pushing comparisons with these, by then, canonized modernist playwrights. There was however one crucial difference: while those dead authors were established as unquestionably serious playwrights, Williams was considered to be a popular, not to say populist, one. The critics themselves contributed to this perception of Williams and, once again, the reception of *Cat* can serve as an example to illustrate this claim.

Although *Cat* was generally well-received, some critics accused Williams of making use of cheap, shocking devices in order to titillate his audiences. As stated above, the play's homoerotic content was far from being uncontroversial, but so were other themes that Williams dealt with. *Morgon-Tidningen* for instance wondered:

"Does Tennessee Williams really need an old man dying of cancer, a limping alcoholic who in addition seems to be homosexual, and a number of relatively featherbrained and repugnant individuals to create dramatic tension?"[37] The same paper also condemned "this grotesque family gallery with alcoholism, homosexuality and cancer as flavoring ingredients."[38] A similar comment appeared in *Arbetet*, whose reviewer disliked the play and disapprovingly listed its themes in a long-winded way:

> the clash between the generations, alcoholism, homosexuality (which after the Kinsey report has become such a popular theme in the United States), female erotic dissatisfaction (a phenomenon that was once taboo, but whose existence during the landslide of the post-war era has dawned for the descendants of the Puritans and is nowadays openly ventilated).[39]

On the one hand, the critical establishment compared Williams to the great modernist playwrights and, on the other hand, it charged him with making use of populist devices to capture his audience's attention, an accusation that disqualified him from being regarded as a high-minded artist. The topics of cancer and alcoholism were already scandalous enough in the mid-1950s and, coupled with the erotic ambiguity of the male lead and the sexual desire of the female lead, seriously affected Williams' reputation and made him appear as an *enfant terrible* of the stage (which also contributed to his popularity with audiences).

Furthermore, while the critics admired how *Cat* respected the three classical unities of time, space, and plot, and specifically praised the powerful second act, they were hardly impressed by the play's forced happy ending. Most Swedish productions followed the script of the so-called Broadway version and thus presented the third act that Williams was convinced to write after the suggestions made by director Kazan and that ends with a clear hint of reconciliation between Maggie and Brick.[40] The highly publicized story, true or not, of Williams giving in to Kazan's demands had reached Sweden and seriously damaged the playwright's critical reputation. One critic deployed a language typical of its time to express the play's "instances of … inconsistency, as if a Negro with a tenor saxophone joined in chamber music." Comparing the Broadway version with Williams' original act (the reading version of which was available at the time), the journalist then stated that "one realizes that the saxophone is Kazan."[41] While this simile was put forward in racially problematic language, it summed up the general assessment of the third act of *Cat*: Swedish reviewers dismissed the Broadway act as the commercial version and quickly pointed fingers at Kazan.[42] It is highly likely that the Swedish Academy was aware of this negative reception of the third act of *Cat*, even though Linde never mentioned it in his report. Regardless of Williams' own motivations for making the changes and regardless of the specific dynamics of the collaboration between him and Kazan, rewriting a play in order to guarantee a commercial success hardly lived up to the "exceptional demands" placed by the Academy to reward an author's literary *oeuvre*.

Regardless of a flattering letter of recommendation and a very sincere critical assessment of his work, Williams' nomination for the Nobel Prize in 1958 was unsuccessful. While he was exceptionally popular with audiences, his dramatic and literary output was deemed as slightly too controversial, slightly too populist, and not quite highbrow or innovative enough. Apart from being accused of titillating audiences with scandalous themes and cheap effects, he was also suspected of sacrificing artistic integrity to commercial success. Moreover, Williams' closet was at this time an open secret. In a generally homophobic climate, critics could use their knowledge of this open secret to make vague (and sometimes not so vague) allusions to his lifestyle. While it is of course possible that Williams was nominated again after the initial nomination in 1958, it is doubtful whether the gothic *Suddenly Last Summer* or the violent *Sweet Bird of Youth* would have appealed to the Swedish Academy. It is also unlikely that any of his more experimental works after *The Night of the Iguana* would have been received favorably, especially in light of the fact that, after *Iguana* in 1962, hardly any new stage works by Williams would be performed in Sweden.

"One man. Three women. One night.

The Night of the Iguana. Since man

has known woman, there has never

been such a night."

PULP WILLIAMS: TENNESSEE IN THE POPULAR IMAGINATION

Thomas Keith

The Madison Avenue aphorism that "sex sells" is even truer when the sex is sensational. Sex combined with violence, or with intimations of violence, sells even better. When Williams wasn't being misremembered as the guy who wrote the song "Sixteen Tons"— written of course by Tennessee Ernie Ford—for decades he was often thought of as a writer of shocking sexuality and violence. Tennessee Williams' image in the popular imagination, beyond Broadway, touring companies, regional theater, countless amateur productions, and far from academia, was established in the marketing of the film versions of his work and in their mass-market paperback tie-in editions. Promotion through various media overlapped to create faulty shorthand about the spirit of Williams' work. In the world of arts and letters he was often given a wider berth; at best considered to be a theatrical genius and a compassionate poet of the outcasts of society. But for many people he was, as theater critic Richard Watts, Jr. wrote, "steeped in passion, hatred, bitterness, and violence."[1] Williams' first published fiction was a fantastic tale of violence and murder, "The Vengeance of Nitocris," published when he was seventeen in the pulp magazine, *Weird Tales*, in 1928. Was it prophetic or, perhaps, merely consistent?

While Williams was enjoying his last commercial success with *The Night of the Iguana*, T. E. Kalem penned a cover story for the March 9, 1962 issue of *Time* magazine in which he declared Williams to be the world's greatest living playwright, "barring the aged Sean O'Casey."[2] Kalem, a great fan of Williams' work and a relatively sympathetic reviewer all the way through the troubled late work and up to *Something Cloudy, Something Clear* in 1981, begins the article with an anecdote from Williams' mother, Edwina, about a pre-school-age Williams making up adventure stories for a rapt audience and frightening himself in the process. Kalem then proceeds to single out and define several of Williams' plays by the salacious aspects of plot and character that had been used for several years to secure Williams reputation as America's most scandalous playwright:

> "[Williams] is the nightmare merchant of Broadway, writer of *Orpheus Descending* (murder by blowtorch), *A Streetcar Named Desire* (rape, nymphomania, homosexuality), *Summer and Smoke* (frigidity), *Cat on a Hot Tin Roof* (impotence, alcoholism, homosexuality), *Sweet Bird of Youth* (drug addiction, castration, syphilis), *Suddenly Last Summer* (homosexuality, cannibalism), and *The Night of the Iguana* (masturbation, underwear fetishism, coprophagy)."[3]

This critical reduction of Williams' work was not new, and it was not entirely unwarranted, but it was previously accomplished one play at a time. Overall, the Kalem article is a well-written portrait of the playwright that focuses as much on the sensational as it does on the literary, biographical, and theatrical aspects of his life. It might seem absurd at this point, as perhaps it would have in 1962, to tag those same plays with labels that focus on some of their more substantial, though often elusive, emotional, spiritual, intellectual, political, and literary themes:

Play	Sensational Plot Elements	Relevant Dramatic Themes
Orpheus Descending	murder by blowtorch	alienation, rebirth, mythic tragedy
A Streetcar Named Desire	rape, nymphomania, homosexuality	sensuality, survival, madness
Summer and Smoke	frigidity	spiritual longing, love, eroticism
Cat on a Hot Tin Roof	impotence, alcoholism, homosexuality	endurance, betrayal, mendacity, repression, mortality
Sweet Bird of Youth	drug addiction, castration, syphilis	celebrity, youth, failure, political corruption
Suddenly Last Summer	homosexuality, cannibalism	obsession, blackmail, free will, existentialism
The Night of the Iguana	masturbation, underwear fetishism, coprophagy	spiritual endurance, depression and panic, compassion

Perhaps no more cheerful than Kalem's list, these literary motifs are valid for these particular plays. By 1962, and in the decades since, it was the alarming elements, such as those from Kalem's list, which defined Williams' popular reputation. However it did not start out that way.

Prior to Hollywood's marketing of Williams, he was introduced to the world as a theatrical and literary phenomenon. Eight of the covers for the first trade editions of Williams' writing published by New Directions were designed by Alvin Lustig (1915–1955), an innovator in graphic design who achieved his greatest fame designing book covers for New Directions, Knopf, Meridian Books, and Noonday Press. Lustig's non-representational images and simple yet inventive use of illustration, color, and typography became the epitome of artistry and elegance. His designs for the

New Directions editions of Tennessee Williams' plays *A Streetcar Named Desire, Summer and Smoke, The Glass Menagerie, The Roman Spring of Mrs. Stone, One Arm and Other Stories, 27 Wagons Full of Cotton, The Rose Tattoo, Camino Real,* and *Cat on a Hot Tin Roof* are considered classics of modern book design and have been admired by generations of readers and designers. From the clean, swift, abstract figures on the cover of *Streetcar* to the photograph of a single magnolia blossom nailed to a barn wall on the cover of *Twenty-seven Wagons Full of Cotton,* Lustig managed to convey both the poetry and the narrative power of Williams' writing, and gave Williams' fiction and plays the right dramatic touch. Founder and publisher of New Directions, James Laughlin (1914–1987) felt, "They brightened the books up.…His beautiful designs [helped] to make a mass audience aware of high quality reading."[4] These chic and often powerful covers also placed Williams within a sphere of serious literature published during the same period. Being part of the New Directions list put Tennessee Williams in the company of modernists such as Ezra Pound and William Carlos Williams, cutting edge poets such as Dylan Thomas and Kenneth Patchen, and international writers including Sartre, Celine, Nabokov, Lorca, Rimbaud, and Octavio Paz. After Lustig's death, covers for Williams' titles remained consistent with the stylish, often abstract, designs of other covers from New Directions, avoiding entirely any implication that the author was anything other than distinguished and significant. The same could not be said, however, for the covers of the mass-market, move tie-in editions of Williams' work that were published beginning in 1952 with *A Streetcar Named Desire.*

From 1950 to 1970, fifteen feature films were produced in Hollywood based on original material by Tennessee Williams, and there have been more film and television adaptations of Williams' work than that of any other modern playwright.[5] The years of Williams' Broadway successes, 1945 to 1961, overlap only eleven of the prolific years of his feature film career. Although many of the films were less potent, watered-down, or bowdlerized cinematic translations of his plays, they reached a significantly larger audience and, with the exception of the Warner Brothers version of *The Glass Menagerie* (1950), they were marketed with an increasingly calculated approach that solidified the image of Tennessee Williams in the public imagination as that of a writer of violence, sex, scandal, and shock. While Williams' critical reputation in the theater remains strong—in spite of wide disagreement as to the value and viability of his later work—his reputation among the generations that grew up on the Hollywood versions of his work is equivalent to that of a writer of pulp fiction.

The mass-market movie tie-in editions of Williams plays published by New American Library under the Signet imprint were descended from the original "pulp fiction" magazines of the nineteenth century, so named because of the poor quality of pulped paper used in their production and their inexpensive cover price. The high-speed manufacturing of the paperback book came out of technology developed during World War II.[6] Combined with the wartime paper shortage, this created the ideal environment for the development of the mass-market paperback from approximately 1945 to 1965. From a sales standpoint, pulp fiction was cheap entertainment; stories of crime and sexuality sold in covers illustrated by pulp magazine artists with colorful, realistic genre paintings depicting dramatic human figures— squared jawed men and scantily clad women—often involved in acts of violence or passion. Classic writers from Shakespeare to Oscar Wilde and from Sophocles to Edgar Allan Poe were given the pulp treatment, as were hundreds of lesser-known authors of romance and mystery, countless unknown writers whose work was considered all but pornographic, and underground writers of straight, gay, and lesbian pornography. However, it is the classic crime, detective fiction, noir, and spy writers of the twentieth century such as Arthur Conan Doyle, E. C. Bentley, Dashiell Hammett, Mickey Spillane, Ellery Queen, Raymond Chandler, Agatha Christie, James M. Cain, John D. MacDonald, Jim Thompson, John LeCarre, and Ian Fleming who still define the genre.[7]

The focus on sex and violence in the film adaptations of Williams' plays, whether actually part of the films or not, offered publicity and marketing a handy hook on which to hang the titillating language and stimulating imagery of pulp fiction and to sell his work on revolving metal racks with other spicy mass-market offerings. Williams was by no means the only contemporary literary writer to receive the pulp treatment of crime and noir fiction. Distinguished writers including Sinclair Lewis, Robert Penn Warren, Erskine Caldwell, Pearl S. Buck, Arthur Miller, Gore Vidal, Edna Ferber, Aldous Huxley, George Orwell, John Steinbeck, William Faulkner, Ernest Hemingway, William Inge, and Truman Capote had books published with the same scintillating covers and on the same sort of cheap paper.

The first Williams film to utilize a mass-market paperback tie-in as part of the publicity campaign was Warner Brothers' film version of *A Streetcar Named Desire* (1951) directed by Elia Kazan. Appropriately sold as a sultry yet serious art film, the preview summarized the plot, "an innocent woman pitted against an untrustworthy, cunning man." However, the producer's battle with the censors became public before the film's release and heightened interest in what was already well known as a titillating story.[8] The Signet paperback used a color reproduction of a painting by Thomas Hart Benton of the Broadway cast that had caused some upset, in particular for Jessica Tandy who found the painting to be an inaccurate and over-sexualized interpretation of Blanche.[9] The Benton painting takes up less than half of the paperback cover and has a mildy pulp fiction feel to it. Though there is a photo on the back cover of Vivien Leigh wearing a slip, if anything the highbrow approach was maintained, the author's Pulitzer Prize being the most prominent cover description.[10] The mass-market edition of *Streetcar* became provocative when a photo of Marlon Brando, naked from the waist up, was printed on the cover of a new edition in 1974.

With the *The Rose Tattoo* (1955), directed by Daniel Mann and produced by Hal Wallis and Paramount, the film advertising took on a somewhat more aggressive tone. As various scenes from the film are strung together in the trailer to introduce the plot, a voice describes the performers while the following descriptions flash over the images: "fiery drama," "package of dynamite," "great performers," "seething violence," "lusty drama," and "startling frankness." A lusty drama to be sure and also a dark comedy, but the film offers no violence and certain no seething violence, and compared to the stage version it did not approach startling frankness. However, these exaggerations must have been effective, because they would grow into astounding claims for later pictures. The Signet tie-in edition of *The Rose Tattoo* has a modestly pulp-like cover illustration that includes a photograph of Anna Magnani tightly holding her bare-chested screen husband (who never actually appears in the film), but the book still advertised the literary reputation of its author and his, by then, two Pulitzer Prizes.[11]

The marketing ante was upped by producer/director Elia Kazan for the trailer of *Baby Doll* (1956), which is likewise more salacious than its pulp tie-in and begins with a low husky voiceover, "This is the story of Baby Doll, a seventeen-year-old bride," as a still photo of Carroll Baker in her crib turns with the title from vertical to horizontal, and the camera zooms in until the screen is filled with the image of her thumb in her mouth. If that wasn't enough to imply that a "dirty picture" was being promised, the following text appeared over shots of Karl Malden, Eli Wallach, and Lonny Chapman: "Dumb Fat Husband," "Shifty Sneaky Italian," and "Big Black Buck." You're not alone if you don't recall the latter character—it was the minor role of Rock, used in the advertising to project a misleading racial component into a film that was already misrepresented as containing scenes of explicit sex, which it did not. The final tag for the preview reiterated the insinuation of underage sex: "sweet as honey...sweet as sin." The Signet paperback tie-in edition took the highbrow road in most of the copy, emphasizing Williams' prizes and theatrical credentials and printing Kazan's and Williams' names in almost the same size font. However, the single, striking cover image is a photographic color close-up of Carol Baker sucking her thumb in the crib— it was likely that by then the major publicity campaign, and the objections of Cardinal Spellman, detailed by Vincent Brook in "Courting Controversy: The Making and Selling of *Baby Doll* and the Demise of the Production Code," had made the title and the central image quite familiar to the general public. Even without the film, this would be a classic pulp fiction cover.[12] While it remains a comic story electrified by a sexual current, the fame of its scandal is what it is still remembered for.

The *Baby Doll* campaign set the tone for ten of the next eleven screen adaptations of original work by Williams. The producers of MGM's *Cat on a Hot Tin Roof* (1958), directed by Richard Brooks, learned from their predecessors the value of a consistent visual tie-in and of sex in advertising. While the trailer promised "shocking impact and uncompromising realism," what it really promised was sex. The character of Maggie is a sensual, cunning survivor, but in the person of a young and beautiful Elizabeth Taylor wearing a tight white lace brassiere, a slip, and pantyhose, in perfect hair and makeup, and kneeling on a brass bed, she was a stunning visual marketing strategy—sexual in a way that straddled artistic and sordid sensibilities. Combined with handsome Paul Newman wearing pajamas and carrying a drink and a crutch, the image was nearly as potent as the one for *Baby Doll*.[13] Compared to the trade edition designed by Lustig, which is essentially a photograph of the Milky Way, the contrast is striking. The fiery graphic of red, orange, and yellow flames painted in behind Taylor and Newman were used on the posters, newspaper ads, lobby cards, the cover of the Signet paperback, and the opening credits of the preview and film as well.

With producer Sam Spiegel's *Suddenly Last Summer*, directed by Joseph Mankiewicz, finally, there was a perfect mix of content and marketing—the film *is* sensational and must have been shocking to audiences when it opened. The offstage events that the character Catherine recounts in the play are horrific, but were left to the imaginations of theater audiences—Williams often insisted they were allegory, not to be taken literally.[14] However, in the film they are acted out and even augmented by visuals of Elizabeth Taylor as Catherine in a sheer white bathing suit in the water, out of the water, walking on the beach, and of the wild band of children chasing a patrician, faceless homosexual, Sebastian, up the hot white streets of Cabeza de Lobo before they mutilate him. Throw in Montgomery Clift, Katharine Hepburn, a private indoor jungle, madness, and the threat of a lobotomy, and it all added up to a "depraved film." Little mention of Williams' writing prowess was made in either the preview or on the mass-market paperback, and both carried the incendiary phrase, "Cathy knew she was being used for [something] evil." On the paperback it reads, "With shattering realism, Tennessee Williams boldly unmasks the corrosive personality of a corrupt sensualist in...*Suddenly Last Summer*."[15] In the preview we hear, "[Williams]...unashamedly writes of a woman's strong wants and a man's strange needs." Evil. Corrupt. Strange needs. It wouldn't have taken a genius to figure out that there was some kind of aberrant sexual behavior in the film—although the homosexuality is merely alluded to, that was sufficiently appalling enough at the time.

With the exception of *Period of Adjustment* (1966), which was sold as a "saucy comedy," all the other films were given some degree of cinematic pulp treatment: *The Fugitive Kind* (1960), *Summer and Smoke* (1961), *The Roman Spring of Mrs. Stone* (1961), *Sweet Bird of Youth* (1962), *The Night of the Iguana* (1964), *This Property is Condemned* (1966), *BOOM* (1968), and *Last of the Mobile Hotshots* (1969).

Fugitive Kind, *Summer and Smoke*, *Roman Spring*, and *Iguana* were fundamentally serious literary and theatrical works that were sold as sexy potboilers. A dark story of the downfall of three outcasts in a racist Southern town, *Fugitive Kind* (adapted from the stage play *Orpheus Descending*) was advertised with photos of the stars, Anna Magnani, Marlon Brando, and Joanne Woodward, posed as if they were in a love triangle, and banners reading, "Their fire...their fever...their desire! And now the screen is struck by lightning!" The mass-market tie-in features a pulp fiction-style illustration of Magnani and Brando on a bed, while Joanne Woodward looks on wistfully from a short distance. The cover copy declares that it is "a passion-lashed motion picture."[16]

Summer and Smoke is the delicate story of a Southern woman who is repressed sexually and emotionally, and whose possible sexual relief is only indicated in the last few moments of the play and the film. Even the unfortunately botched screenplay by James Poe and Meade Roberts doesn't warrant the sexual tone of the advertising, primarily a pulp-style painting of stars Geraldine

Page and Laurence Harvey which appears to be the scenario of a handsome man forcing himself on a reluctant woman. The back cover copy reads, "Tennessee Williams' tragic drama of two ill-starred lovers: an idealistic girl/ and a wildly passionate young man—one hungering for the spirit, the other hungering for the flesh." [17] A good example of how far removed this pulp treatment takes the work from its more serious literary roots is a comparison of the Alvin Lustig cover of the New Directions edition of the play from 1948 with the mass-market movie tie-in cover published by New American Library in 1961. [18]

Roman Spring of Mrs. Stone, This Property is Condemned, and *BOOM* received rather half-hearted pulp treatment. Adapted from Williams' novel, *Roman Spring* was sold in the trailer as a highbrow film about "A Strange Romance," and advertised on the paperback as a "daring [novel] of a frustrated woman who turns to younger men for love," with a blurred and retouched photo of a very young Warren Beatty falling vaguely into a mature Vivien Leigh's bosom. Miss Leigh's head is resting on the pillow the way it might in a coffin. [19]

The trashiest promise made for *This Property*—almost nothing of which but the title comes from a one-act play by Williams—is found on a poster and refers to a seductively clad and posed Natalie Wood, "Call her what you want. Do with her what you will. But remember…THIS PROPERTY IS CONDEMNED."

BOOM, which has reached nearly legendary status as a "bad film," is a campy retelling of the more serious play, *The Milk Train Doesn't Stop Here Anymore.* Although there was no mass-market tie-in edition, the posters showed the leads, Elizabeth Taylor and Richard Burton, yelling at each, separated by the line, "They devour each other," or in a passionate clutch with the punny headline, "Taylor and Burton Explode In BOOM!"

Most outrageous was the pulpization of *The Night of the Iguana,* a poignant drama about lost souls who converge on a hilltop over the Gulf of Mexico looking for, variously, understanding, control, compassion, love, emotional balance, and spiritual grace. Out of a black screen the trailer begins as the rapid pounding of drums is heard, then dropout-white sketches of the faces of the stars of the film come out of the blackness—first Richard Burton, then all together Deborah Kerr, Ava Gardner, and Sue Lyons emerge—then suddenly the screen switches to footage of lightning illuminating a beach in a tropical storm, then a sketch of Burton and Lyons floats under the title of the movie as it quickly fills the screen. Over all this, the deep rich voice of a young James Earl Jones is heard to intone, "One man. Three women. One night. *The Night of the Iguana*. Since man has known woman, there has never been such a night." If that doesn't imply that there's going to be an orgy, nothing does. The mass-market edition offers the same mathematical possibilities, but the graphics are more contemporary, like those used for perhaps an Ian Fleming novel; the grainy white sketches of the leads are below a geometrical drawing of an iguana-like man with his arms around a naked, orange woman, and they border the title.[20]

Perhaps a more legitimate ad campaign was matched to the film version of *Sweet Bird,* directed by Richard Brooks and produced by Pandro S. Berman. "He Used Love Like Most Men Use Money," read the movie posters. The implications of the older woman, Geraldine Page, coupled with the younger man, Paul Newman, were inherently potent; not only was Paul Newman's character prostituting himself, but both actors were sexually charged, the stakes high, and the chemistry between them came through on the screen. The urgent voiceover in the preview trailer tells us:

> Never before, even in the unconventional world of Tennessee Williams has there been anyone like the Princess who understood Chance Wayne / Never before, even in the love-hungry world of Tennessee Williams has there been a girl like Heavenly, who loved Chance Wayne / Never before, even in the savage world of Tennessee Williams, where there are no rules and no limits, have people tasted deeply of life's pleasures and of its frustrations.

Unconventional. Love-hungry. Savage. No rules. No limits. And the cover of the mass-market tie-in paperback shows an illustrated photo of the two leads in bed, obviously naked but wrapped in sheets, and the cover copy promises, "Two self-corrupters recklessly courting the SWEET BIRD OF YOUTH with evil, hatred, and wild, passionate love"—a trashy description worthy of any pulp fiction romance.[21]

The last Williams film released during this period, *The Last of the Mobile Hot-shots*, is based on the 1968 play, *Kingdom of Earth*, which ran on Broadway under the producer David Merrick's preferred title of *The Seven Descents of Myrtle*. To further complicate the matter, Gore Vidal's original title for the screenplay was *Blood Kin*, under which title the film was released in the United Kingdom and Australia. *Mobile Hot-shots*—involving two half-brothers, one black and one white, the latter of whom is dying and returns home with a woman he married on a game show—had the potential to be a controversial film due to racial and sexual ingredients in the original play, but the screenplay was a confusing muddle and it engendered a slow, and rather dull, film. The pulp aspects in the marketing were modified to fit the aesthetics of the late 1960s. There was no mass-market tie-in from Signet, but the film promotion involved posters of the two men, James Coburn on a brass bed and Robert Hooks standing behind it, while in the foreground Lynn Redgrave looks back over her shoulder wearing low-slung jeans and removing her bra. The copy reads, "Tennessee Williams' story of two brothers… and the woman they shared." In a large circle nearby there is a warning: "SUITABLE ONLY FOR ADULTS." Any casual observer could reasonably assume it was pornography.

While other writers from outside the film industry received the same lowbrow, pulp treatment, Williams was the only literary writer who it stuck to. This is in part because of the nature of his plays, but much more due to his prolifigacy and commercial viability—the films just kept coming and the producers kept utilizing proven advertising and marketing techniques for getting bodies in the seats. To what extent Williams thought about how the pulp marketing would affect his reputation, whether he was amused by it or paid much attention to it all, he certainly approved the sale of his work to Hollywood and welcomed the income.

Had the films of Tennessee Williams' plays never been made he would still be known as a groundbreaking and sometimes shocking author. But his work might not so consistently be thought of by the extreme plot elements in T. E. Kalem's list. The pulp fiction-style advertising and marketing that accompanied these films for over fifteen years solidified a negative shorthand about Williams' work and hence, his character, which was only reinforced by the critical theatrical failures of his later years, his public battles with drugs and alcohol, the negative reaction to his *Memoirs* (1975), and the ongoing truism that sex and violence sell.

"
Why, rather than be banal

and hysterical and absurd,
"
doesn't he keep quiet?

MR. WILLIAMS IS ADVISED TO STAY SILENT

David Kaplan

DESERVING THE FLICK AIMED AT A PESTIFEROUS INSECT

On Sunday November 5, 1961 *The New York Times* published an article by its then chief drama critic, Howard Taubman. The occasion was the Broadway run of *We've Come Through,* a play written by Hugh Wheeler and directed by José Quintero, with an unknown Burt Reynolds in the small role of a rough-trade sailor. This was Wheeler's second play. The plot centered on a gay man, as did Wheeler's first play, *Big Fish, Little Fish.*[1]

Two weeks before, on Thursday, October 26, Taubman had given *We've Come Through* a qualified review with good quotes: "it has fine tender honest things" and Hugh Wheeler is "a writer of uncommon freshness and integrity." There was, however, something more Taubman wanted to say besides the review. By the time he got to it, *We've Come Through* had closed after five performances.

Though Tennessee Williams is mentioned, in passing and with approval, Taubman's article, about "the increasing incidence and influence of homosexuality on New York's stage," passed into common use what would explain, define and demean Tennessee Williams for decades to follow. With or without conscious intent from Taubman, using the authority of *The New York Times*—in 1961

184 TENN AT ONE HUNDRED

the most powerful of American newspapers, on par with national magazines such as Henry Luce's *Time* or the *Saturday Evening Post*— the article's effect was to make respectable and public what we now recognize and label as homophobia: the judging of someone's work on the basis of who they are, not what they have done. Taubman goes a step beyond George Jean Nathan's derisively calling actors and playwrights "pansies" and queers. It is impossible to explain away Taubman's desire to reveal a "homosexual infiltration" of the American theater during the Cold War. By any interpretation it is the revelation of a threat that must be fought against. Taubman's comparison of homosexuality to a pestiferous insect implies the necessity of extermination. That *The New York Times* would print what follows required approval from its editors and owners.

NOT WHAT IT SEEMS
Homosexual Motif Gets Heterosexual Guise

It is time to speak openly and candidly of the increasing incidence and influence of homosexuality on New York's stage—and, indeed, in the other arts as well.

The subject is too important to be left forever to the sly whisperers and malicious gossips. Criticism, like playwriting, is crippled by a resort to evasions. The public is deluded and misled if polite pretenses are accepted at face value.

The infiltration of homosexual attitudes occurs in the theatre at many levels. It is noticeable when a male designer dresses the girls in a musical to make them unappealing and disrobes the boys so that more male skin is visible than art or illusion require. It is apparent in a vagrant bit of nasty dialogue thrown into a show or in a redundant touch like two unmistakably mannish females walking across a stage without a reason or a word of comment.

These intrusions are private jokes turned public in a spirit of defiance or in the fun-and-games exuberance of a mischievous student testing a teacher's patience and acumen. They may be nuisances, deserving the flick aimed at a pestiferous insect, but do not merit serious discussion.

What demands frank analysis is the indirection that distorts human values. Plays on adult themes are couched in terms and symbols that do not truly reflect the author's mind. Characters represent something different from what they purport to be. It is no wonder that they seem sicker than necessary and that the plays are more subtly disturbing than the playwright perhaps intended.

Exaggeration

The unpleasant female of the species is exaggerated into a fantastically consuming monster or an incredibly pathetic drab. The male is turned into a ragingly lustful beast or into a limp, handsome neutral creature of otherworldly purity. No doubt there are such people, and it is the dramatist's business if he is fascinated by them. But when his emphases are persistently disproportionate, it is because he is treating a difficult, delicate problem in the guise of normality.

The insidious result of unspoken taboos is that sincere, searching writers feel they must state a homosexual theme in heterosexual situations. They convince themselves that what they wish to say will get through anyhow. But dissembling is unhealthy. The audience senses rot at the drama's core.

Taubman then discusses some recent plays in which the "problems of homosexuality were probed with directness and integrity," among them Tennessee Williams' *Cat on a Hot Tin Roof*.

Although these are examples of successful plays on delicate themes, there can be no blinking the fact that heterosexual audiences feel uncomfortable in the presence of truth-telling about sexual deviation. And there can be no denying that playwrights interested in such themes continue to attack them tangentially, even disagreeably and sneakily.

Falsehood

> That is why the work of some talented writers seems tainted. That is why studies ostensibly devoted to the tensions between men and women carry an uneasy burden of falsehood. One suspects what is wrong. But how can one question a writer's professed intentions or impugn motivations hidden in his heart, if not his subconscious?

The last few paragraphs of the article discuss Hugh Wheeler's play—the "fundamental flaw" of which, according to Taubman, "was that one did not believe in the pivotal boy-and-girl relationship as the thing it looked to be," and concludes:

> Mr. Wheeler has been brave to go as far as he has in writing about homosexuality with probity. His way is infinitely preferable to the furtive, leering insinuations that have contaminated some of our arts.

FESTERED FOOLISHNESS

Taubman's November article—with its vocabulary of *tainted, unhealthy,* and *contaminated*—carried forward a debate in print from the previous season's *New York Times Magazine,* described by Richard Sharp in *The Village Voice*:

> another bit of festered foolishness appeared in the *Times* where Tennessee Williams and Marya Mannes some months ago flung lemon slices at each other like two overbred Siamese cats at an animal tea. Miss Mannes examined what she called "the public appetite for the theater of violence, aberration and decay."[2]

Miss Mannes was married, three times. Her first husband had been Jo Mielziner, the designer of *The Glass Menagerie* and *Streetcar.* By 1960 she was married to her third husband, a British businessman. She was born in New York where her parents, David Mannes and the former Clara Damrosch, founded the Mannes

School of Music. Their daughter wrote about culture in general, not just theater, and is described as a social critic in her deposition against Lenny Bruce in 1964. Shrieks that Tennessee Williams was sick issued from her at intervals like a little girl startled by looming shadows in her doll-strewn bedroom, though Miss Mannes never did specify what illness she meant.

Miss Mannes' usual pulpit was not the *New York Times Magazine*, but a bi-weekly magazine called *The Reporter*, which stayed in business from 1949 through 1968 until its hawkish support of the Viet Nam War was so repulsive to advertisers its owner was forced to shut it down. In 1955 the title of the Mannes review of *Cat on a Hot Tin Roof*, "The Morbid Magic of Tennessee Williams,"[3] sums up the rest of what she thought: she praised Williams as artist, and went on to say that in his plays so far—from *Glass Menagerie* to *Cat*—"His people are mostly sick people."

In 1959 on WNEW TV, a new media for her and America, she had a conversation with the improbably named Virgilia Peterson in which Miss Peterson described *Sweet Bird of Youth* as "a sick play by a sick man." Miss Mannes concurred. Her own review of *Sweet Bird of Youth* in *The Reporter* was titled "Sour Bird, Sweet Raisin."[4] The sweet raisin of the headline is for another play, *A Raisin in the Sun*; her comments on *Sweet Bird* are a case of sour bewilderment:

> The laughter at the Martin Beck Theatre in New York these nights is made, I think, of…a fascination with and amusement in depravity, sickness, and degradation which makes me equally disturbed at the public, the playwright, and those critics who have hailed *Sweet Bird of Youth* as one of Tennessee Williams' "finest dramas" and "a play of overwhelming force."

The *New York Times Magazine* knew what it would get well before it published her May 29, 1960 article. Her argument was summarized by the magazine this way: "The unrelieved gloom of evil and corruption on Broadway's stage calls for a little light along the erstwhile Great White Way."

PLEA FOR FAIRER LADIES

During the course of the theater season now coming to a close the constant playgoer has kept strange company indeed. Only a psychiatrist or a nurse in a mental institution would have spent several hours of so many nights in the company of addicts, perverts, sadists, hysterics, bums, delinquents and others afflicted in mind and body...Very unpleasant people doing some very unpleasant things and using very unpleasant language. This is a phenomenon that deserves attention.

She begins with *Sweet Bird of Youth,* mentions plays long forgotten, except for "a revolting mother in *Gypsy*" and off-Broadway's "sniveling, hawking old wreck of *Krapp's Last Tape*."[5]

Mannes' plea concludes with questions, "What has made *My Fair Lady* the hit of all time?" [Do] "you need to be sick to be dramatic?...More than anything we want to believe in those qualities that make human beings so much more than animals and so much more than case histories?"

Williams was given space to respond in the *Times* with an essay "TW explains his POV":

I dare to suggest, from my POV, that the theater has made in our time its greatest artistic advance through the unlocking and lighting up and ventilation of the closets, attics, and basements of human behavior and experience....It is not the essential dignity of man but the essential ambiguity of man that needs to be stated."[6]

The paper published Williams' photograph facing off with a photo of Miss Mannes. Letters were sent in by the public, many of them siding with Miss Mannes. Other critics commented, including the *Times* of London correspondent, J. Donald Adams, that for a writer: "if he surrenders to man's 'ambiguity' and makes no effort to identify himself with the wholeness of man's spirit, he is doing only half his job as man and artist."[7]

Richard Gilman, writing in *Commonweal*, the New York-based journal of religion, politics, and culture edited by lay Catholics, had this to say:

> Of course the bourgeois theater, the theater of *Theater Arts, Time* and Marya Mannes, the *serious* bourgeois theater as distinct from all that crass commercialism, is not really interested in ennoblement, but in optimism. When Miss Mannes scolds Tennessee Williams for his sordidness, or when Howard Taubman hopes that Genet will some day write about blacks and whites who love one another, we are in the presence of those old balloons filled with the gas of middle-class propositions about life.[8]

Richard Sharp responded in *The Village Voice*: "Miss Mannes asked that we be given what we 'want to believe' in the theatre, and I am left with the impression that she prefers *Peter Pan* and *Life With Father* to *Oedipus Rex* and *Othello*. And so, farewell to her."

Sharp, in his own way, agreed with Taubman when it came to Williams, and was no less homophobic:

> Williams' inability to make a play into anything more than a camp dooms him to work a minority vein which is narrow and ugly, but dramatically teeming—and he works it to exhaustion, of both its dramatic possibilities and the audience's patience.[9]

EXHAUSTION

The claim that Williams was exhausting his own talent, and the patience of the audience, had been circulating for a while among more thoughtful critics who did not yet believe Williams' work was camp or doomed, but did believe he was depleted. One of the more eloquent observations about this change in Williams, published in the Summer 1959 *Hudson Review*, was written by Robert Brustein in his first review of a play by Williams, *Sweet Bird of Youth*. This was not a quick review written in haste to meet an overnight deadline. The *Hudson Review* is a quarterly, and its ability to affect box office was and is marginal. The play had opened in

March, the review appeared that summer, while *Sweet Bird* was still performing on Broadway. Robert Brustein, who had graduated two years before from Columbia University with a PhD in Drama, and who had directed plays in England, was part of the new group of critics—Richard Gilman was another—who had expectations that the American theater could be a serious, refined art and its literature, including its plays and criticism, a defining aspect of national thought.

Brustein begins his review by dismissing the play as unreal:

WILLIAMS' NEBULOUS NIGHTMARE

Sweet Bird of Youth is a highly private neurotic fantasy which takes place in a Terra Incognita quite remote from the terrain of the waking world. There all events have a mechanically sexual construction, everyone is caught up in extravagant depravity, success and failure alternate with astonishing swiftness, letters are sent but never delivered, and people not only get threatened with castration but have this threat executed and do nothing to avoid it when it actually comes. That this world is to be regarded as real or meaningful is a surprise sprung too often to promote much confidence in the author's vision.

The details of the criticism remind us of what audiences didn't like about *Camino Real*, that the director—the same one, Elia Kazan—hadn't clarified the style of the production for the audience so they might easily distinguish whether what they were watching was meant to be taken as a dream or a waking reality. Brustein called attention to just that:

Uncomfortably suspended between his traditional realism and a new theatricalism he is experimenting with, Kazan has underlined rather than disguised the play's defects. People act against each other as if alone in a room, but they also aim their remarks at the audience. Some of the business is pantomimed, and some is executed with real props. There is a phone on the stage but it is not attached by any wires, and the sets include real furniture but no walls. Thus Kazan unwittingly confirms a suspicion that the play, written in a predominantly realistic style, contains something disturbingly unreal; if Kazan's suspicion has been a conviction, it might have had more fortunate results. For, in the world of this play, it is no use pretending that time and space exist. The phone on the set is purely gratuitous when you have only to think bad thoughts in order to be heard, and all those thoughts are known anyway to the dark forces which plot your destruction.

Soon after, the review stops talking about the play, and begins to talk about the playwright:

The wild and fertile imagination which conceives has far outstripped the mind which shapes. With his fancy leading him into areas which he does not seem completely able to enter or leave, Williams is losing his ability to examine either the internal or external worlds with any real penetration. Williams has been often criticized for his sensationalism, but I find him still not sensational enough, for there is nothing more daring than the truth. He continues to disguise his true sexual concerns much as Miller obscures his political themes; and O'Neill remains the only American dramatist who has doggedly pursued his furies to their lair. There is a place in our drama for the nightmare and no one seems more qualified than Williams to write a good one. But his work will founder in formlessness, incoherence and dishonesty if he does not soon prove himself the master of his dreams.

Brustein's second critique of a play by Williams was his review of *The Night of the Iguana*, subtitled "A Little Night Music," and published in *The New Republic*, January 22, 1962. The play had opened December 28:

With this play, Williams has returned once again to the primeval jungle, where—around a ramshackle resort hotel near Acapulco—the steaming tropical underbrush is meant to evoke the terrors of existence. But he has explored this territory too many times before—the play seems tired, unadventurous, and self-derivative. Furthermore, the author's compulsion to express himself on the subjects of fleshly corruption, time and old age, the malevolence of God, and the maiming of the sensitive by life has now become so strong that he no longer bothers to provide a substructure of action to support his vision. *The Night of the Iguana* enjoys no organizing principle whatsoever; and except for some perfunctory gestures towards the end, it is very short on plot, pattern, or theme.

As with *Camino Real*, the lack of comprehension of a form is perhaps due to a directorial and acting style that could not deliver what the play required. The direction was credited to Frank Corsaro, well known, as was Kazan, for his Acting Studio connections (though Brustein saw little evidence of it in the production). It is obvious even from the photos, though, that Bette Davis was playing Bette Davis, and the revelation in one of her memoirs that she banned Corsaro from commenting on her performance is not a surprise.

The last paragraph is, once again, an analysis of Williams himself, not the play:

A rich atmosphere, a series of languid scenes, and some interesting character sketches are more than Williams has offered us in some time, but they are still not enough to sustain our interest through a full evening. Perhaps Williams, identifying with Nonno, has decided to think of himself as only "a minor league poet with a major league spirit," and there is enough fatigue in the play to suggest that, again like Nonno, he feels like "the oldest living and practicing poet in the world." But even a minor poet fashions his work with more care and coherence that this; even an aged eagle occasionally spreads its wings. I am inclined to persist in my heresy that there is at least one more genuine work of art left in Williams, which will emerge when he has finally been able to objectify his personal problems and to shape them into a suitable myth. Meanwhile, let us put down *The Night of the Iguana* as another of his innumerable exercises in marking time.

Brustein was in the minority about *Iguana*. Taubman at *The New York Times* gave it a rave ("Tennessee Williams is writing at the top of his form").[10] *Time* magazine put Williams on its cover that March and called him the "world's greatest living playwright."

Yet this acclaim was short-lived. His next major play, *The Milk Train Doesn't Stop Here Anymore,* met with responses that ranged from limited approval to more accusations of exhaustion, summed up by Walter Kerr's review in the *Herald Tribune*: "uncertain, drained [and] out of breath."

Williams did have periods of personal exhaustion, though it is dubious to say that about his writing. Throughout his life, he suffered from intense feelings of doubt and depression, what he personified in his notebooks[11] and letters—and in the demons that beset the Reverend Shannon in *The Night of the Iguana*—as his blue devils. Shortness of breath, heart palpitations, panic, and crippling self-doubt were signs of the blue devil's grip, against which Williams pitted the words he put down on paper. At a crucial time in his life, when he did feel exhausted and overwhelmed, he sought and received professional help, but for himself, not for his writing.

In March of 1957 *Orpheus Descending* opened on Broadway to disappointing reviews.[12] Five days later Williams' father died. Acknowledging that this was more than he could handle on his own, Williams went to see a psychotherapist, Dr. Lawrence S. Kubie, a strict Freudian analyst, who was, according to Gore Vidal, "seen by people at the time as—a slick bit of goods on the make among the rich, the famous, the gullible."[13] As a strategy to get him to concentrate on the pleasures of analysis, rather than distract himself with pleasure from anything else, Dr. Kubie advised Williams to stop writing. More, and not unconnected to this, the unwriting writer should aim for heterosexuality.[14] He should do that by distancing himself from his partner, Frank Merlo.

Williams did distance himself from Merlo, temporarily, but it was not an attempt to go straight, and in the months following the doctor's advice, far from "lying fallow" as had been suggested, he wrote *Suddenly Last Summer* and worked on the one-act version of *The Night of the Iguana*, while tinkering with several texts published posthumously, including the screenplay for *The Loss of a Teardrop Diamond* and *The Day on Which a Man Dies*.

This last text, *The Day on Which a Man Dies*, written from 1959 through 1960, though not published till 2008, has perhaps the most direct reference to Williams' months in therapy. At the climax of the play a painter who has abandoned his previous, popular style of painting with traditional brushes, in order to experiment with a spray paint gun—an obvious parallel to Williams' desire to abandon his own traditional style—is about to kill himself, having reached the limits of what he can endure in pursuit of new forms.

Williams, experimenting with dramatic form, handles the scene as a confessional within a Japanese Noh drama-inspired ritual, in which the painter, known simply as Man, is handed the props of his death by onstage stagehands. But, first he confronts his feelings of emptiness as an artist:

> MAN: Where are they, where did they go, the images, the visions?

> [*A Stage Assistant opens [a] panel...to reveal an abstract design of birds in flight.*]

> MAN: —They say if you wait for them, they'll come back. — Sometime, by something or someone, something was broken in me and to repair the break I used a—what?—imitation of—what?—a frantically and fiercely aggressive imitation of a pride I could only feel under liquor and drugs, and out of this I—created, attempted to—create. Consequently, what am I? A painter, now, with a spray-gun.

> [*A Stage Assistant rushes up to him with the spray-gun.*]

MAN: The paid-for wisdom and kindness of a doctor that said rest, rest! —It will come back; meaning they would come back, the visions, the images, and the power to paint them on canvas with something more orderly than this— [*He accepts spray-gun from a Stage Assistant.*] —Spray-gun… [*He clasps violent hands to either side of his head.*]

Images!—Come Back! [*He turns about, giggling crazily, and whistling for them* (*his lost visions*) *as if they were dogs.*]

In the play, the artist then kills himself by swallowing Lysol, fulfilling Williams' long-ago plans for a play about Vachel Lindsay, who committed suicide in just such a painful way.

If *The Day on Which a Man Dies*, with its unseen doctor who "said rest, rest!" is the private, unpublished, reflection of Williams' experience with a therapist, *Suddenly Last Summer*, written during the August hiatus while Williams was in therapy, is the public reflection, performed Off-Broadway in 1959 as part of a double bill titled *Garden District*. Central to *Suddenly Last Summer* is the enigmatic role of Dr. Cukrowicz, "Doctor Sugar." This underwritten character stands in judgment outside of the action of the play, says relatively little, and reveals little of his own life or emotions. Kubie attended a performance and wrote the playwright a letter praising the actor playing the role saying "of the many portrayals of the role of the psychiatrist that I have seen on stage and film, his rang truest." [15] As Michael Paller points out in his article "The Couch and Tennessee," this is what Freudians call projection. No where in the text is Dr. Sugar identified as a psychiatrist—he is a brain surgeon.

Williams' time with Kubie lasted six months and, as with most of Williams' experiences, sparked images for his writing. The Freudian contribution to Williams' self-knowledge was shrunk down—defensively—to the playwright's wonderful and often-quoted remark from a *Playboy* interview: "I wouldn't break up with Frank, of course, so I broke up with [the doctor]." Besides, if I got rid of my demons, I'd lose my angels." [16]

MR. WILLIAMS IS ADVISED TO STAY SILENT

Williams' time with his Freudian analyst was in the late 1950s and the analyst's diagnosis and advice given in the privacy of the therapy session. Among drama critics, rather than medical practitioners, personal analysis of Williams with a diagnosis of exhaustion and a prescription to remain silent became a public proclamation. In 1963 Richard Gilman's review of *The Milk Train Doesn't Stop Here Anymore*, published in the February 8, 1963 issue of *Commonweal*, the headline referred to Williams as the character of Kurtz, a revered demigod among the Africans in Joseph Conrad's *Heart of Darkness*, revealed in the novel as hollow and empty, a living corpse.

Mistuh Williams, He Dead

Sitting among the ashes of Tennessee Williams' latest play, his erstwhile defender, the veteran sufferer who has stayed with him through the entire cycle of extinctions and resurrections, now thinks: this time it's finished, he has had it and I have had it too. There is no point looking for another rebirth, because whatever it is that gives back to consumed birds their wings, plumage and beating hearts is not going to listen to another word.

Why, rather than be banal and hysterical and absurd, doesn't he keep quiet? Why doesn't he simply stop writing, stay absolutely unproductive for a long time in Key West, or the South of Spain, or the corner of any bar, and just think? We know this is what he has been trying to do, but how is it possible in the midst of that self-created din, the clatter of the somersaults he keeps turning in front of us, like a spoiled child who needs to have his existence continually justified, indeed ascertained, by our glances, which show admiration, fear, disgust and troubled love.

How many plays in how few years? How terrifying it must be to feel that a season cannot pass, as for that child an evening cannot, without your name being on clucking tongues and your reflection in the encircling eyes. But

Williams seems unable to let go; he is wedded to his fear and compulsion, which are bringing about his creative suicide because they are the very things that make a silent, fertile period in the desert, his possible salvation, so unthinkable. Unlike D. H. Lawrence, one of the sources of his sensibility, Williams cannot "shed his sicknesses in his books," because to write them has become a malady itself.

Gilman's dismissal of *The Milk Train Doesn't Stop Here Anymore* continues, ending with:

About Williams, one more thing. Perhaps it is still too soon to write him off, since no creative death is irremediable. Yet how often can the phoenix rise, and must there not be some source of grace intact, some channel of air kept open for the bird to be summoned up into? In using the stage not to solve his dilemmas esthetically but to exhibit them in their inchoate form, he is bringing about the permanent death of his art, intruding himself into the space it should occupy and thus drawing the sickness it is meant to heal more airlessly and irrevocably around him.

This was in 1963. It took two more years for another drama critic— at *The New York Times*—to connect the dots of exhaustion, sterility, and add the claim that any homosexual's pursuit of creativity was inevitably fruitless.

THE FINAL EQUATION

On January 23, 1966, Stanley Kauffmann, who replaced Taubman as the daily theater critic at *The New York Times*, undertook a detailed diagnosis of homosexuals in the theater. The occasion for his article—again, not a review, but something Kauffmann felt he needed to say—was the Broadway production of Joe Orton's *Entertaining Mr. Sloane*, which closed after thirteen performances. In that play's conclusion a murderous young man is shared sexually by a middle-aged brother and sister. Mr. Orton's sexuality was no secret, unlike some American playwrights Kauffmann hints at in his article, but does not name.

Unlike Taubman, Kauffmann does not prescribe extermination or removal. What he does is pass along as truth the then current myths about homosexuals, among other things, calling homosexuality the equivalent of alcoholism.

Homosexual Drama And Its Disguises

A recent Broadway production raises again the subject of the homosexual dramatist. It is a subject that nobody is comfortable about. All of us admirably "normal" people are a bit irritated by it and wish it could disappear. However, it promises to be a matter of continuing, perhaps increasing, significance.

The principal complaint against homosexual dramatists is well-known. Because three of the most successful American playwrights of the last twenty years are (reputed) homosexuals and because their plays often treat women and marriage, therefore, it is said, postwar American drama presents a badly distorted picture of American women, marriage, and society in general. Certainly there is substance in the charge; but is it rightly directed?

When Kauffmann wrote coyly "three of the most successful American playwrights of the last twenty years are (reputed) homosexuals" his readers would have supplied the names: Edward Albee, Tennessee Williams, and William Inge. The author of *Our Town*, Thornton Wilder, was very much in the closet. Kauffmann continues:

The first, obvious point is that there is no law against heterosexual dramatists, and there is no demonstrable cabal against their being produced. If there are heterosexuals who have talent equivalent with those three men, why aren't these "normal" people writing? Why don't they counterbalance or correct the distorted picture?

But, to talk of what is and not of what might be, the fact is that the homosexual dramatist is not to blame in this matter. If he writes of marriage and of other relationships about which he knows or cares little, it is because he has no choice but to masquerade. Both convention and the law demand it. In society the homosexual's life must be discreetly concealed. As material for drama, that life must be even more intensely concealed. If he is to write of his experience, he must invent a two-sex version of the one-sex experience that he really knows. It is we who insist on it, not he.

Two Alternatives

There would seem to be only two alternative ways to end this masquerading. First, the Dramatists' Guild can pass a law forbidding membership to those who do not pass a medico-psychological test for heterosexuality. Or, second, social and theatrical convention can be widened so that homosexual life may be as freely dramatized as heterosexual life, may be as frankly treated in our drama as it is in contemporary fiction.

If we object to the distortion that homosexual disguises entail and if, as a civilized people, we do not want to gag these artists, then there seems only one conclusion. The conditions that force the dissembling must change. The homosexual dramatist must be free to write truthfully of what he knows, rather than try to transform it to a life he does not know, to the detriment of his truth and ours.

The cries go up, perhaps, of decadence, corruption, encouragement of emotional-psychological illness. But is there consistency in these cries? Are there similar objections to *The Country Wife*, *Inadmissible Evidence*, *The Right Honourable Gentleman* on the ground that they propagandize for the sexually unconventional or "corruptive" matters that are germane to them? Alcoholism, greed, ruthless competitiveness are equally neurotic, equally undesirable socially; would any of us wish to bar them arbitrarily from the stage?

Only this one neurosis, homosexuality, is taboo in the main traffic of our stage. The reasons for this I leave to psychologists and to self-candor, but they do not make the discrimination any more just.

Fault Is Ours

I do not argue for increased homosexual influence in our theater. It is precisely because I, like many others, am weary of *disguised* homosexual influence that I raise the matter. We have all had very much more than enough of the materials so often presented by the three writers in question: the viciousness toward women, the lurid violence that seems a sublimation of social hatreds, the transvestite sexual exhibitionism that has the same sneering exploitation of its audience that every club stripper has behind her smile. But I suggest that, fundamentally, what we are objecting to in all these plays is largely the result of conditions that we ourselves have imposed. The dissimulations and role-playings are there because we have made them inevitable.

Homosexuals with writing ability are likely to go on being drawn to the theater. It is the quite logical consequence of the defiant and/or protective histrionism they must employ in their daily lives. So there is every reason to expect more plays by talented homosexuals. There is some liberty for them, limited, in café theaters and Off Broadway; if they want the full resources of the professional theater, they must dissemble. So there is every reason to expect their plays to be streaked with vindictiveness toward the society that constricts and, theatrically, discriminates against them.

To me, their distortion of marriage and femininity is not the primary aspect of this matter; for if an adult listens to these plays with a figurative transistor-radio simultaneously translating, he hears that the marital quarrels are usually homosexual quarrels with one of the pair in costume and that the incontrovertibly female figures are usually drawn less in truth than in envy or fear. To me, there is a more important result of this vindictiveness— its effect on the basic concept of drama itself and of art in general.

Homosexual artists, male and female, tend to convert their exclusion into a philosophy of art that glorifies their exclusion. They exalt style, manner, surface. They decry artistic concern with the traditional matters of theme and subject because they are prevented from using fully the themes of their own experience. They emphasize manner and style because these elements of art, at which they are often adept, are legal tender in their transactions with the world. These elements are, or can be, esthetically divorced from such other considerations as character and idea.

Thus we get plays in which manner is the paramount consideration, in which the surface and the *being* of the work are to be taken as its whole. Its allegorical relevance (if any) is not to be anatomized, its visceral emotion (if any) need not be validated, and any judgment other than a stylistic one is considered inappropriate, even censorious. Not all artists and critics who advance this theory of style-as-king are homosexuals, but the camp has a strong homosexual coloration.

What is more, this theory can be seen, I believe, as an instrument of revenge on the main body of society. Theme and subject are important historical principles in our art. The arguments to prove that they are of diminishing importance—in fact, ought never to have been important—are cover for an attack on the idea of social relevance. By adulation of sheer style, this group tends to deride the whole culture and the society that produced it, tends to reduce art to a clever game which even that society cannot keep them from playing.

But how can one blame these people? Conventions and puritanisms in the Western world have forced them to wear masks for generations, to hate themselves, and thus to hate those who make them hate themselves. Now that they have a certain relative freedom, they vent their feelings in camouflaged form.

> Doubtless, if the theater comes to approximate the publishing world's liberality, we shall trace in plays—as we are doing in novels—the history of heterosexual romantic love with an altered cast of characters. But that situation would be self- amending in time; the present situation is self-perpetuating and is culturally risky.
>
> A serious public, seriously interested in the theater, must sooner or later consider that, when it complains of homosexual influences and distortions, it is complaining, at one remove, about its own attitudes. I note further that one of the few contemporary dramatists whose works are candidates for greatness—Jean Genet—is a homosexual who has never had to disguise his nature.

The openly gay Jean Genet, who has, as Kauffmann correctly prophesied, risen to acknowledged greatness, was not—and never has been yet—performed in a Broadway theater. Genet's work was shown in downtown theaters, at Circle in the Square, at the Saint Mark's Playhouse, at Tempo Theater (also on Saint Mark's Place) but never above 14th Street, the Mason Dixon line separating "downtown" from the rest of theater in Manhattan. The "café theaters" Kauffmann refers to were also downtown, in particular Caffé Cino, the first of the off-off-Broadway theaters, on Cornelia Street in Greenwich Village, from 1958 to 1968: where an 8' x 8' performance area was literally the platform that helped launch the careers of the first group of American playwrights to openly write about gay people. This was especially so after the breakout success in 1964 of Lanford Wilson's *The Madness of Lady Bright*, about a lonely, aging queen. The first Caffé Cino hit, it ran for over 200 performances.

That run went unreported in *The New York Times* until well after it was over. Downtown theater—specifically off-off-Broadway—was beneath notice, in part, because of its technical limitations, but also because it was considered ghetto theater: of limited interest to the mainstream audience of *The New York Times*.

Kauffmann wrote for the uptown audience. His bases—his base of readers and the base of his own identity—were the liberal politics of the time: civil rights—for black people—were supported without qualification and McCarthyism was repulsive. The liberal concern for homosexuals was compassionate, as it would be towards a compulsive alcoholic. As Doug Arell points out in his 2002 article "Homophobic Criticism and Its Disguises: The Case of Stanley Kauffmann," the liberal veneer Kauffmann gives to the prejudices of the time help make them more believable by providing a motive ("If you were treated this way, you'd seek to undermine the straight world, too.")[17]

Reactions to Kauffmann's article were strong. Many letters were written in response, pro and con, so many that two weeks later Kauffmann wrote another article headlined "On the Acceptability of the Homosexual." In this second article, Kauffmann expressed compassion for the plight of homosexuals put into positions where they would inevitably turn angry, vicious, and subversive in society. That to Kauffmann these things were inevitable—a long hatred of women and the compulsion to undermine marriage—could, at that time, be backed up with medical and legal definitions and even a recent *Time* magazine article (from which he probably got the idea for his first article) that concluded homosexuality "deserves no encouragement, no glamorization, no rationalization, no fake status as a minoritysss martyrdom, no sophistry about simple differences in taste—and, above all, no pretense that it is anything but a pernicious sickness."[18]

By medical definition at that time, homosexuals were intrinsically neurotic and self-hating. In 1966 the reference manual of the American Psychiatric Association (APA)—from which diagnoses were derived—termed homosexuality a pathological sexual deviance. In 1966 homosexuality was still illegal according to the sodomy laws of the country. In New York City, there had been since 1927 the Wales Padlock Law which provided jail terms and fines for playwrights (and producers)—and the taking away of the license of a theater for a year—for those "depicting or dealing with the subject of sex degeneracy or sex perversion."[19]

So, Stanley Kauffmann was not adding anything new to the current views on homosexuality. Instead, he was shoveling the manure of his received ideas about homosexuality onto Broadway—using the height of his power at the *Times* to do so and get a good spread. Behind the scenes at the paper, turmoil followed Kauffmann's second article. The positive headline so annoyed

204 TENN AT ONE HUNDRED

Iphigene Sulzberger, the mother of the publisher of *The New York Times*, that she wrote her son a letter of complaint.[20] The gist of her grievance was that such things shouldn't be on the front page of a newspaper section where her grandchildren could see them.

The *Times* has changed its policies since then, as the photos of smiling gay couples in the "Weddings and Celebrations" section of the paper demonstrate. Psychological theory about homosexuality has changed since 1966, too. After 1973, homosexuality was no longer classified by the American Psychiatric Association as a disorder. After a 2003 Supreme Court decision, anti-sodomy laws between consenting adults have been declared unconstitutional. The Wales Padlock law ended in 1967.

Kauffmann's article, however, has had implications that continue to this day for the reputation of Tennessee Williams. Of the other two playwrights Kauffmann hints at—but doesn't name for legal reasons—the effects were different. Inge had entered a creative slump, and ended up killing himself. For many years, Albee distanced himself strongly from gay identity. Thornton Wilder, of course, stayed more firmly than ever in the closet. For Tennessee Williams, though, Kauffmann provided the axioms that served as a starting point for an equation of deduction and inference.

The equation is this:

- **Williams repeats himself = exhausted**
  (see Gilman and Brustein)
- **Exhausted = sick**
  (see Miss Marya Mannes)
- **Sick = homosexual**
  (see Taubman)
- **Homosexual = inevitably fruitless and unsuccessful creativity**
  (see Kauffmann)

This logical enough sequence concludes that Williams wrote no successful plays after *Iguana*, because he had not the discipline, being exhausted, nor the mental health, being gay, to bring his vision into an understandable dramatic form. A parallel "proof" might be done, which would yield the same results, by applying a psychoanalysis analysis of Williams' life as the key to understanding the value of his work. This spurious method would conclude that, unable to resolve the conflicts of his life, Williams was unable to resolve and give form to the complexities of his writing.

Just as Cardinal Spellman condemned *Baby Doll* without having seen the movie, this truism—it certainly can't be proven true—that Williams wrote no more valuable work after *Iguana*—is passed on still by journalists, critics, and "scholars" who haven't read any of the work after *Iguana*, including the more than fifty plays and one-acts published after the playwright's death—nor have they seen any performances of the plays Williams wrote after *Iguana*. But they do know the short summation. It is more efficient to quickly harvest a memorable reductive statement from an online source—or flip through respectable books of fifty-year old opinions, spurious then, ludicrous now. Critics reviewing the most often-produced Williams plays *Glass Menagerie* or *Streetcar* have enough to do to keep up with what they're talking about from the 1940s, without trying to think about the complexities of new dramatic structure or the unconventional metaphors of Williams' later plays.

And so, the flower of ignorance is handed off without consideration—or knowledge, perhaps—of its roots in homophobia and a psychoanalysis, itself outdated, of Williams' life, rather than the individual plays. Recent books, newspaper articles, and online graffiti repeat it still.

Applying American-style Freudian analysis to Williams' plays is like having a Rabbi visit an Amish family to determine if they keep a kosher kitchen. In 1966, and in 2011, the application of psychoanalytic theory to the work of Williams is a measure with a predictable final evaluation. One applies such an appraisal when one already knows the answer one wants. Williams' work will always come out poorly when explained away as symptom rather than metaphor, just as the elongation of the figures of El Greco's paintings lose spiritual significance when claimed to be the result of an astigmatism of the painter's eyes. All works of Williams are artifacts, the images in them are metaphors, distorted sometimes as much as the work of El Greco, and for the same reason: these artists see the world on fire, yearning towards something with so much force that bodies and the world itself stretch grotesquely. The structure of Williams plays is neither classical nor realistic because the author's vision of the world is neither.

Robert Brustein and Richard Gilman's writings, while not intrinsically homophobic, were used by Taubman and Kauffmann as building blocks in their arguments. Not that all the sources from six decades ago still believe Williams' writing to be a symptom of homosexuality, if they ever really did. In the fall of 2010, looking at an early draft of this chapter, Robert Brustein, who still writes for *The New Republic*, remarked while reading Taubman's and Kauffmann's articles that their definitions of homosexual writers were understandable now as simplifications and distortions influenced by the prejudices of the time—and that, "the validity of Tennessee Williams' plays is proven by their quality. Far from distorting women, Williams loved women, and revealed their psychology with insight and compassion."[21]

Over time, Williams' inability to abide by conventional dramatic structure is understandable as something other than lack of discipline or exhaustion. Again, more than fifty years later, Brustein spoke of Williams' "way with form" as a means to articulate the complexity of his themes: "a conflict between what is delicate and poetic in American life and that which is unfeeling, brutalizing, and coarse. That the plays took on the form of dreams seems inevitable, and if not always satisfying in production, worthy of respect as dreams."[22, 23]

In 1977, as *Vieux Carré*, his penultimate play on Broadway, was about to open, Williams published an essay in *The New York Times* on the figure he had become in the popular press:

> Of course no one is more acutely aware than I that I am widely regarded as the ghost of a writer, a ghost still visible, excessively solid of flesh and perhaps too ambulatory, but a writer remembered mostly for works which were staged between 1944 and 1961....Once his critics, his audience and the academic communities in which his work is studied have found what they consider a convenient and suitable term for the style of a playwright, it seems to be very difficult for them to concede to him the privilege and necessity of turning to other ways.[24]

"Everybody wants me to write another *Streetcar*," Williams is said to have cried out in exasperation—but he no longer experienced the world in the way he had in the late 1940s. What was exhausted for him were the traditional forms of dramatic construction, and he was trying to find new ones with which to express his living experience and vision of the world. To what degree he was successful has yet to be proven, but the challenge will inevitably be taken up in the future by creative theater artists.

D. H. Lawrence, very much one of the sources of Williams' sensibility, had this to say, as good a final word on the subject as any:

It is hard to hear a new voice, as hard as it is to listen to an unknown language. We just don't listen. There is a new voice in the old American classics. The world has declined to hear it....

Why?—Out of fear. The world fears a new experience more than it fears anything. Because a new experience displaces so many old experiences. And it is like trying to use muscles that have perhaps never been used, or that have been going stiff for ages. It hurts horribly. The world doesn't fear a new idea. It can pigeonhole any idea. But it can't pigeon-hole a real new experience. [25]

Richard Gilman. "Mistuh Williams, He Dead." *Commonweal*, 8 February 1963. © 1963 Commonweal Foundation, reprinted by permission. For subscriptions, www.commonwealmagazine.org

Robert Brustein, "Williams' Nebulous Nightmare." Reprinted by permission from *The Hudson Review*, Vol. XII, No. 2 (Summer 1959). Copyright © 1959 by The Hudson Review, Inc.

Robert Brustein. "The Night of the Iguana: A Little Night Music." *The New Republic*, 22 January 1962. Reprinted by permission of the author.

Howard Taubman. "Not What Is Seems: Homosexual Motif Gets Heterosexual Guise." New York Times, 5 November 1961: X1. From The New York Times, © 1961 The New York Times All rights reserved. Used by permission and protected by the Copyright Laws of the United States. The printing, copying, redistribution, or retransmission of the Material without express written permission is prohibited.

Stanley Kauffmann. "Homosexual Drama and Its Disguises" from The New York Times, Arts & Leisure section, 23 January 1966: 93. From The New York Times, © 1966 The New York Times All rights reserved. Used by permission and protected by the Copyright Laws of the United States. The printing, copying, redistribution, or retransmission of the Material without express written permission is prohibited.

" I am so tired of reading about the

sad homosexual Tennessee. I never

knew anyone who reveled more in his

"

sexuality than Tenn did.

TENNESSEE AMONG THE BIOGRAPHERS

Kenneth Holditch

In a very real sense, it all began—the art of the biography—with James Boswell when he became obsessed—there is no other appropriate verb for it—with that great man of letters, Samuel Johnson, and began tagging along at the heels of the lexicographer like an alert and devoted dog, his ears pricked to catch every utterance from his master's voice. What led this unknown, untrained, even undisciplined Scotsman to shadow his idol, jotting down his every act, his every gesture, his every word? Whatever Boswell's motivation, succeeding generations of readers owe him a debt of gratitude for representing for them Johnson as a living, breathing entity, warts and all, brought to us, as it were, "like Alcestis from the grave." Had Boswell not been thus obsessive, thus attentive, it is doubtful whether Johnson's reputation would have been as great as it is today. In the process, of course, Boswell also made himself a famous man.

Although Boswell's position in relation to his subject was a rare one, since he was in almost constant attendance upon Johnson for an extended period of time, he nevertheless set the standard and even established the methodology for those who followed in his profession for the next two and a half centuries. Despite his adoration of Johnson, Boswell retained an amazing degree of objectivity, it seems to me, for even in the midst of canonizing his monumental friend and portraying his strengths, he reveals the human weaknesses that accompany them. The Johnson of Boswell's re-creation is a living breathing human being, which is, after all, the *summum bonum* desired by any competent biographer secure in his craft: to present the subject being memorialized with all the virtues and all the vices, if not revealed, at least suggested.

Unfortunately, not all subjects of biography have been as well served as Samuel Johnson. Consider poor Edgar Allan Poe, whose life was full of more than enough struggle and pain, only to be defamed after death by an enemy, appropriately named Rufus W. Griswold, who created a fantasy Poe as drunkard and drug addict, neither of which reflected the reality of the poet's life. As a sad result, generations of readers have conceived of Poe as a dissolute reprobate rather than the hard-working—indeed, over-worked—genius he actually was. Consider also the case of another great poet of the American Renaissance, Emily Dickinson, many of whose biographers have wasted much time, ink, and paper in speculation as to the love life of the genius of Amherst, unwilling to believe, as Allen Tate observed in his essay on Dickinson, that within the narrow bounds of her father's house and garden, hers was one of the richest lives ever lived in America. True, but even today there are researchers endeavoring to find a lover, male or female—or demon—for the spinster lady with the powerfully creative imagination.

More recently there is the biography of Elvis Presley by Albert Harry Goldman, who clearly does not like or even approve of the man whose life he has undertaken to write; the result is a "hatchet job" that makes a sad and misguided life seem more miserable and even useless. Why, one wonders, would an author choose to spend the necessary time and effort required to produce an even barely credible or adequate life history, particularly if the biographer does not like the subject? Fortunately, subsequent books, especially the two volume biography of Peter Guralnick, have dispelled the false image of Elvis produced by Goldman, but surely the harm that he did remains, as long as copies of his book continue to exist in personal and public libraries.

An egregious example of biographical incompetence, or perhaps even viciousness, involves two women who had never published a book, much less a biography, but were assigned by Louisiana State University Press to produce a much needed life of novelist John

Kennedy Toole, author of *A Confederacy of Dunces*. The result—implausibly called *Ignatius Rising*—was a travesty, filled with factual errors, misquotations, and the most egregious falsehoods about the personal life of Toole. One of the authors even confessed to having consulted a medium in a wasted effort to reach the novelist to discover the reason for his suicide. The offensive volume produced by their suspect research makes for amusing reading, ludicrous as it is, but at the same time it has done a grave injustice to the memory of an extremely talented young man.

The preceding examples of biographies, ranging from the classic to the viciously or stupidly inaccurate, are offered to indicate the spectrum of life studies devoted to Tennessee Williams. As the examples indicate, perhaps the most pertinent question to be asked is do these biographers benefit the reputations of their subjects or do they detract from same—or, again, are they simply of no significance at all?

Unfortunately, the first biography of Tennessee Williams to be published—if we place his mother's *Remember Me to Tom* (1963) in a separate category as "family memoir"—is perhaps the least reliable, Donald Spoto's *The Kindness of Strangers* (1985). Reading it, one can understand Oscar Wilde's cynical observation that biography is "adding to death a new terror." It is not that the work is unreadable, for in fact the narrative flows very well, but, it is too often inaccurate and demonstrates evidence of having been written in haste in about a year. There is the famous (or infamous) instance of his referring to Margo Jones, the "Texas Tornado" as Tennessee dubbed her, as a lesbian. When he was questioned about the source for that information by Helen Sheehy, the biographer of Jones, his response was a cavalier "Well, perhaps it's not true," or words to that effect. He spent little time in New Orleans, despite the tremendous influence the city had on the dramatist and his work. He interviewed me and one of my colleagues and I gave him a tour of sites in the French Quarter associated with Tennessee, from which he extracted the following statement:

> The renovation of the French Quarter was continuing in the early 1940s, under the inspired supervision of Lyle Saxon and Elizabeth Werlein, with whom Williams often took breakfast at the famous Morning Call Coffee Shop; they were sometimes joined by Roark

Bradford, to whom Williams first told the story of his meeting with two bizarre people at the Athletic Club—a sadistic black masseur who had found a willing partner in a frail white masochist.

Tennessee did make friends with Lyle Saxon and Roark Bradford, but there is no record that he ever met Elizebeth (note that Spoto misspells her name) Werlein nor that the three of them ever drank coffee together in the French Market. I did indeed inform Spoto that Tennessee was reputed to have gotten the inspiration for "Desire and the Black Masseur" from an employee of the New Orleans Athletic Club, but there was no indication that he even conveyed the story to Roark Bradford. This strange mingling and confusing of facts makes one doubt the veracity of more important passages in *The Kindness of Strangers.*

This is one of several biographies that portray Tennessee as a sad, lonely malcontent who produced great dramas despite his dysfunctional lifestyle. Spoto exhibits, to his discredit, little of the "kindness" of his title in his portrayal of the playwright. There is a strangely puritanical tone in his account of Tennessee's private life—one is reminded of the Griswold biography of Poe. Despite its shortcomings, Spoto's book is one of the few complete records of Tennessee's life, and it is an engrossing narrative that provides a partially accurate portrait of the playwright, and if approached with extreme caution, it may certainly serve some useful purpose.

What it has to say as an assessment of Williams' work as a whole is out-of-date, since Spoto did not, of course, have knowledge of the plays written by Williams published posthumously after 1985, which include such important work as *Not About Nightingales, The Parade,* and *And Tell Sad Stories of the Death of Queens.* It seems to be, of late, the one biography most often cited in published essays and books on Williams, a fact that is troubling.

The second serious biography, *Everyone Else Is An Audience* (1993), served the playwright little better, although Ronald Hayman's attitude toward Tennessee was a bit more positive than that of Spoto. There are, however, a number of factual errors, evident to anyone who knows much about the subject; for example, he perpetuates the original error that the prefrontal lobotomy was performed on Rose

Williams in 1937, when in fact it did not occur until 1943. In an even more egregious error, the biographer states that refusing to believe Rose's assertion that her father molested her, Edwina had punished her with a lobotomy, an unsubstantiated, unlikely, and cruel charge against the mother. Hayman also makes some strange judgments about his subject, as when he asserts that Tennessee's plays have "no serious intellectual content," a rather glaring failure to acknowledge the philosophical considerations that mark the actions of many of the characters. Another problem in Hayman's work is the large amount of space devoted to plot summaries rather than analysis of the entirety of the plays, and sometimes his summaries miss the mark, as in his comments on *A Streetcar Named Desire*, in which he asserts that "Blanche affects a greater gentility than she has ever had"; that "she sold the ancestral home," when in fact she lost it; and that she had found her husband "in bed with a young boy." In writing about the family of *The Glass Menagerie* he gets the family name wrong, calling them the Winghams, not the Wingfields. Hayman seems convinced that every character and every action and every theme in every play is cut directly from the fabric of Tennessee's private life, and he spends too much time trying to prove it—and to what purpose? As a result of the time wasted on such misdirected elements as those listed above, *Everyone Else Is an Audience* seems a rather slim and watery account of Tennessee's life and career, as if it had been written in haste and, indeed, without much faith in or commitment to its subject.

Finally, Hayman, even more than Spoto, is committed to the characterization of Tennessee as a sad, guilt-laden homosexual, drunkard, and drug addict. He writes, for example, "From *The Glass Menagerie* onward, self-criticism and self-hatred had bulked large in motivating Tennessee's writing," a Puritanical pronouncement calculated to turn the uninformed reader away from reading or attending any play written after that first successful effort. The remark is ridiculously uninformed and inept, enough alone to make Hayman's study worthless as an aid to understanding a great dramatist's canon.

It may seem a bit of a stretch to suggest it, but I think that in many respects Tennessee Williams can be said to have found his Boswell when he met Lyle Leverich in California in January 1976. Like Boswell, Leverich was not a recognized writer when he first met the playwright, nor had he ever envisioned himself in the role of chronicler of anyone's life. Their first fortunate encounter occurred in January 1976 when Lyle was still performing his role as a producer, and the meeting led Leverich to request Tennessee's permission to produce two of his dramas—*The Glass Menagerie* and *The Two-Character Play*—in San Francisco, a desire that became reality in October of that year. The next year, Tennessee was so impressed by a rebuttal Lyle had written to Robert Brustein's savage review of *Tennessee Williams' Letters to Donald Windham* that he labeled the piece "marvelously good" and added that, "No one has ever written a more powerful and eloquent defense of my work and character." When Lyle and Tennessee were both in Atlanta for the production of *Tiger Tail* in 1978, Lyle told the dramatist that he felt the *Memoirs* did not offer an accurate portrayal and that someone should write about his relationship to the theater, to which Tennessee replied, "Baby, you write it!" The die was cast. The next year, 1979, at the Kennedy Center Honors, Tennessee told his brother Dakin that Leverich was the "authorized biographer" and later gave Lyle two letters acknowledging him to be the chosen one— the second on the last day that Tennessee ever spent in New Orleans; the next month, he was dead.

The fact that Leverich learned to be a good writer and mastered the essential elements required of a good biographer—reading, researching, interviewing, analyzing, interpreting, synthesizing— is an amazing accomplishment, but even more astounding is the fact that the one volume of a proposed two-volume life is the best account of Tennessee's life from 1911 to 1983, which is, I think, damned near a miracle. Like Samuel Johnson, Tennessee seems to have known or at least have met anyone who mattered in the world of theater and other spheres, even politics, a fact that magnifies the task of the biographer, who, in order to do a good job, must interview as many of those friends, associates, and even enemies as possible to glean whatever bits of information, no matter how small, each can contribute to the portrait of the subject in question. Having fulfilled all these functions, Leverich then had to assemble an abundance of material into a unified, insightful, informative, and, yes, entertaining work. The dedication with which he prefaces the finished volume makes it clear how seriously Lyle took his obligation and what he conceived it to be: "For Tennessee, who asked me to report, in truth, his cause aright."

Once the actual writing began, following Tennessee's death, Leverich worked with vigor and devotion, putting aside the other tasks to which he had previously been committed, namely producing plays, including those of Tennessee Williams. Part of his work involved the preparation of a carefully detailed timeline of Tennessee's life and career, which served as an indispensable guide in the writing of *Tom: The Unknown Tennessee Williams*. In the early period of his work, Lyle made excellent progress until he suddenly ran into a brick wall, or perhaps more accurately the Kremlin Wall named Maria Britneva, a Russian adventuress, and friend of Williams, who managed to marry into an aristocratic British family and retitle herself the Lady St. Just. A thorny British hedgerow named in Tennessee's will to care for Rose Williams, she had appropriated unto herself duties far beyond the scope set by the document itself. Among other excesses she perpetrated was a refusal to allow Lyle to use material from the letters and the journals of the playwright, effectively blocking the completion of a competent biography. As John Lahr details in "The Lady and Tennessee," her other actions in a similar vein involved her refusal to allow a Broadway theater to be renamed for Tennessee unless the owners paid her for the right. As a sad result there is to date no Tennessee Williams Theater in New York City. Despite Lyle's struggles against Maria's strictures and the support he received from many powerful people in the theater and publishing worlds, his forward progress was thwarted until her tight-fisted control of almost all activities that involved Tennessee's works or even his name ended when fate intervened in the form of the death of the Lady St. Just.

Because Leverich had been so long delayed in the publication of his first volume—he did not receive a go-ahead from the estate until November 1994, more than eleven years after Tennessee's death—he did not live to complete the second half of his work, but the timeline he left could be of inestimable value to whoever takes up the gauntlet and completes the difficult task he so admirably began. However, what he did accomplish was to reveal the genius that underlies the creation of Tennessee Williams' greatest plays and the unifying threads of the factual and the imagined that bind the works to the creator and his vision.

Tennessee has not been well served by those friends—or those claiming to be friends—who have put pen to paper to memorialize him. Two such cases are Dotson Rader and Bruce Smith. Rader, it is true, was acquainted with and often in the company of the playwright for a number of years and does offer, in the midst of *Cry of the Heart* (1986), a work that seems derivative of earlier sources and largely self-serving, a number of brief flashes of the real Tennessee in all his complexity and "infinite variety." Rader peppers his recycling of elements from Dakin Williams' biography, itself already derivative of Edwina Williams' *Remember Me to Tom*, with portraits of Tennessee in particular and significant scenes and settings—December 1971 anti-war rally at The Cathedral Church of St. John the Divine at which Tennessee, Willem de Koonig, and Norman Mailer all spoke; the opening night of the ill-fated *Clothes for a Summer Hotel*, Tennessee's last full-length drama to reach Broadway; and Tennessee at home—in New York, in Key West, and in New Orleans.

There is considerable sloppiness in the writing of *Cry of the Heart*—all the more troublesome because Rader is a professional author of considerable skill. There are careless errors, as when he attributes classic remarks and jokes to the wrong person, when he botches names, or misspells words—or perhaps creates new ones, "fellatiate," for example. He professes to have known John Uecker, actor and friend of Tennessee, for years and to have introduced him to Tennessee, yet persistently misspells his name as "Uker." There are frequent bits of misinformation, as when he states that Tennessee was born *in* the rectory in Columbus (he was born in a clinic), and that Clarksdale, Mississippi, is on the Tallahatchie River (in fact it is on the Sunflower). Such lapses, minor though they may seem, tend to make the reader skeptical of more important material. Although the dialogue Rader attributes to Williams rings true to any reader who ever heard the dramatist speak, one is troubled by the amount of it, much allegedly recalled from a dozen or more years before it was recorded. Since Rader was apparently not as conscientious as James Boswell, obsessively jotting down the master's words of wisdom at the time they were spoken, one may doubt their accuracy. Some of the material, especially that involving Tennessee's sexual life and things revealed to Rader in confidence, would surely have been better kept unrevealed. However, despite these shortcoming, it seems to me that reading *Cry of the Heart*, albeit with some degree of scepticism, one can acquire a sketchy and uninteresting picture of Tennessee.

Bruce Smith's *Costly Performances* (1990), though cut from somewhat the same cloth as Rader's book—that is, a personal reminiscence from an employee-companion of Tennessee's—is a bargain basement item, offering little of any substance for the reader anxious to know some truth about the playwright. First of all, Smith's tenure as a part of Tennessee's household was a brief one, and he seems to stretch a little material a long way. The reader may feel this book would more aptly have been entitled "A Year in the Life of Tennessee Williams." A considerable amount of space in *Costly Performances* is devoted to retelling old material from other books and an unnecessary reviewing of Tennessee's life prior to the time span of the narrative. Given the amount of space Smith devotes to himself, perhaps the book should have been entitled "A Year in the Life of Tennessee Williams Starring Bruce Smith." There are errors aplenty, for example, the misspelling of names: Poe's middle name is rendered "Allen"; Willem de Koonig becomes "Wilhelm"; Billy Barnes becomes "Billie." The first two pages contain a sentence calculated to drive an English professor or a proofreader—and I have in my time served in both capacities—into apoplexy: Smith describes an early Sevier forebear of the playwright's as "The man whom, as Tennessee observed, was 'credited with the quixotic conversion of many Chinese....'"

On the plus side, however, Bruce Smith, like Rader, is very good at recreating Tennessee's distinctive voice, that deep Delta drawl, which turned almost everything, even invectives and insults, into lyrical language. One prime example is the occasion when Tennessee, speaking of Poe, refers to himself as "the other relic of the old South." So good is this remark, and so authentically like Tennessee's pronouncements, that one assumes that it must be an accurate recollection. Besides, Smith does not seem to be capable of creating such a *bon mot* on his own. In defense of Bruce Smith, it should be acknowledged that the book that was published was not the complete book he wrote, due to the interference of the

Lady Maria, who insisted that certain very important passages be excised, and the original, though by no means a major biography, was considerably more forceful than the expurgated version.

After the publication of *Memoirs* (1975) there were, and are, many who feel that Williams did not do himself any favors by baring his soul or the particulars of his life that way. Not to be relied upon for factual detail, *Memoirs* is nevertheless a fascinating portrait of the artist during the last decade of his life when his darkest period had passed, but at a time when daily life was still difficult and his always nagging feelings of failure had become a chronic disease.

Other possibilities for those in search of a useful and accurate life of Tennessee Williams are not biographies *per se* but rather the voluminous journals, diaries, and letters he wrote through the years. Collections of his letters have been published by New Directions in two volumes: *Selected Letters of Tennessee Williams, Volume I 1920–1945* (2000) and *Volume II 1945–1957* (2004), edited by Albert J. Devlin and Nancy M. Tischler. Both volumes deserve the high praise they have received and *Volume I* was given an award by the Modern Language Association for "a distinguished edition of letters." The diaries and journals have been meticulously edited with exhaustive footnotes and explanatory material in Margaret Bradham Thornton's admirable *Notebooks* (2006). Because Tennessee was very observant and attentive to the events of his life and to the people that he met, his personal records offer an accurate and comprehensive self-portrait of the man. With Thornton's explanatory notes and transitional material, this volume provides much more accurate information about Tennessee's life and work than several of the other works examined above. However, even more than in the *Memoirs*, Williams' writing in the journals is intensely subjective and his assessments of everything from his talent to his mental condition on any given day are not necessarily going to be accurate. The jacket flap of the *Notebooks* indicates that they cover the period from 1936 to 1981 even though the journals to which Bradham had access only cover a period from March 1936 through September 1958. The rest of the years are filled in with unqualified quotes from negative critical assessments of the later plays, a dark, unfinished essay, "Mes Cahiers Noir," and, finally, a few diary fragments from 1979 and 1980.

People who knew Tennessee Williams well often complemented Lyle Leverich for what he accomplished in his *Tom: The Unknown Tennessee*, which was, as they saw it, to recreate within six hundred pages the living breathing man they had known in life. One notable exception to that judgment came from Donald Windham, who first met Tennessee in the 1930s and spent much time with him in subsequent decades, even collaborating with him on a play. In the past twenty years, I had several conversations with Windham, who was always a friend of Tennessee's, no matter the bad blood between them at various stages of their lives. We spoke of many things, but primarily of how Tennessee had been served by those who wrote about him. "I am so tired of reading about the sad homosexual Tennessee," Donald would say. "I never knew anyone who reveled more in his sexuality than Tenn did." We agreed that the Spoto, Hayman, Rader, and Smith books were guilty of this, but Windham insisted that Lyle Leverich was equally culpable in misportraying Tennessee, a judgment with which I must respectfully disagree, much as I admire Windham's opinions.

Tennessee Williams was very jealous of what his reputation would be after his career was finished and put away, along with his life, among the petals of yesterday's roses. He was sensible in being so, because biographers are a motley crew if ever there were one, and many are the dangers that lie in wait for the celebrity—politician, actor, or writer, for example—at the hands of those who relate their life stories as they understand them. The art of the biographer is to other branches of literature as the autopsy is to other branches of medicine, and just as often as not, once the biographer has done his job, one is left with nothing more than the dissected subject, lifeless and revealing no secrets, just as is the case when the coroner's invasive examination provides no assistance to the detective—or just as the song remains unexplained in Emily Dickinson's magnificent poem in which the lark is dissected to find what makes it sing, alas, to no avail. For those trying to understand the complex character of our greatest American playwright, readers should go to Lyle Leverich and consult Margaret Thornton's detailed research in *The Notebooks* for additional information. The two of them, I think, contribute to our understanding of Williams both as a man and an author.

" If Maria didn't kill

the thing she loved,

which was Williams' art,

"
she unwittingly wounded it.

THE LADY AND TENNESSEE

John Lahr

"He taught me not to lie."
  —Lady Maria St. Just, on Tennessee Williams

Lady Maria St. Just, who, it was said, was neither a lady nor a saint nor just, died, in England, on February 15, 1994. She was famous for her high spirits and her high-hat ways, which won her many friends and many enemies. She was a resourceful hostess and a good cook, but humble pie was not on her menu. Once, at a dinner party I was attending, she was summoned to the telephone to take an emergency call from Wilbury, her palatial country estate in Wiltshire and the oldest Palladian building in England. When she returned, she was agitated. "The dining-room ceiling has fallen in!" she said. "But God was with us, only the servants were hurt!" Her outrageousness delighted many. Sir John Gielgud, whom she dubbed King Wallah from their theater tour of the Far East just after the war, was a devoted friend, and so was Gore Vidal. But Maria's deepest and most long-standing attachment was to Tennessee Williams. She was the model for the fierce survival spirit of Maggie in *Cat on a Hot Tin Roof* (1955). She was also the manic, self-dramatizing, "two-faced" Countess of suspicious pedigree in the 1976 play *This Is (An Entertainment)*, whose title at one time went on to include her maiden name—"For Maria Britneva"—in its

222 TENN AT ONE HUNDRED

parentheses. And it was Maria whom Williams named, along with the lawyer John Eastman, as co-trustee of the Rose Williams Trust, established for his adored and lobotomized sister, who is eighty-five this year. As an actress, Maria worked only occasionally, but, because of confusions in Williams' clumsily drawn will, from 1984 to the end of her life she was cast as a player on the world stage. "She was to be the muse," Gore Vidal explains. "She was the surviving relic and keeper of the flame. It gave her something to do, which was very sweet of Tennessee. She had no purpose in life."

From the outset, Maria's survival was problematic. She was born on July 6, 1921, in St. Petersburg, Russia; but thirteen months later, as she tells it, under the threat of famine, her mother, Mary, escaped to England with Maria and her older brother, Vladimir, leaving their father, Dr. Alexander Britnev, apparently to the hands of the murderous Bolsheviks. "Little Mary…was so tiny that no one could believe that she was over a year old," Mary Britneva writes in *A Stranger in Your Midst*, her autobiography. According to Maria in her own Book, *Five O'Clock Angel*—primarily a collection of letters from Williams, which I was briefly engaged to compile, and which Maria ultimately decided to put together herself—she arrived in England with rickets. She remained a tiny figure (she grew to be about five feet tall), with a mane of brown hair, huge gray-brown eyes, and a beaky nose, which she turned up at the world. But another quality also remained—a combination of sadness and terror, which her mother had brought to their new life in England, and which was, along with Maria's nostalgia for a lost aristocratic world, a large part of her inheritance. English life belied a Russian saying frequently repeated in the Britnev household: "A person is met according to his clothes; but he is escorted according to his brains." In her autobiography Mary Britneva writes, "Here, you are both met and escorted 'according to your clothes,' alas! If a person is badly dressed, or has not acquired the English table-manners—be he ever so brilliant, he is not to be considered—and remains a *quantité negligeablé*." The appearance of substance was what counted—a bluff posture Maria instinctively adopted as the Britneva family renegotiated its social position in England. Inevitably, the family ambition and the family finances were at odds. In order to send her children to good schools (Maria was, as she said, expensively if not extensively educated), Mary Britneva gave lessons in French and Russian and did line translations of Chekhov.

She was ambitious for her daughter; she recounts shuttling Maria to and from ballet lessons, which Maria attacked with characteristic single-mindedness. When, in 1933, a young dancer with Monte Carlo's Ballets Russes was found to be under the statutory age of twelve, Maria stepped in. After three seasons, she had to give up dance, because of foot trouble and, she later told Richard Eyre, the head of the Royal National Theatre, because "my bosom was too big." She transferred her desire to be a star to theater. She got herself into Michel Saint-Denis's acting school, and set about making a career.

Maria's frenetic energy—her ability to act out her anxiety as momentum—was something that Williams teased in *This Is (An Entertainment)*, in which the Countess refers to "my spectacular velocity through time." Maria was driven, and she found a way, by sheer force of personality, to scale both the English aristocracy and the aristocracy of success. Maria spoke loudly and carried a big shtick. "She scared people," Gore Vidal says. As Maria admitted in a letter to Eyre when she was in her sixties, her roar masked a timidity, which she felt she must conceal. "She had a terrified heart," the singer-comedienne Paula Laurence says. "Terrified."

Maria was adamant about living to the limit of her dreams—a hard thing to accomplish at any time, and especially hard in threadbare postwar Britain. But she faced down the world, with what Elia Kazan, in his preface to *Five O'Clock Angel*, calls her "unswervable, desperate grip on what she valued in life." And, when life didn't present her with the right scenario, Maria reinvented it. "Never travel to Paris alone; it's a lovers' city," Maria told Dotson Rader, a friend of Tennessee Williams' and the author of a memoir about him, *Tennessee: Cry of the Heart*. "And I'll give you another tip. Always have a double bed. Tennessee and I always have a double bed." Rader recalls that Williams, who had been off in one of his druggy daydreams, suddenly grew alert to the conversation: "Yes, baby, we always have double beds. But they're always in separate rooms."

In *Five O'Clock Angel* Maria practices the same kind of narrative trick. Here, in an astonishing act of ventriloquism, she is both the subject of the narrative and the omniscient narrator: "The Tartar imperiousness; the theatrical panache; the dislike of the bourgeois, the stuffy, or the second-rate; above all, the savagely mordant sense of humor; the spirit is the same. It was that spirit which proved enduringly attractive to a man whose own character seemed very different—the American playwright Tennessee Williams." This transparent mythmaking allows Maria to direct a well-choreographed drama of her idealized self, in which fantasy goes unchallenged and glides effortlessly into the presumption of fact.

Almost everyone, including Williams, was seduced by Maria's moving portrait of the daughter of noble White Russian émigrés whose paternal grandfather had been physician to "Dowager Empress Maria Fedorovna at Tsarskoe Selo," and whose father had stayed behind in Russia in 1922 to be "shortly afterwards…shot by the Soviets." But recently released K.G.B. files and government papers show that most of this was revised history, of Maria's fabrication. Maria's mother was born an English citizen and had been partly educated in England; and Maria's maternal grandfather, Charles Herbert Bucknall, was English on both sides. (He had been the business partner in St. Petersburg of the French wholesale gem dealers Leo and Georges Sachs—a particularly unappealing legacy to someone of Maria's anti-Semitic persuasion.) So the Britnevs didn't actually flee the marauding Bolsheviks; they had English papers. And, according to Russian researchers, the Britnev family line was made up of *raznochintsi*—intelligentsia who were of plebian descent. The Britnevs were descended from petty-bourgeois merchants from Kronshtadt, where they owned tugboats and diving equipment and public baths. There was no record of her grandfather's association with the Tsarina. As for Maria's father, his K.G.B. file reveals that far from being executed by the Bolsheviks he served in the Red Army. Dr. Britnev was actually executed in 1930, by the Stalinists; then, on April 18, 1969, he was "rehabilitated" by the Communists. Britnev's link to the Bolsheviks explains the privileges that the Britnevs enjoyed during the particularly brutal Stalinist years of the twenties: they travelled back and forth between

Russia and England with relative ease. All this puts paid to Maria's being a White Russian, or even an Off-White Russian.

Maria gave credibility to her story, and to her aura of artistic entitlement, by associating with the rich and famous, who acted as a kind of hedge against loss. "She always had to have some adored figure whom she was fiercely loyal to, even when the great figure did not *need* loyalty, much less fierce loyalty," Vidal says. In 1945, she attached herself to Sir John Gielgud, who served as her protector and her entrée into the theater. 'I was the dogsbody," Maria told *Interview.* "I did everything! I dressed John....I was a terrific favorite of John's. And consequently everybody hated me because they were jealous." To win favor, Maria was capable of acts of enormous rashness. Of a 1946 production in which Maria was elevated from understudy to walk-on, Gielgud says, "When Edith Evans, as the consumptive wife in *Crime and Punishment*, coughed too constantly during one of my best scenes, Maria pushed her face in a cushion to keep her quiet. This, as you can imagine, was not well received by the Dame." Nor was it well received by Hugh (Binkie) Beaumont, who was the panjandrum of H. M. Tennent's, the powerful West End Management company that produced the play. He cancelled Maria's contract.

"I never thought her much of an actress, but she longed to succeed as one," Gielgud recalls. Maria had won a place forever in Sir John's heart but lost her toehold in the mainstream of English theater. "She wasn't a good actress," says the English drama critic Milton Shulman, who was a neighbor of Maria's. "She was too much a fantasist offstage to be a fantasist onstage." Maria also had neither the conventional looks nor the reserve for the clipped English-drawing-room drama that was the staple of the West End from the mid-forties to the mid-fifties. She had an artistic temperament, but she couldn't produce art. She was up against it. Then she met Williams and hitched her wagon to his star.

The romance of the Williams-Britneva friendship is built on the cornerstone of their first meeting. In her story, Maria casts herself as an ingénue of "eighteen or nineteen." (She was just shy of twenty-seven.) She and Williams met at a dinner at Gielgud's home on June

11, 1948. Maria told Dick Cavett on his talk show, "I was invited to this wonderful party. Noël Coward playing the piano. Vivien Leigh, Larry Olivier, the most wonderful people…I suddenly saw in the corner this crumpled little man, very alone—one red sock and one blue sock. I thought he must be another understudy." Since Gielgud was directing the debut of *The Glass Menagerie* in London, it's hardly likely that Williams, who had just won the Pulitzer Prize for *A Streetcar Named Desire* (1947), went unnoticed at the party. But there were a few things that assuredly did go unnoticed by Maria. The Oliviers were not there: according to their biographers, they were in Australia most of the year. And it must have been the blithe spirit of Noël Coward who was tinkling the ivories, since Coward himself was in New York, meeting with his publishers, and didn't arrive back in England until nearly two weeks later.

Gore Vidal, who hung out with Williams in Paris after the playwright bolted from the prospect of a disastrous London opening, starring Helen Hayes as Amanda Wingfield, believes that the two must have met several weeks later, at a party given by Binkie Beaumont. But, wherever the meeting took place, it made boon companions of Maria, Vidal, and Williams. Vidal recalls the three of them walking along the Strand the following day: "Maria ate and ate. She and her mother were poor. They were still on ration books. She had some toffees, and she gave me one. I had a pivot tooth—a false tooth—which immediately came out. Riotous laughter from Maria. Could've killed her. The three of us became friends. And then she attached herself."

Williams recognized in Maria what Elia Kazan called a "symbol, an archetype, of the 'rebellious spirit' at bay." He knew an embattled romantic when he saw one. Thomas Lanier Williams, who was ten years older than Maria, had also invented himself as an artist, adopting the name Tennessee Williams in 1938. By rights, he should have called himself Mississippi Williams, since until his family moved to St. Louis, in 1918, he'd been raised in a series of Episcopal rectories where his grandfather was pastor, most of them in Mississippi. But the name Tennessee evoked the lost heroic heritage of his hated, hard-drinking father—a traveling salesman called C. C. Williams, whose ancestors were among the founders of that state. Williams shared with Maria a difficult beginning (in his case, diphtheria and kidney infection at the age of six); the trauma of dislocation (the shift to St. Louis was the alienation around which *The Glass Menagerie* was built); and a sense, no matter how well disguised, of being under siege. Williams had been writing since his youth but had only just broken through when he met Maria; the purity of her aspirations and the poverty of her circumstances moved him. In 1949, he wrote from London to his friends the writer Donald Windham and the actor Sandy Campbell:

> She detests London and has fallen out completely with the Beaumont office so she has no prospect of work here. Only a television job, three weeks rehearsal and entire salary amounts to one hundred dollars. (One performance.) Seems to have no interesting friends here, nobody she likes much and her family is quite poor, except for an aunt who treats her rather coolly. Poor child.

Maria played the devoted, adorable (and needy) girl; Williams was the benevolent sugar daddy, always ready to spring for vacation tickets, hotels, loans, jewelry, even an occasional dress or fur. "I felt I was in a state of grace when I was with him," Maria later said, and she was: protected by the big magic of Williams' talent and renown from a world whose security, in her case, had a habit of collapsing.

To a woman of Maria's overweening social and artistic ambitions, an important marriage was crucial, and one of the first men she set her cap at was Williams himself. "She was madly in love with Tenn, madly, madly in love," says the journalist Harriet Van Horne, who knew Maria in her vagabond days in the fifties, in New York, where she was pursuing her stalled acting career and cooking supper in a one-room apartment for, among others, William Faulkner and Marlon Brando. (Maria was said to have bedded Brando, and in her twilight years she was a staunch friend to members of the star's family during their legal troubles.) Although there is no evidence that Maria and Williams had sex, Van Horne heard the sound of genuine passion in Maria's talk about him: "Her description— 'Tennessee is so tanned. His head is like a brown nut. I just love to run my fingers through his hair.' You don't say that unless you've got a physical attraction." Maria wrote in her diary, "I do love Tennessee and don't think there is anyone alive who is more sweet and gentle, kind and generous and so full of talent…His companionship and support are what I value now most in my life." Maria went to a psychotherapist about her relationship with Williams, and, despite sensational evidence to the contrary, wanted to believe that he was a lapsed heterosexual. "To go around saying Tennessee wasn't a faggot is madness," Vidal says. But at times Maria went around saying even more than that. "She called me up and said, 'I've got to see you right away,'" Arthur Miller says. "She showed up and she said, 'Tennessee and I want to get married'—not *are going* to get married. 'What do you think?' I was floored. I said, 'Are you sure you're both of the same mind?' I sensed a large element of fantasy in it. She was playing some kind of role, flying around the room and being extremely romantic and excited, like a fourteen-year-old girl. All I could do was stall and think whether I'd heard right. I think she wanted me to talk to Tennessee and get him to marry her."

"She liked to fuck," says Paula Laurence, who, with her husband, the producer Charles Bowden, was among Maria's best American friends. But Laurence adds, "she didn't throw it around. She had to be sure what kind of a bargain she was striking with it." In 1951, Maria had an abortion, and Williams wrote in a letter to his good friend Paul Bigelow that she was suffering 'the immemorial trouble of warm-hearted ladies.' (Williams went on to say, "Keep this under your Borsalino, pet! It is not supposed to be anything more exotic than ulcers.") But the next year, almost to the week, Williams was piping a happier tune, to his agent, Audrey Wood, about "our little secret": Maria had been having an affair with Williams' patrician American publisher, James Laughlin, known as Jay—the handsome millionaire who had founded New Directions. Williams wrote:

> We left Maria in Paris, impecunious and gay and charming as ever…not too depressed over the fact that our friend Jay has apparently resumed his American affair. She makes me think of a joke about a Brooklyn "queen" whose lover had gone to sea.

A friend said how are you feeling, and the response was "I am inconsolable! I've only had five sailors since supper!"

Maria was seeking consolation with John Huston when I left. I introduced them on the set of "Moulin Rouge."...I had not been here a day when I received a wire from Maria. "AT IT LIKE KNIVES. HUSTON A STEAMING HOT CUP OF TEA. WANT TO STAY IN PARIS. CALL ME."...I do hope she gets a job out of this, which was the original purpose of the meeting, and not just another one of her peculiar misadventures. She says she "always forgets to be careful," whatever that means, and nature seems determined to make use of her!

By 1954, Maria had managed to hook Laughlin: their engagement was announced in the London *Times*. But Laughlin got cold feet, and several months later broke it off. This was an enormous humiliation for Maria. According to her, it was her extravagance in buying Laughlin eight silk ties that spooked him. "My God! What are you going to do with all my money?" she quotes Laughlin as saying in *Five O'Clock Angel,* which is dedicated to him. She goes on, "I was genuinely surprised. 'Why, have you *got* any?— I'll spend it, of course!" Maria knew perfectly well that Laughlin was wealthy. A press release she later composed with the help of a New York P.R. man refers to her having "broken her engagement to a multimillionaire steel heir." Williams wrote to Laughlin, implicitly suggesting that he settle money on Maria for "disappointment as a result of being discarded like this, in such a public fashion."

What had terrified Laughlin was Maria's essentially volatile nature. "I think you are one of the world's more attractive girls," he admitted to her in his Dear Maria letter. "But I'm also afraid of you— afraid of how you might wreck my life with all that misdirected energy pouring out of you like a giant Russian dynamo." In a five-page handwritten letter to Williams he spelled out his fears more directly. "She is so strong-willed and dominating and, to use her phrase, 'makes such rows' when I assert myself against her wishes," he wrote. "If anything, in the years I have known her, she has become *more* vital and active, more ready to get caught up in the interests and doings of people who do not really fit into the center of her picture." He added, "I doubt if she is really 'crushed,' as you say. I don't think you really understand what a vitality she has. *Nothing* could or would crush her."

On July 25, 1956, Maria married Peter Grenfell, Lord St. Just, the son of Edward Grenfell, who was the English banking partner of J. P. Morgan, with whom he had formed Morgan Grenfell & Co. Peter, who suffered from a manic depression that led to frequent bouts of uncontrollable shaking and crying, had a love of country pursuits (shooting, sailing) and of the ballet and the opera. His mother, the dowager, was a patron of the arts, and entertained Diaghilev's Ballets Russes at Wilbury; as a child, Peter was encouraged to admire all things Russian. He was a handsome man with a long, Slavic-looking face. Mark Birley, an old friend of Lord Peter's and a godson of the Dowager's, says, "There was even a story that Peter's real father was one of the dancers at their slightly bohemian weekends." Maria not only was a link to Peter's past but, in her promises to help cure him, was perceived as a link to his future. "He thought she could help him," Bobby Henderson, a trustee of Lord Peter's estate, says. "She had an effect on him. She bemused him. Her amusingness distracted him. It was an escape. He certainly had strong feelings for her. He seemed to want to be near her; and then he didn't." Lord Peter's love/hate for Maria was apparent from the outset. "He bolted from outside Harvey Nichols when she was buying gloves for the wedding," Margaret Anne Stuart, St. Just's frequent companion in the late fifties, says, "He went into a clinic. He called her up and apologized—this is what he told me—and the next time he saw her the marriage took place."

Maria's New York press release told a Cinderella story with a twist: that she was sacrificing the promise of a big career for the promise of a big bankroll. "Thus, Maria said goodbye to her friend Tennessee Williams' hope of having her play the lead in his next play," the release said. "The poor but proud British actress had been warming up here taking Southern accent lessons on Tennessee's orders." Poverty was now something to joke about. The lead paragraph quoted her as saying, "I'm probably the only girl to ever wed a peer, in a dress from Gimbel's basement, a dollar hat, with a ribbon from Woolworth's, standing in a pair of ten cent shoes!"

According to Clarissa Heald, a family friend of the Grenfells, Maria had met Peter through her paternal aunt, who worked as a paid companion to the Dowager after the first Lord St. Just's death, in 1941. Maria, in other words, had been below stairs and was now marrying the lord of the manor. The Dowager, who later referred to her as "the little Bolshevik," and who was, in turn, hated by Maria and dismissed by her as "really rather common, you know," began by putting a good face on her son's marriage. "I believe you will bring love and salvation to Peter," she wrote to Maria at the time of the wedding. "He has suffered cruelly, and his great courage in not turning to drink or drugs has amazed the doctors." Peter St. Just turned to drink soon enough, but his position and his problems were on a scale that appealed to his new wife's grandiosity. According to the press release, St, Just had greeted Maria when she arrived in England for a European holiday with the daughter of the head of M.C.A., Jean Stein, and said, "Darling, will you marry me?" In fact, Maria had taken Peter St. Just out of the sanitarium to marry him. They spent their wedding night at Claridge's, but they had a furious row, and the next day Lord Peter ran off for a fortnight. "He was in kind of strange shape," Stein recalls, and goes on to explain Maria's impulse. "To be Lady St. Just and to have some money. Are you kidding? She had nothing. Desperate. And to have that beautiful home in the country and to be legitimate." But as long as the Dowager was alive Maria was only a visitor to Wilbury, and had to bide her time to claim it.

Vidal remembers Peter St. Just as "great charmer when he was in good form." But Maria's talk about her husband was increasingly bitter, and her bitterness has led Vidal to conclude that—despite Williams' public utterances—she was not the model for Maggie in *Cat on a Hot Tin Roof.* "She probably got him to say it—I mean, Tennessee would say anything," Vidal says. "Maggie was in love with Brick; Maria was not in love with Peter, to put it simply. And Maggie desired Brick physically, which Maria did not Peter St. Just."

Their union proved a marriage of inconvenience. "He came back to her often when he was ill," Lady Stuart says. "But when he was healthy she didn't see him for dust." Though the marriage produced two children—Natasha and Katherine—St. Just also fathered at least one and possibly two illegitimate children. And the Dowager treated Maria badly; even the implicit promise of generosity proved false. (In her letters, Maria frequently drew a witch on a broomstick next to the Dowager's name.) Lord Peter and Lady Maria were put on a minimal allowance by his trustees. "Maria was living in a tiny, tiny flat with her two babies in London," says Harriet Van Horne, who visited her there in the late fifties. "They bought the house in Gerald Road for Maria, but they would not put it in Maria's name. It was in the name of the girls. She lived there by grace and favor."

Maria tried to put a droll spin on her husband's frequent breakdowns. "Oh, Peter's in the bin again," Van Horne remembers her saying. "He loves it. He's learned to make ashtrays." Van Horne explains, "Other people had messy marriages. She didn't. She had an unfortunate husband who was a little mad." Maria always displayed what Williams called, in reference to another disenchanted romantic, Chance Wayne, "that terrible stiff-necked pride of the defeated."

Maria projected onto Tennessee Williams all the passion and romantic idealism that were absent in her marriage. He was an improbable St. George who came to her aid in the increasingly frequent times of separation and tribulation. "She used to find herself without any money," the journalist Drusilla Beyfus says. "I remember what Maria told me when I went to stay at Wilbury and commented on the pretty wallpaper—William Morris wallpaper, I think. She said, "Isn't it wonderful? Tennessee's paid for it. Every time I lie in bed and look at it, I thank God for Tennessee.'" Where St. Just shrugged off her attentions, Williams welcomed them; where St. Just viewed her as a burden to be endured, Williams, from his transatlantic vantage point, saw her as a character to be enjoyed; where St. Just abused her with occasional outbursts of violence (Maria miscarried a child after one fight, she told a friend), Williams, always the courtly Southern gent, was solicitous of her, at least to her face. Lord Peter's depression led him down unproductive byways, but Williams turned his suffering into something public, something that could be, as he says in *Sweet Bird of Youth*, unveiled: "a sculpture, almost heroic." Increasingly, in Maria's mind Williams became the husband manqué, and she was the unkissed bride. "It was a friendship," she writes in the introduction to *Five O'Clock Angel,* betraying the unabashed and barmy depth of her romantic fantasy, "that they managed successfully to keep private for over thirty years."

Maria's worship at the altar of Williams' talent paid off in a number of appearances in his plays: a walk-on role in the London production of *Summer and Smoke* in 1951; an Off-Broadway stab at Blanche in *Streetcar* in 1955, about which Brooks Atkinson said, "Maria Britneva, an English actress, is not able to express the inner tensions of that haunted gentlewoman"; a cameo in *Suddenly Last Summer* in 1959, as the mute, demented woman with a doll in the opening sequence who undergoes a lobotomy; and bit parts in *Orpheus Descending* at the Royal Court in 1959 and in the London and Vienna productions of *The Red Devil Battery Sign* in 1977. Sometimes Williams tried to temper Maria's theatrical ambitions. "You *must* be realistic about what you should do and what you shouldn't do in theatre," he wrote her in 1952, spurning her plea to play Esmeralda in *Camino Real.* But at other times he championed her cause. "Doll," Williams wrote her in 1954, "I have mobilized the city in an all-out campaign to find "WORK FOR MARIA!" Such was Williams' thralldom to Maria that by the nineteen-seventies he was referring to them both ironically as "her Ladyship and slave."

"She was so extraordinary about weaving her way into people's lives," Paula Laurence says. "Before you knew it, you were entirely surrounded. But it was done with tremendous affection, the most flattering kind of interest, outrageous presents, and loving attention. How could you not want that?" Certainly the distracted and disorganized Tennessee Williams did. "I am quite incapable of learning the relative values of all these crazy coins, bobs, half crowns, ten shillings, quids, etc.," he wrote to Audrey Wood from London in 1948, just before Maria came into his life. "When Margo"—the director Margo Jones, who also adored Williams—"deserts me I shall be in total chaos!" Maria made herself indispensable. She sent him gifts, did his laundry, and dispensed a lot of brusque maternal straight talk ("Read, mark, and inwardly digest"). In fact, Maria had the physical outline and all the emotional attributes of Williams' mother, Edwina, who was also petite, domineering, strong-willed, and filled with nostalgia

234 TENN AT ONE HUNDRED

for a vanished aristocratic heritage. The unconscious authority and appeal that this resemblance gave Maria helps to explain the strange power she seemed to exert over Williams.

Maria also turned Williams' social life into a fiesta. The actor Keith Baxter, who appeared with Maria in *The Red Devil Battery Sign*, says, "That's one of the things Tenn found absolutely thrilling about her: that she was the life force. Where Maria was, there was energy; and Tenn's energies were very much depleted." She brought incidental comedy to Williams' melancholy existence. "In a single night & morning the Lady St. Pig has made an indelible impression on Buffalo & especially the management and players of the Arena Theatre," he wrote to Gore Vidal in 1973, in a joint letter with Maria. "With our plane booking at 2 p.m., she decided at 11:30 to go see Niagara Falls and it took a taxi driver, myself, and the assistant hotel manager to convince her the project was unrealistic time-wise. It was with noticeable reluctance that she returned me the fare." (Here Maria adds, "He hadn't given me enough anyway, Scrooge.")

From the outset, Maria's hold on Williams was noticed with amusement by his friends. Donald Windham wrote in his memoirs, "She is one of the few people who, with a combination of flattery and mockery, good humor and shyness, can sometimes cajole Tennessee into seeing his absurdities and dropping them. At the same time, she consolidates herself in his good will by mischievous endorsements of the desires he wants to be encouraged in." Even toward the end of Williams' life, after the sixties, which he called the Stoned Age, Maria—although she deplored his homosexual world and his drugged haze—kept control over him by providing what he wanted. "She was supplying or trying to supply him not only with boys…but with drugs," claims Bruce Smith, a P.R. man whose memoir *Costly Performances* is an account of his friendship with Williams between 1979 and 1981. Smith refused to stay with Williams after discovering a set of needles in a brown paper bag in Williams' apartment. In an unpublished passage from his memoir, Smith writes of cornering Maria and telling her, "I've seen the needles in this morning's package. Let's not play holier than thou," and he adds, "Her eyes widened and she stepped back into the kitchen." Dotson Rader, who was no stranger to drugs, and occasionally stayed in Williams' Key West home, also "became convinced that she was acting as his pusher." Rader goes on:

> He couldn't get Seconal. The doctors wouldn't give him pills…I became convinced that she was giving him the pills because whenever she would show up he'd suddenly have them.…I thought she was getting prescriptions in her name and giving him the stuff. I got really angry two days before the opening of *Clothes* because he was in no shape. We all had dinner at Vas Voglis's, who was another piece of work, and Tennessee was with her. He'd been with her all day long, and he was absolutely stoned. He'd missed a rehearsal. She was sitting there smug. I suddenly started attacking her. I said, "You filthy cunt! You're pushin' drugs on him! You're killing him, you son-of-a-bitch!" To which she got terribly British, terribly upper-class. She turned to Tennessee and said, "Aren't you going to defend me, darling, against this ruffian?" I said I was going back to the hotel, and that anything I found I was going to flush down the toilet. And if he had drugs again, I said I was going to call the police and get her deported…I think that's one of the reasons why he was always so happy to see her…She facilitated his addictions."

Another one of Williams' addictions was the contact high of celebrity. And Maria acted as his champion and protector, facing down the world for him when increasingly he was too drugged or drunk to hold his head up. Once, after attending the opening of Martin Sherman's *Bent* (1979) on Broadway, they went backstage with Rader to see its star, Richard Gere. He was slumped in his jockey shorts at the dressing table when Williams held out his hand in congratulation. "Gere just stares at Tennessee and won't take his hand," Rader, who was no fan of Maria's, recalls, "I must say I was proud of her. 'Don't you know who this is, young man? Don't you know who'd extending his hand to you? It's Tennessee Williams, the world's greatest playwright. How *dare* you not take his hand!'"

The power of celebrity emboldened and even sanctioned Maria's tyrannical nature. "She tried to kill me," alleges Williams' younger brother, Dakin, referring to Maria's pushing him off a catwalk at

New York's Lyceum Theater after the opening of *Out Cry* (1973) when Dakin was in disfavor with Williams, in large part for having him institutionalized in 1969. "There was a two-foot-wide aperture in the railing," Dakin says. "Seventy-five feet onto concrete. The lady maneuvered me right in front of that opening. She said, 'Step back, Dakin,' and she shoved me with both hands on my shoulders.… Luckily for me, there was a spiral staircase out of sight beneath this opening; and, of course, my arms were flailing about as I was falling and I caught hold of it." In 1979, Dakin saw Maria at the Watergate Hotel, in Washington, where Williams was to receive a Kennedy Center Honors Award. Dakin recalls, "I came up to her and said, 'Now, Maria, why did you do that?' referring to the attempt she made on my life. She said, 'Well, Dakin, you were behaving so beastly.' My brother asked her about it, and said, 'You might have killed my brother Dakin.' And she said to Tennessee, "Oh, that was the intention, luv.'"

Williams, who was inclined to be conciliatory except when liquored up, was both amazed and appalled by Maria's forthrightness. "You seem to say all the things that discreet people only think," he wrote to her in 1949. "I do most earnestly advise and beseech you to curb it, like the fancy little dogs on Fifth Avenue." But Maria couldn't resist. With a few accurate verbal strokes, she could winkle out the defining aspect of a personality. "No-neck monsters," the first phrase of *Cat*, was her coinage, and she invented a whole lexicon of mischievous nicknames to amuse Williams. His regal agent, Audrey Wood, was Lady Mandarin; his jowly friend Carson McCullers was Choppers; the suave Berlin-born agent Robert Lantz was Mitt Schlag. In the early fifties, when Maria had a studio apartment in New York, Drusilla Beyfus remembers coming to meet her for the first time, only to find a bloodstained handkerchief and a note pinned to the door. "Suicide upstairs—Be with you soon," it read. Beyfus says, "I never knew if there actually was a suicide. We all went out for a jolly dinner afterward, and it was never mentioned again. I felt as if I was in a Chekhov play." The playwright John Guare, who visited Maria at Wilbury, says, "You understood why Tennessee must have liked her. Every moment was high melodrama. Completely manic humor. All good guys and bad guys. She lived by her nose. She lived on instinct.

Dangerously. She would size people up in a second and be totally wrong or totally right."

Over the years, Williams took increasing pleasure in aiming Maria's grapeshot vitriol at various imposing friends and watching the showdown. When Maria complained of being unable to understand Brando in his definitive portrayal of Stanley Kowalski in *Streetcar*, Williams took her backstage to tell him so. He imported Maria to Florida under the assumed name Miss Bow to watch Tallulah Bankhead make a hash of Blanche in a 1955 production that was being tried out at the Coconut Grove Theatre before coming to New York, and for which Maria had unsuccessfully auditioned as Stella. It was a recipe for mayhem. "From the moment Miss Bankhead saw Maria, she would have none of her," Sandy Campbell writes in "B," a privately printed epistolary account of the production, in which he had a small part. "Tenn is licking his lips with the prospect of an encounter between B and her." Williams, who was secretly disgruntled with Bankhead's performance, brought Miss Bow to the opening-night party ("Maria, naturally...talking violently against B's performance"). Inevitably, the next day there was some sniping between Bankhead and Williams, who, having hypocritically praised her, now told her she'd given a bad performance. Campbell, who was present, recounts the scene:

> "And you had the nerve to say that after getting down on your knees to me in the dressing room," B said.
> "Are you calling me a hypocrite?. . ."
> "And bringing that bitch, Maria, to the party is shocking," B said.
> Tenn, standing up: "My dear, I do not have to stand for this anymore. Calling...my best friend a black bitch is more that I can take!" And he marched out.

"She would give him backbone," Gore Vidal says of Maria role in Williams' life and career. He would rather slide off to the nearest bar and forget about it. He had a thing of really talking very obscenely, and it got worse as he got older. He'd be in perfectly respectable mixed company, and he'd start in, "Oh, I saw this boy on the Strand, and he had…" The whole room would be riveted. And Maria's voice could be heard: "Oh, Tennessee, do shut up!" I told Maria that should be the title of her book. Sometimes he liked it; but he was a perfectly shrewd strategist of his career, and there were times when he would tell her to shut up and stop it. And she would immediately become as meek as a lamb."

Maria's caustic wit effectively eroded several of Williams' allegiances. It also created a sense of collusion that passed for intimacy. "Once she got the inkling that Tenn was beginning to get suspicious of someone, she would pee in his ear," Rader says. Maria apparently played a part in stoking the paranoia about Audrey Wood that led, in 1971, to Williams' final split with his agent of thirty-two years. Maria had taken a dislike to Wood from her earliest days in New York, when she was made to wait in Wood's outer office, at ICM, to receive a weekly stipend of twenty-five dollars that Williams had arranged for her. According to the agent Bridget Aschenberg, who worked with Wood, Maria was the only person who ever made the steely doyenne of American theatrical agents cry. "It was some kind of terrible scene with Tenn and her and Lady Maria, in the dressing room," Aschenberg says of Williams' tirade at Wood, which occurred backstage during *Out Cry*. "She came into the office the next day. She was wearing dark glasses. She said, 'I don't want to talk about it.' She hated this woman. She hated her." Later, in 1979, the agent Mitch Douglas took over the representation of Williams, and Wood would sometimes stick her head in his office door to inquire, "How's he doing?" Douglas recalls her popping in one morning: "Well, dear, have you met Maria yet?' I said, 'Not yet.' And she says, 'Well, watch her, dear, she's a bitch.' Audrey didn't say things like that." (The first time Douglas heard from Maria, she phoned to say, "Mitch, I am in Tennessee's apartment, and it's filthy. The floors are filthy. The windows are even dirtier." Douglas recalls, "I said, 'Maria, I don't do floors.'") It was Wood's prowess as both critic and confidante for Williams that galled Maria, and which she felt compelled to trash in *Five O'Clock Angel*. She writes, "The manuscript Tennessee had sent to Audrey, to which she had reacted so negatively, was a new play—*Cat on a Hot Tin Roof*. Audrey could not understand its plot, which Maria had to explain to her." The claim is dizzying in its absurdity. *Cat* is dedicated to Wood, and she certainly understood the plays; she made criticisms of them that Williams incorporated into his final scripts. "I'm glad you wrote me so candidly about it," Williams said in a letter to Wood about her notes to *Orpheus Descending* (1957). "Your reaction to a script means much more to me than anyone else's."

In revising history, Maria was revising her place in Williams' story, which since the publication of his *Memoirs*, in 1975, had been a bone of contention between them. As Maria frequently told the press, she had thrown *Memoirs* in the wastebasket. She was offended, she said, by his louche tales. She was even more offended by Williams' making a scant eleven mentions of her, calling her "an occasional actress," and promising the reader "I will write more about Maria later." The most memorable remark thing about her in the book is that "the lady is afflicted with *folie de grandeur.*" Maria put the screws to Williams, and his apology was a few typewritten pages about their relationship, which he promised would be published in the British edition. In the end, they were published in *Five O'Clock Angel.* Williams wrote, "In the American edition of my memoirs, this richly sustaining attachment was, for some reason, reduced by the editors to the point where it seemed to be little more than an acquaintance, practically unexplained." But had the St. Just-Williams *amitié amoureuse* really been blue-pencilled out by others? "The answer is no," Kate Medina, the editor of the book, says. Williams himself had virtually left Maria out of the official story of his life. She had absorbed him, but had Williams, as she claims in *Five O'Clock Angel,* absorbed her? "I suppose in a way he had," Gore Vidal says. "Although he was a *very* solitary cat. He appreciated, to a degree, what she did for him, which was just kind of looking after him. But I don't think he ever had any affection for anybody."

When, at the end of his life, Peter St. Just was very ill and Maria was his devoted attendant, Harriet Van Horne remembers asking her, "Suppose both Peter and Tenn were terminally ill? At whose bedside would you sit?" Maria relied, "Well, Tennessee's, darling, of course." As it happened, Williams died in 1983, a year and a half before Peter St. Just. Over the remaining years of her life, Maria frequently asked Paula Laurence, "What do you think? If Tennessee had lived, how would this have ended?" Laurence explains, "She wanted us to reassure her that he would be with her somehow. Maybe not in a legal marriage, but together. You felt so sad about that. 'Get real, girl.' Jesus!"

Maria's fantasy of being Williams' widow and her own artistic frustrations coalesced in her role as co-trustee of the Rose Williams Trust, which accounted for the majority of Williams' estate, amounting to five million dollars. She did an imaginative job as Rose's caretaker—frequently visiting her in the sanitarium where she lived, and furnishing her new apartment there with a canopied bed, white wicker furniture, and flowered pillows. "It's a room for a teen-ager," says Laurence, whose husband helped Maria look after Rose. "It's the room she never had."

Williams, who built a shrine to Rose in his Key West house, enshrined her memory in many plays, perhaps most notably in the part of Laura in *The Glass Menagerie* (1945). Like Laura, Rose exhibited an almost morbid shyness, which was connected to the repression of sexual feeling in their mother's puritanical household and to their father's tyrannical behavior. As Rose reached adulthood, her behavior grew increasingly erratic. She had delusions of being murdered and poisoned. She became abusive and violent. (She once had to be stopped from carrying a kitchen knife to a psychiatric appointment.) After a psychiatrist warned that Rose might murder her father, the family institutionalized her; they later consented to a lobotomy. Unlike Williams, for whom work provided "outer oblivion and inner violence," Rose had no way of exorcising pain. Her outer violence was transformed through the operation to inner oblivion.

In her care of Rose, Maria was appropriately warm and dutiful, but in her extracurricular involvement in Williams' literary affairs she was fanatical. She took to the job like a moth to light, and held sway with a ferocity that even her solicitor, the legendary Sir Arnold Goodman, told her was out of bounds. He writes in his memoir, *Tell Them I'm On My Way* (1993), "She was engaged in vigorous battles to maintain the integrity of various productions, despite my constant remonstrances that it is no part of her duty as a trustee to engage in casting the play. However, remonstrances to Maria are about as futile as persuading a charging bull of the error of its ways." Because the trust was vested with the copyrights to the plays, Maria's role increasingly allowed her to give or deny permission to produce them, and to insist in other ways on her idea of Williams—and of herself—for posterity. Her imperialism extended even to Williams' grave, marked—improbably, since he was an Episcopalian—by a Russian Orthodox cross.

The only authorized voice about Williams was to be Maria's. As she writes in the penultimate paragraph of *Five O'Clock Angel*, again giving her fantasy the ring of fact, "Tennessee's two great loves had been his work and his sister Rose. In his Will, he entrusted the care of both to Maria." How well she succeeded in purveying this myth could be seen in her obituaries. "THE ARISTOCRATIC HELLCAT WHO LOVED TENNESSEE WILLIAMS," the *Evening Standard* said. The *Guardian* spelled out her story in calmer detail: "She was William's closest woman friend, and her almost familial devotion was acknowledged upon his death, when she was named as his literary executor. His artistic heritage could not have been entrusted to a more vigilant administrator."

Obituaries and her pronouncements to the contrary, Maria became Tennessee Williams' literary executor only by default. "Maria was never named as literary executor," the estate's other co-trustee, John Eastman, says. "Tennessee and I talked about it. He said, 'My only concern is Rose.'" And in at least one regard Williams' will is explicit in its intention to separate the co-trustees, who had fiduciary power, from the people evaluating his literary remains; in a codicil to his will he designated Harvard University to be the sole arbiter of such judgment.

The will had been the focus of much ambivalent feeling between Maria and Williams. "She was always whining about money," Rader says. "About her future. She was getting old. He'd say, 'Oh, baby, don't worry. You're in the will.'" But, Rader notes, "Tennessee was always telling people they were in his will." Maria argued with Williams— and even fell out with him for a number of years, friends say—over being made an heiress. This estrangement accounts for the meager twenty letters from Williams to Maria between 1959 and 1967 that appear in *Five O'Clock Angel*. "Ultimately, money was at the root of her evil," Paula Laurence says. "She loved money. Money was all tied up with security, with love, with emotions." With a large estate to manage, two daughters in private school, and an erratic husband, financial security was always an issue for Maria. She wanted Williams to leave her a percentage of the royalties to one of his major plays—a gesture he'd made to other important caretakers, such as his mother, who got half the royalties from *The Glass Menagerie*, and his great friend and lover Frank Merlo, who got a percentage of *The Rose Tattoo*. When Williams died, he left Maria the proceeds of his rarely performed *The Two-Character Play* (as *Out Cry* was later titled)— which in fiscal terms was as impudent a joke as Shakespeare's leaving his wife the "second best bed." Williams also made Maria's co-trusteeship—and the not insubstantial stipend that eventually came with it—dependent on Rose's life span. According to the will, when Rose died the co-trustees' role and their salary and benefits would stop. It was a guarantee, beyond Maria's avowed devotion to Rose, that proper care would be taken.

In the most literal sense, the trustees fulfilled their mandate— which was to increase the economic value of the trust. "We did that," Eastman says, "led by Maria." In 1984, Maria and Eastman began to assist the will's executor—the Southeast Banks of Florida—in administering the estate, and in the next five years Williams' earnings jumped from $349,000 to $545,000 a year; between 1989 and 1993, they rose to $809,000 a year. But Maria, who had no academic training and no understanding of how a literary reputation is made or sustained, encouraged productions and discouraged discussion. Williams' royalties went up, but the dialogue about his work went down. Scholars were refused the right to quote from Williams' unpublished writings, or even to Xerox material from Williams' early papers, which occupy a hundred boxes at the University of Texas at Austin. "These are the people who keep Williams' reputation alive by writing about him and by teaching him in their classes," the librarian who oversees the collection, Cathy Henderson, wrote to Maria in 1992. "Denying this group of users the option of doing at least a portion of their research from photocopies discourages critical attention and sets the stage for there being less

THE LADY AND TENNESSEE

of an audience for his works." And today, more than a decade after
Williams' death, his letters have not been edited; his journals have
not been published; there are no standard editions of his great plays;
his private library is unavailable; and no publishing schedule has
been organized for his unpublished work. (Maria cancelled the
New Directions publication of *Something Cloudy, Something Clear*,
in 1993, presumably because of its homosexual content.)

Since Lady St. Just's social and public persona was an elaborate
house of cards, any scrutiny was a threat; and Maria was determined
to influence the choice of a Williams biographer. "His personal image
had been appallingly tarnished," she said of the spate of inadequately
researched memoirs about Williams—including his own—that have
emphasized drink, drugs, and homosexual promiscuity. "I couldn't
bear this image for posterity." She considered a number of writers. I
myself was approached—not by Maria but through an agent—and
decided against working on a Williams biography, because of family
commitments. Maria also approached several literary biographers,
such as A. Scott Berg, Judith Thurman, and Margot Peters, who had
the kind of reputation that could add luster to a Williams enterprise.
But, ultimately, literary excellence and Maria's terms proved to be at
odds. No reputable writer would give five to ten years to a project
only to abdicate control to a third party.

Gore Vidal says, "I explained to her, 'All you care about is how
you come out of the story. Any biographer will give you the right to
censor anything about yourself, since the biography is not of Maria
but of Tennessee.'" This, of course, was the galling problem.

Maria did make an arrangement with Margot Peters, the
author of biographies of Charlotte Bronte and the Barrymores, and
between 1989 and 1991 Peters worked on the project. It did not
go smoothly. "She definitely wanted to vet the manuscript." Peters
says, "I just kept telling her, 'Maria, this is my own biography. You're
giving me the rights, but it's mine. I can't work if you're going to vet
the manuscript.' There were some things that she wouldn't even let
me examine. First I could use quotes, then perhaps I couldn't." The
project was off; then it was on again. Finally, the two women parted
ways in a bitter transatlantic phone call. "I would never trust you
with him," Peters recalls Maria telling her. Peters still seethes at the

memory. "You have ruined Tennessee Williams!" she screamed at
Maria. "You're ruining him! You're ruining his reputation! You're
ruining scholarship for him! I wouldn't work on him or with you
for anything in this world!" And she slammed the telephone down.

Maria, an admirer of Margaret Thatcher, adopted the former
British Prime Minister's tactic when faced with opposition to her
will: she took no prisoners. She boasted to Virginia Spencer Carr,
who has a contract with Scribners—now on hold—to write a
biography of Williams, that she had already managed to "squash
two" biographies, and then ventured to make it a hat trick by
telling Carr that she would not be given permission to quote from
Williams' work. As both Peters and Carr discovered, obliteration,
not negotiation, was Maria's style. She had never mentioned
even to the "authorized" Peters that for five years prior to his
death Williams had cooperated on a biography with the theater
producer Lyle Leverich. Leverich, who was planning a two-part
biography, possessed two letters from Williams naming him as the
authorized biographer and allowing him "full access to my private
correspondence and journals."

Williams first met Leverich in 1976, when Leverich was
managing a small San Francisco theater called The Showcase and
successfully produced *The Two Character Play*. The following year,
Leverich wrote a long letter to *The New York Times* in response to
a wrongheaded review by Robert Brustein of *Tennessee Williams'
Letters to Donald Windham: 1940–1965*—published in 1977, it
remains the best book about Williams—and Williams wrote to
thank him for his support. The next year, over dinner, Leverich
complained that Williams' own *Memoirs* had done him a disservice,
and suggested that a book should be written about Williams' work
in the theater, whereupon the playwright said, "Baby, you write it!"
In January of 1979, Williams instructed his then agent, the late Bill
Barnes, to represent Leverich. And subsequently Williams decided
that Leverich should be his biographer—a task Leverich accepted.
In 1984, shortly after Williams died, Charles Carroll—who, as the
personal representative of the Southeast Banks of Florida, was the
sole executor of Williams' estate until the will was probated, in June
of 1988—reconfirmed Leverich as Williams' official biographer.

Leverich worked on his first volume in ten years of relative tranquility, though the manuscript of *Tom: The Unknown Tennessee* was as peripatetic as its subject, moving from the bankrupt publishing firm of Congdon & Weed to William Morrow, and finally landing, in 1990, at Grove Weidenfeld, where it was scheduled for the 1991 fall list. By mid-1988, however, Williams' will had come out of probate; Maria and Eastman had become the co-trustees, and Maria ascended to her self-proclaimed role of Williams' literary guardian. She took to it with a vengeful enthusiasm reminiscent of her overhaul of Wilbury once the Dowager had died and Maria had installed herself, her children, and her two pugs at the estate. ("BANG, BANG BANG, and out like stout go the following," she had written gleefully to Williams about firing the cook, the butler, the pantry boy, and the chambermaid.) Like Mrs. Goforth in *The Milk Train Doesn't Stop Here Anymore* (1963), Maria consigned anyone who wouldn't do her bidding to the "oubliette"—that place in medieval times where, Williams wrote, "people were put for keeps to be forgotten." She set out to retroactively deny Leverich permission to publish, on the ground that Williams' two letters of authorization did not specifically say that Leverich could quote from correspondence and journals. Leverich contended that he had indeed obtained the required approval from the Southeast Banks of Florida, and had proceeded in good faith since then, but Maria dismissed Leverich's work as just another "pirate book." She took the matter up with Andreas Brown, the owner of the Gotham Book Mart and an appraiser of literary archives, who had been hired by Audrey Wood in the sixties to catalogue and appraise Williams' papers, and had resumed the task after Williams' death. In a letter Maria upbraided Brown for helping Leverich and assured him that Leverich would never be the authorized biographer. Brown's response was brusque. "Yes," he wrote to Maria, about assisting Leverich. "I first did so for five years prior to Tennessee's death because Tennessee asked me to do so."

Maria continued her attempts to scupper Leverich's biography. Williams' will stipulates that "all my papers shall be available to such persons writing my biography of whom my Executors and/or Trustees shall have approved." But Maria convinced Leverich that she had the authority to rescind the executor's decision to appoint him as biographer. In a vain effort to prove the quality of his work and obtain the estate's assurance that there would be no costly legal challenge to his right to publish, Leverich asked several eminent literary and theatrical figures to read the manuscript. One of them was Arthur Miller, who wrote, "It is plainly a work of distinction… with a narrative flow of its own. I think it will be a great service to Williams' reputation and among other things may bring more of the young to an appreciation of his achievement and his profoundly idealistic attitude toward humanity." As for Grove, its lawyer thought that Leverich had a strong case, but the company was not prepared to take on a potentially expensive crusade against the quixotic Lady St. Just. As the end of 1990, Grove dropped plans to publish the book until Leverich could secure recognition from the estate of his prior authorization, or until Rose Williams died and the trust was dissolved.

Maria pleaded innocence. In another letter to Brown, she laid the responsibility for the estate's hard line on James Laughlin's judgment. Leverich had submitted an early, unedited draft to Laughlin for comment, but Laughlin had returned the manuscript in the spring of 1989, explaining that he had been unable to read it because he was coping with fire damage to his Connecticut home. He added, however, that he didn't think it would "fit into Maria's plans," because "she wants something far shorter and with a different slant." Subsequently, Laughlin wrote to the estate's lawyer:

> I am writing to confirm that Lyle Leverich submitted his Williams manuscript to me for my opinion of its quality as an authorized biography.
>
> I admired the depth of its research but did not feel that the book had the literary qualities requisite for designation as an authorized biography of Tennessee Williams.

What had happened? Brown, who knew both Leverich and Laughlin well, wanted to know. "As I recall," he wrote Laughlin on June 27, 1990, "Lyle submitted his early unedited draft to you for general comment, not as a screening process for Maria and the estate to accept or reject Lyle's work as 'authorized.' Further, I do not recall your saying at any time during those occasions when the two of us discussed Lyle and his manuscript that you had concluded that his biography did not 'warrant' authorization." Brown got his explanation from Laughlin in a handwritten postcard, postmarked July 5th: "The answer is spelled blackmail. Sorry!"

Maria had played her ace. As holder of the copyrights, she could always move future Williams books to another publisher and, coincidentally, block Laughlin's plan to publish a volume of Williams' letters to him. (In the end, she worked out a deal with Laughlin insuring that his book would come out well after hers.) In May of 1992, Laughlin wrote to Leverich, "I must remain friends with the estate because we have business to do with them, but I don't like the censorship bit at all."

Others, including Gore Vidal, lobbied Maria on behalf of Leverich and academic freedom. Vidal says, "I've denounced her. I've bawled her out. She knew (a) that he was very thorough and (b) that he was onto the abortion thing. And I said, 'Everybody has abortions, for chrissake. What's the big deal? It's not as though you're in line to be Queen of England, and this might be bad P.R. You're just an actress—actresses go in for that sort of thing.'" Leverich, in fact, wrote to Maria offering to "submit for your review and comment" such sensitive material as he'd uncovered. She never replied. Although Maria rightly railed against the misinformation and shoddy scholarship in much other writing about Williams, she went to her grave with Leverich's project stymied. "Maria wreaked havoc on this man's life," Brown says. "It's a real moral crime."

"I feel a sadness," the seventy-four-year-old Leverich told me just after Maria died. "Tennessee gave Maria an opportunity to make friends around the world, and she made so many enemies."

The English actress Sheila Gish became a particularly aggrieved enemy in 1983, when Maria, acting with an authority that was spurious, tried to stop her from starring in a production of *Streetcar* at the Greenwich Theater, in London. Williams had been enthusiastic about having the highly regarded actress play Blanche. "You'll be marvelous in it," he wrote Gish on February 26, 1982, adding ruefully, "For me, time is running out and I'm almost glad that it is." A few months after Tennessee's time had indeed run out,

Maria was threatening to close down the play and ruin the theater because of Gish, whom she said Williams disliked as an actress. But Gish's name was stipulated in the contract that allowed the theater to do the play, and, because Maria's co-trusteeship hadn't yet come into existence, the theater's director, Alan Strachan, called Maria's bluff. The production went ahead and moved with great acclaim to the Mermaid Theatre. Gish's success would be her downfall. She later found herself stonewalled from starring roles in *Cat on a Hot Tin Roof*, *The Glass Menagerie*, and *The Night of the Iguana*. She talked to Equity and to her lawyer about taking legal action against what she calls Lady St. Just's "personal McCarthyism," and enlisted such friends as Sir Alec Guinness, the director John Dexter, and the playwright Martin Sherman to plead her case with Maria. She got nowhere. "I did go through some very, very bad times over this," Gish says. "When you find something that you can really do—and do better than anybody else around—it's like saying to Ian McKellen, 'Sorry, luv. You can't do any more Shakespeare.'" News of Maria's death reached Gish in the South of France. "I hardly believed it," she says. "I got very drunk the next night with an enormous, *enormous* sense of relief, because she'd been someone I'd lived with for ten years. I hadn't realized how heavy the weight of her had been."

When Jeanne Newlin, the curator of the Harvard Theatre Collection, arrived at Wilbury in August of 1984, Maria was distraught. Williams was dead. Lord Peter was about to be hospitalized. Her mind was not on the Williams estate, but Newlin had come to discuss the handling of the manuscripts and encouraged her to attend an estate meeting in October. Maria had played a large part in getting Williams to sign a codicil to his will withdrawing the bequest of his papers to the University of the South—the alma mater of his beloved grandfather Walter Dakin, in whose name a literary fund was to be established—and giving them to Harvard. (Behind closed doors, this legal hornet's nest was resolved with the University of the South receiving the assets of the trust—including the earnings of the published works—and Harvard getting clear title to the manuscripts.) Lyle Leverich had been in New Orleans with Williams when Maria called him about the will. "Tell her I'm asleep,'" he recalls Williams saying to his companion. "Then he turned to me and said, 'They want me to change my will.' Those were exactly his words. He mumbled something about not wanting to do it. He shook his head." But, under continuing pressure in the last months of his life, Williams signed the codicil, and Newlin wanted Maria to come to America and participate in the management of the Williams estate, although, she remembers, "John Eastman was terribly opposed to having her."

Eastman was something of a public figure, having negotiated the breakup of the Beatles in the early seventies, and he had an impressive list of rich clients. His sister, Linda, had married Paul McCartney, for whom Eastman now acted. He also represented Andrew Lloyd Webber, David Bowie, Billy Joel, and the Willem de Kooning estate. The Eastman firm (a father-son team) had drawn up Williams' will, but John had known Williams for only a few years before he died. "He really wasn't interested in Tennessee," Newlin says. But she adds, "I had known Maria. I knew that she was the one who knew Tennessee, and I was beginning to be worried about the material." The October meeting was postponed when Lord Peter had a relapse, and later in the month he died. Lord Peter's estate came to four million and sixty-five thousand pounds, the bulk of which was left to his daughters Natasha and Katherine, but his will was immediately contested by his illegitimate offspring, and Maria was strapped. "She did feel desperate after the deaths. She didn't know what to do," Newlin recalls. "'Do I stay in Wilbury? Do I have to sell it? I won't sell it.' It was just like *The Cherry Orchard*. Chop. Chop. Chop. Coming after you." The co-trusteeship held out to Maria the promise of money and perhaps some direction in a life that seemed in shards. Newlin pressed her hard to get involved. "And I'll tell you something," she says, "It was necessary. A Tennessee Williams person was necessary, who was familiar with the work."

At the first estate meeting, Maria was demure. "She was a listener," Charles Carroll says. "But that was probably the only time." Maria was a mouse studying to be a rat. She was nearly twenty years older than Eastman and had knowledge of theater and of Williams. "He doesn't know anything," she complained to Paula Laurence when she and Eastman were at odds. Eastman, according to Carroll, who was present at these early business meeting, "tried to appease" Maria. "Maria was the greatest cheerleader Tennessee Williams will ever have," Eastman says now, but he adds, "Sometimes cheerleaders aren't so pretty once you get them off the field."

Even so, Eastman basically paints a picture of a happy and equal collaboration. "I had no trouble working with Maria. I may be the only one who didn't," he says. "We just talked over every major decision. She and I both signed every single contract." To those who worked with the estate, Eastman seemed only too glad to have Maria oversee the literary side of Williams' affairs. "Eastman is perfectly willing to get out of any aspect which is not going to bring in money, which means the literary aspect of it," Gore Vidal says. Robert Lantz, who represented the Williams estate between 1985 and 1989, noticed that "in the case of Tennessee's executors it was very odd. The balance wasn't kept."

Indeed, Maria tipped it in her favor. She tried to stop many of the productions that the Southeast Banks of Florida, in the first nine months after Williams' death, had set up. "She wrote nasty letter after nasty letter," Carroll says. She balked at Ann-Margret's being in a cable-TV production of *Streetcar*—a project that had been initiated in Williams' lifetime. When a Broadway house wanted to call itself the Tennessee Williams, Maria demanded money for the honor. "She got everybody kind of turned off," Carroll says. "So we ended with nothing." Rocco Landesman, the head of New York's Jujamcyn Theatres, also wanted to use Williams' name for a theater. He says, "I wanted to name what is now the Walter Kerr Theatre after Tennessee. I called Maria St. Just. She talked quite a lot and listened not at all. The gist of the conversation was that if we'd produce *Orpheus Descending* on Broadway she'd arrange this. Which was too bad, because Tennessee would have had the most beautiful theater in New York named after him. But I wouldn't submit to blackmail."

The bank, before the trust was fully vested with the copyrights, continually reminded Maria that she had no legal right to act as the estate, but Maria dismissed Carroll and his explanations of her function as regally as she would dismiss any servant. While worrying about the depleted funds of the Rose Williams Trust (the grand total of professional fees for administering and litigating the five-million-dollar estate was $1,370,437), Maria rapidly helped diminish them. "Maria kept coming over on the Concorde." Carroll says, "She would check in at the best hotel, and she'd be there for thirty days. Finally, because of her status, we said we would honor a first-class round-trip ticket from London, and only for those meetings which we called. She didn't like it, but she did adhere to it after a while." Maria's aggrandizing temperament extended to Williams' property as well. "She took a lot of stuff with her all the time, even things out of the apartment that Tennessee had here in Manhattan Plaza, which he had rarely ever occupied," Paula Laurence says. "That's how Maria was. She plundered." In the summer of 1988, Laurence's husband, Charles Bowden, found a more congenial sanitarium for Rose. "There were a few bits and pieces of jewelry that Rose had," Laurence says. "When Rose moved, Maria took them. In her mind, I don't think it was stealing." Even unimportant artifacts were treated by Maria as part of her domain. Earlier in her life, Rose had got quite good at drawing and used to hang her work on a kind of clothesline. "Every time Maria went there, she made a clean sweep of them and took them off her," Laurence says. "She has piles of Rose's drawings. Why? What was she going to do with them? Tennessee had quite a few paintings here in New York. At one point, she was able to get hold of them. She said, "Oh, you've got to have one of these. You'll love it.' Well, they're at Wilbury. She just took them. But her rationale was that if she didn't guard these treasures they would fall into the hands of these 'predators'—as she called the homosexual coterie who surrounded him."

According to Maria, the moment that she learned of Williams' death marked the great physical change that dominated the last decade of her life and became a metaphor for it. She was watching the television news with Lord Peter at his sanitarium. "She went to pick up the telephone," Elaine Dundy, the novelist and the first Mrs. Kenneth Tynan, remembers Maria telling her, "and this incredible pain shot through her arm to her fingers, and the telephone fell from her hand." From that moment, Maria claimed, her hands were crippled with rheumatoid arthritis. She couldn't open a door, turn a doorknob, or turn off a spigot. As she did with all the negative elements in her life, Maria chose to ignore the arthritis, but for those last years she was in constant agony. Laurence believes that "arthritis is a disease of control freaks—people who have to manipulate and grasp, and that was all true of Maria." The onset of the pain coincided with her rise to power as Williams' literary guardian, and, according to Jeanne Newlin, "The more she got involved, she didn't want anything distributed to anybody."

In February of 1984, Williams' former agent at ICM, Bill Barnes—whom Williams had credited with giving his floundering career the kiss of life in the early seventies—invited Maria and James Laughlin to his penthouse to read two Williams journals from the late thirties and early forties, which, Barnes said, Williams had given him out of gratitude for his hard work. Barnes was planning to publish the diaries with Simon & Schuster. Laughlin found the pages "wonderful," but in a note to Barnes a few days later he added that both he and Maria felt that the book should be published in an understated *"literary* way." The two journals, according to Leverich, who had been allowed by Williams to read them, are "the most important of all his journals that I've seen. As a mirror of a young artist attempting to seek some artistic level, they are particularly poignant and revealing." But Barnes had no letter to prove that they were a gift, and in 1985 the estate slapped him with a two-million-dollar suit accusing him of malfeasance, on the ground that handling the diaries was part of his "fiduciary duties" as Williams' agent and therefore he had no right to sell or possess them. *Variety* reported the story and made it sound as if Barnes had stolen the journals. "It destroyed him," Leverich says. "He was never the same after that."

Possession of the journals wasn't as important to Maria as suppression of their content. "I don't think it should be published," Vidal remembers Maria telling him when he remonstrated with her. "Because, reading it, I am convinced that he was mad. I don't want the world to think of him as someone insane." Vidal says, "She really was protecting some sort of image she has of him that she wants the world to have." Maria, who was now Williams' widow without a ring, also didn't want to be perceived in the world as having another demented husband. Although she claimed a victory, the two parties settled out of court, agreeing to split the baby; Barnes got thirty thousand dollars from the Rose Williams Trust for his share of the diaries, which were appraised at sixty thousand dollars.

There was an outstanding issue, however: if the journals were considered part of Tennessee Williams' papers, then they would go to Harvard, along with his other manuscripts, once the probate period had ended. But the Barnes settlement fudged this question, and, in any case, the trustees were dragging their feet about Williams' manuscripts. Their argument, and one that was frequently raised by Maria, was that Williams' papers were "assets" and might need to be sold to boost the Rose Williams Trust. (Rose's upkeep, according to Charles Bowden, is approximately a quarter of a million dollars a year.) Harvard objected to this, and a court ruled that the objections be partly sustained and that all Williams' manuscripts—except for the two journals, which were classified as personal property and thus belonged to the trust—be handed over to Harvard outright. Maria was furious.

To someone who has only a hammer, everything is a nail. Because of the court ruling, Maria couldn't finally control Williams' physical manuscripts, but she continued to work doggedly to control productions of his plays. In this arena, she was a force of nature. "Either you let her in or you dealt with chaos," says Elizabeth McCann, the American co-producer of Sir Peter Hall's successful revival of *Orpheus Descending*, in 1989. Hall, who staged the first English productions of *Camino Real* and *Cat on a Hot Tin Roof*, was an old friend of both Williams and Maria. For the New York production of *Orpheus*, he and Vanessa Redgrave decided to intensify the erotic charge between Lady and Val, by letting Redgrave drop her kimono and appear naked in the half-light as Lady goes behind the curtain to make love to Val for the first time. Maria strongly objected, on the ground that "Tennessee would never have liked it." Hall recalls, "She said, 'You've simply got to cut it.' I said, 'I won't. You gonna take the rights away? You gonna close the play down because I have this moment? You simply can't.' In the end, she gave way." Williams' will stipulated that not one word of his plays could be changed, but Maria was prepared to ignore the will in order to kiss the hem of theatrical power. The most courtly and influential

English directors—Hall and Richard Eyre and Harold Pinter—got their way. "Certainly Richard and I were favored," Hall says. "Both of us were pushing Maria into allowing the widest possible playing of Tennessee." Maria did not want Julie Walters in Hall's version of *The Rose Tattoo*; did not like Lindsay Duncan, who won the *Evening Standard's* Best Actress Award for her Maggie in Howard Davies' version of *Cat on a Hot Tin Roof*; and did not even know of Alfred Molina, the fine actor whom Eyre cast in his successful revival of *The Night of the Iguana*, or of Jessica Lange, who played Blanche in Gregory Mosher's 1992 Broadway revival of *Streetcar*. Eyre and Hall knew how to handle her. "She just longed to be part of the group," Eyre says. "She longed to sit around rehearsals and drink coffee and gossip in the breaks and tell stories about Tennessee." But younger directors who had neither the social cachet nor the charm to keep her in her place were in for heavy weather. Simon Curtis, the head of BBC television drama, tried to persuade Maria to let him produce a film script that Williams had written, called *Stopped Rocking*. Curtis says, "She pretended an awful lot. 'Who's going to write the screenplay?' she said to me. 'It *is* a screenplay,' I said."

Howard Davies, whose production of *Cat on a Hot Tin Roof*, in 1988, was the most astute of the recent revivals, refused to charm Maria, and, despite his expert adaptation, which later had a well-received Broadway run, was prohibited by Maria from ever doing another Williams play. She also scotched a deal to film the Broadway version for television. Davies, whose production of *Cat* amalgamated various versions of the play, says, "I couldn't bear the thought of getting into a dialogue with her about anything. She was just all over the place, absolutely scattered." Davies told Maria he needed to make minor changes, mainly in the tricky third act. "In fact, what I did was a major, major compilation of whatever I could get," Davies says. "Then I sent it to her, having led her to believe—I mean I did lie and I did cheat—that they were minimal changes." Maria approved the adaptation. "I can only assume she didn't read it," Davies says. And when Maria saw one of the London previews she was thrilled. "She was jumping up and down with joy, as if, somehow, through acting and directing I'd made it work," says Davies, who was proud of the seamlessness of his changes. But by opening night Maria had read the original and was incensed. "She accused me of being a cheat and a liar," Davies says. I said, 'Yes, but it works. You liked it last week, so what you're not liking about it now is that you couldn't spot the difference.'"

When *Cat* opened in New York, starring Kathleen Turner as Maggie, Maria insisted on attending rehearsals. Davies refused to have her. "I said, 'If you set one foot inside this theater, I will ask my cast to leave and I certainly will leave.' Davies recalls. Inevitably, Maria tried to go behind his back and give notes to Turner herself. Turner would have none of it, Davies says, "I could hear her down the corridor; it was something like 'Get that woman out of my room and make sure she stays out!'"

Gregory Mosher also turned Maria out of his *Streetcar* rehearsals. He recalls, "I was on the stairs, and I heard Maria giving very specific notes to Jessica Lange—trivial stuff about the gestures and the laugh. She came out, and I said, 'Maria, why are you giving notes?' She said, 'I'm not.' 'Well, no, I'm sorry. I heard you. I was sitting right here. You were giving notes.' She said, 'You can't speak to me in that way!' I said, 'I'm not speaking to you in any way at all. You know you're not supposed to be talking to the actors.' She said—she started screaming in the way she does—'I will not be spoken to, I will *not* be spoken to in that way. I'm going back to England!' And she went back to England."

Mosher had been the artistic director of Chicago's Goodman Theatre and of the Lincoln Center Theater, and was the original director of all the major plays of David Mamet, but to Maria, who had no knowledge of the American theater scene, he was a nonentity. Maria was also unaware that there were at least three different published texts of *A Streetcar Named Desire*. "You couldn't win," Mosher says. "If you went with the regulation text, she would say, 'Well, that's not what Marlon said.' But if you used the Dramatists Play Service version she would say, 'That's not what Tennessee wrote.' Kazan made hundreds of changes in the script—just rewrote lines. Why is that version still out there?" Mosher only gradually began to make the connection between the sloppiness that surrounded Williams' literary affairs and Maria. "I didn't put her together with the fact that you *still* can't tell which is the definitive edition of *A*

Streetcar Named Desire," he says. "Or with the fact that *A House Not Meant to Stand* in its full-length form is not published and is not produced in New York. How is that possible? Well, because she doesn't like it, quote unquote. She wouldn't let me do the play at Lincoln Center. She said, 'The play is not doable.' I said, 'You didn't even see it. How do you know if it's doable or not?' She said, 'It's a bad play.' I said, 'It's a good play, actually. It's not *Streetcar*, but it's a good play.'"

Mosher complains that Maria assumed the role of the police in dealing with the cast—that she would say to the actors, "Accents don't matter. Tennessee told me." Mosher explains, "'The accent doesn't matter,' *always*, a hundred per cent of the time, means 'You're never going to get it, so stop worrying.' It never means the accent doesn't matter. You would just be so touched by this woman's innocence." Maria even brought a photograph of Wilbury to a rehearsal and told the cast that it was the house that had given Williams the notion of Belle Reve—a factual tidbit that boggled the imagination, since the play was written in 1945–46 and she didn't meet Williams until 1948. To her consternation, the cast laughed.

One ongoing battle was the color of Blanche's peignoir, which Williams describes in his stage directions as scarlet, but which Maria insisted should be pale pink. "I said, 'No, it's dark red. That's the whole point of this production.'" Mosher recalls. "And she said, 'No, you're just wrong. You're just wrong!' I said, 'Maria, all I know is what I read.' She said, 'Well, excuse me. I know it sounds immodest to say this, but who are you? And this is, after all, the best American play of the twentieth century.' And I realized that she thinks she wrote it. What else could 'I know it sounds immodest' mean? It's the widow problem."

In order to protect the actors and himself from the weight of the play's legend, Mosher banned all discussion of Kazan's original production and of Brando's performance. But Alec Baldwin, who played Stanley, says that Maria took to finagling rides uptown with him in order to give him notes. "The No. 1 thing you strive for in acting is to be unself-conscious," Baldwin says. "She made everybody self-conscious." Baldwin got Mosher to call her off, but before the show he'd get on the loudspeaker for the cast's amusement:

"Attention, everyone. This is Maria. May I have your attention, please!" Baldwin mimics Maria's grandness with a surprisingly accurate English inflection. "I'm going to be having champagne and strawberries in Jessica's dressing room after the performance tonight. And please, everyone, try to pick up the pace. Jessica, darling, please louder, darling. You can't be heard past the fourth row. And Alec, darling, try to be more sexy if you can. And please join me for champagne and strawberries afterward. I love you all." Baldwin's prank also mocked the vacuity of Maria's view of the play. For all her passion about Williams' work, she had no informed perspective. "She had no view of Tennessee," Mosher says. "You know that theater joke about the guy who gets cast in the original production of *Streetcar* and he writes home to his mother and says, 'So I'm in this wonderful play about a doctor who comes to save a woman'? That's her view. That Tennessee was a man for whom the most important thing in his life was that he loved her.…But it was about her glorification, not his. I would accept her behavior if Tennessee Williams were an infinitely more celebrated person in the culture, but he's not."

At the finale of *This Is (An Entertainment),* Williams' spokesman, the General, offers an affectionate envoi to the Countess (and to Maria); "My last request is a last command. Give the lady safe passage through the mountains! Will you? For old times' sake?" In a sense, Williams' will offered Maria the safe harbor in life that the play hoped for in make-believe. But in the fifteen years between the play's writing and his death, Williams' relationship with Maria had continued to decline. Williams' last, garbled story, "The Negative," written in November of 1982, tells of a has-been poet who can't finish his poem and is about to be sent to a nursing home. He gets a phone call from the mysterious Lady Mona, who seems to know all his difficulties, and wants to be his muse. They meet in a dark café. Lady Mona wears a black veil. The poet lifts the veil. The poet lifts the veil and is horrified by the woman's rapacious eyes, and he throws himself into the Thames. "He knew that she had exaggerated and exploited the level of their friendship beyond all recognition," Bruce Smith says, noting that at the end of Williams' life "he was weaning himself away from her. There were unopened letters from her even when I was around there and she was back in London. He was emotionally through with her. He said to me, 'I don't know why she bothers to come over here for these openings because she isn't needed and she really isn't wanted.'"

Mitch Douglas confirms Williams' courtly dismissal of Lady St. Just. "Maria was very much a presence," he recalls of the rehearsals for Williams' last Broadway play, *Clothes for a Summer Hotel.* "There were lots of notes, and, if I may respectfully say so, she was getting in the way. Tennessee would smile and be very nice to her and then turn around to the people at hand and say, 'Well, you know, she really doesn't understand this kind of theater.'" According to Charles Carroll, Williams was considering striking Maria's assignment as a co-trustee from his will, but "he was a procrastinator, and he never got it done." And Elizabeth McCann says that Maria "wasn't really interested in the scholarship or the longevity of Williams for the future. She was only interested in what was in it for her. Now. This moment." McCann attended Maria's funeral, where, at the end, following Russian Orthodox custom, mourners kissed the corpse. "I remember thinking as I watched these people parade up to kiss the corpse that there was no way I could approach Maria St. Just even in death," McCann says. 'I'd had my last run-in as far as I was concerned. 'Thank you a lot, Maria, not this trip.' She was a pistol."

If Maria didn't kill the thing she loved, which was Williams' art, she unwittingly wounded it. Williams' great labor—he wrote from four to eight hours a day for a good forty years—is a national treasure, and one of the century's great chronicles of the romance and the barbarity of individualism. Its value as a financial asset has been honored by the estate, but its value as an intellectual asset, as a defining part of our century's sense of itself, has been overseen haphazardly. Now that John Eastman alone has the responsibility, common sense has begun to prevail. The estate has lifted Maria's censure and given New Directions permission to publish *Something Cloudy, Something Clear*; and just last month negotiations with Lyle Leverich were concluded that will allow his two-part biography to proceed to publication. "There's less here than meets the eye," Eastman says. "It's a happy ending."

Perhaps it will be, but there's also more to it than meets the eye. Williams belongs to the world, not to the lawyers, and it behooves the estate to set up a procedure whereby accredited writers, academics, and theater artists can make reasonable use of Williams' published and unpublished papers. The conversation between our greatest playwright and the world still languishes in misinformation. "It's going to take over two generations of scholars to ascertain the significance of the papers he held at the end of his life," Jeanne Newlin says. "And that work must be begun." Meanwhile, brazen and bumptious to the end, Lady Maria St. Just, who helped create this quagmire, rests peacefully at Wilbury; buried not with the Grenfell clan, with whom she was always at war, but with those loved ones who obeyed her every whim and believed her every word—her dogs.

"The Lady and Tennessee" by John Lahr. Copyright © 1994 by John Lahr. Originally appeared in *The New Yorker* (December 19, 1994). Reprinted by permission of Georges Borchardt, Inc., on behalf of the author.

"
I was convinced that

Tennessee Williams had lost his mind.
"
I mean, really lost his mind.

TOO GROTESQUE AND TOO FUNNY FOR LAUGHTER: PUBLISHING THE LATE TENNESSEE WILLIAMS

Annette Saddik

"As some things are too sad and too deep for tears, so some
    things are too grotesque and too funny for laughter."
    —George du Maurier, Trilby (1894)[1]

"...something too pitiful for humor, and too strange for pity."
    —Norman Nadel, review of Tennessee Williams' The
    Gnädiges Fräulein, New York Telegram and Sun
    (February 23,1966)

Whearer I first read the 1982 play *The Remarkable Rooming-House of Mme. Le Monde*, I was convinced that Tennessee Williams had lost his mind. I mean, really lost his mind. I had always been a defender, even a champion, of Williams' late work for several years, and I appreciated his experimentations with a more presentational, anti-realistic style, combined with an outrageous, often grotesque, sensibility. But this was too much. The play begins with the entrance of a "lasciviously" grinning young man, one of Mme. Le Monde's sons who is "hung like a dray horse" and "kept on the place for…incestuous relations" with his mother. He opens the play by dragging Mint—"a delicate little man with a childlike face" whose "legs are mysteriously paralyzed"—behind the curtain and raping him, a "sexual assault" that Mint seems to both dread and enjoy. Mint's paralysis forces him to swing from hooks implanted on the ceiling of Mme. Le Monde's attic, the "rectangle with hooks" where he lives as a tenant. When the Boy is finished with him, he tells Mint that their visitor, Hall, is downstairs with Mme. Le Monde and will hook him back up "if he ever hauls himself out of that ole buffalo waterin' hole of Mom's," alerting him that "it takes Mom a long time to come." Throughout the play, Mint's desperation is evident and cruelty permeates the atmosphere, as a world of instability and meager resources is marked by the ruthlessness of individuals in their fight for self-preservation. I didn't know what to do. Or think.

After reading the play several times to try and make sense of the bizarre excesses, I started to realize that its uncanny power emerged precisely from the fact that it *was* too much. Just as life is too much. Language, images, all forms of representation are inevitably inadequate, and cannot contain emotion, impulse, desire. Williams always knew that in order to illustrate a truth about reality, he needed to distort and exaggerate our experiences of that reality. That's what he had been doing all along in his work, only now he was taking us to the brink of unbearable pain and horror, where the only place to go, the only way of dealing with such intense experience, was laughter. Somehow, in all its perverse ugliness, I started to sense that *The Remarkable Rooming-House of Mme. Le Monde* was a very funny play. I remembered that this was written by the man who, rumor has it, would sit in the back of the theater during performances of *A Streetcar Named Desire* and laugh hysterically at the final scene when Blanche gets taken away to an insane asylum. For Williams, the comic and the tragic were inseparable.

Williams' work had never been tame—rife with forbidden desire, madness, castration, rape, cannibalism, all forms of emotional and physical violence—yet the relative innocence and outright censorship of the 1940s and '50s were able to keep these themes just barely under control. The playfully dark humor of Williams' late plays was therefore a logical and mature continuation of his earlier work, employing what he called "freer" forms that engaged the "madness" of political and social chaos during the late twentieth century.[2] With plays such as *The Remarkable Rooming-House of Mme. Le Monde*, however, Williams succeeded in pushing the boundaries of good taste to the extreme, challenging conventional notions of what can be shown onstage, and thereby revealing a more primitive, primary side of human nature. Making the rape in *A Streetcar Named Desire* (1947), the homosexual subtext in *Cat on a Hot Tin Roof* (1955), and even the cannibalism in *Suddenly Last Summer* (1958), the dismemberment in *Orpheus Descending* (1957), and the castration in *Sweet Bird of Youth* (1958)—all of which take place offstage—appear subtle and almost quaint, *The Remarkable Rooming-House of Mme. Le Monde* went still beyond what the public had come to expect of Tennessee Williams in terms of shock value and violent imagery.

Extreme, excessive, grotesque, campy, cartoonish, pop-art, burlesque, slapstick, grand guignol—these are just some adjectives that begin to describe the sensibility of Williams' late work. His late plays reflect the freedom to finally be "too much," to laugh at the absurdity of life and its inevitable suffering with a laughter that surpasses tears. These later plays continued to exhibit the kind of risks that had always made Williams exciting and inspirational, yet by the 1960s he was starting to more blatantly ignore the boundaries of social and dramatic convention, as he boldly embraced excess as a vehicle for artistic expression.

The late "outrageous" plays that Williams was writing during the 1960s, '70s, and '80s were his response to a critical establishment that swung from hailing him as "America's Greatest Playwright" during the 1940s and '50s, to viciously dismissing both him and his work after *The Night of the Iguana* in 1961. During the 1960s, the critical reception of Williams' work was brutal, and often took the form of personal attack. Richard Gilman titled his 1963 review of *The Milk Train Doesn't Stop Here Anymore* in *The Commonweal*: "Mistuh Williams, He Dead." Robert Brustein's reaction to *Milk Train* was that "the writing is soft, the theme banal, the action sketchy, the play unfinished—and since there is no drama, why should there be a review, especially when the directing, the decor, and the acting…are as indifferent as the text?" In his May 23, 1969, review of *In the Bar of a Tokyo Hotel*, T. E. Kalem wrote in *Time* magazine that Williams "is lying on the sickbed of his formidable talent," and that his work "has become increasingly infirm," so "grave" that the play "seems more deserving of a coroner's report than a review."

While some of the reviews of Williams' late work did acknowledge his experimentation with new styles and were insightful, most were extremely and unfairly negative. Several critics were content to accept their own lack of comprehension, and simply lamented Williams' abandonment of the Aristotelian formula on which dramatic realism is based, harping on a nostalgia for *The Glass Menagerie* or *A Streetcar Named Desire*. Reviewing *Slapstick Tragedy* (a double-bill of two one-acts, *The Gnädiges Fräulein* and *The Mutilated*) on February 23, 1966, John McClain acknowledged in the *New York Journal-American* that although it was "extremely funny much of the time," he "hasn't the foggiest idea of what Mr. Williams has to tell us," and so he wished that he "would give us something old and square like *Streetcar Named Desire*." Others, like Norman Nadel in the *New York World-Telegram and Sun*, simply called the plays "bizarre" and "embarrassing," even though he admitted there were "times when this outlandish play is uproarious." Some reviews of Williams' late plays, however, did acknowledge—begrudgingly—that Williams' work was headed in a new, relevant direction. Even though Clive Barnes wrote in *The New York Times* in 1969 that *In the Bar of a Tokyo Hotel* "repelled [him] with its self-pity," he did believe that the play was "avant garde" and would be "appreciated in the theater of the future."

Personal attacks on Williams from the reviewers were also becoming more common, as they used his plays to offer their opinions of the playwright's lifestyle. Martin Gottfried's review in *Women's Wear Daily* (February 23, 1966) of the two plays that comprised *Slapstick Tragedy* was nothing short of cruel, claiming that Williams is "a playwright in trouble," as, "[h]aving years ago abandoned his natural inclinations to write money-making self-parodies, he finds himself wandering in pathetic circles." Gottfried called Williams' "instincts themselves confused." The apparent incomprehensibility of the art was, more and more, being imposed onto the artist. Michael Smith wrote in *The Village Voice* on March 3, 1966, that the plays of *Slapstick Tragedy* "are direct metaphorical enactments of Tennessee Williams' concern for his own life," as "he can't quite distinguish these 'mutilated' characters from his own self-image." And Henry Hewes reported in the *Saturday Review of Literature* on May 23, 1969, that the failure of *In the Bar of a Tokyo Hotel* was "unimportant compared with our concern for its author." By June 1969 *Life* magazine was describing Williams as a "burned out cinder" after taking out a full-page ad in the *New York Times* that featured a head-shot of Williams. Printed below in huge type was the caption: "Played Out?"

The Milk Train Doesn't Stop Here Anymore was to be the first of many failures with critics and audiences that would send Williams into a tailspin of depression and substance abuse. Yet he still wrote diligently every morning, often waking up as early as 5 A.M. to work. Williams was just as prolific in the last twenty-four years of his life as he had been in the previous twenty-four; in the forty-eight years from 1935 to 1983 he completed at least thirty-three full-length plays and at least seventy one-acts.[3] Williams continued to write and oversee productions of numerous new plays until his death in 1983. Ultimately, he was not backing down and he was not going away. He was still here, he was most definitely queer—in every sense of the word—and he wanted to make sure that everyone knew it.

So when I was approached in 2003 by New Directions Publishing, Williams' publisher since the beginning of his career, editor Thomas Keith and president and publisher Peggy Fox asked about about the possibility of my editing and introducing a collection of Williams' previously uncollected (many of them unpublished and unproduced) late plays. I thought about what was going on in these plays' stylistically, thematically, and politically and why they remained unpublished. Aside from *The Day on Which a Man Dies*, a play that Williams sold to UCLA in 1970, all of the plays that were eventually included in the volume, which was finally published in 2008 as *The Traveling Companion and Other Plays*, were ones that Williams had at one time presented for publication or production. These were neither manuscripts that were found in a secret box under his bed, nor plays that he never intended anyone to see. Williams wanted these plays to be performed and read. Many of them had been put on hold by New Directions in the years after his death for several reasons: the overwhelming amount of plays, one-acts, stories, poetry, letters, journals, and screenplays that had yet to be edited and published; the objections of his literary executrix, Maria St. Just; an incomprehension or lack of appreciation in relation to Williams' earlier style; the often negative critical reception surrounding these plays when they had been produced; their graphic and risqué nature; or more general logistical concerns of competing production demands, budget, audience tastes, and saleability. With changes in the theater and in our culture over the last twenty to thirty years, however, along with the growing understanding of Williams' late dramaturgy that scholars and theater directors brought to his work in the years after his death, New Directions was ready to take another look at these plays during the new millennium.

I wanted *The Remarkable Rooming-House of Mme. Le Monde* to be included in the volume because I believed that it had something important to say about Williams' vision of the world, something to show us, and I thought that with the right production, it would work well in performance. It had originally been published in a limited edition of 176 copies in 1984 by the Albondocani Press in New York. George Bixby, the publisher, recalls that he requested permission from Williams' agent, Luis Sanjuro, to publish a limited edition of the one-act play *The Traveling Companion* in 1982. Williams' reply was that if Bixby were to publish something, it might as well be something brand new, as *The Traveling Companion* had been published in 1981 in *Christopher Street* magazine. So Sanjuro sent Bixby *The Remarkable Rooming-House of Mme. Le Monde* at Williams' request. This was a play that Williams wanted the public to know, he wanted it to be read and performed. Even though it had been published in a limited edition, it had never been published in a trade edition, and so few people outside the community of Williams scholars knew of its existence until it was published by New Directions in 2008.

No doubt due, in part, to both its obscurity and the extreme content that made it a risk to stage, *The Remarkable Rooming-House of Mme. Le Monde* was not performed until September 2009 at the Provincetown Tennessee Williams Festival by Boston's Beau Jest Moving Theater, directed by Davis Robinson.

When I went to see this production, I was prepared for the worst. This was not an easy play. Even if the director, the cast, and the staging did manage to translate Williams' vision truthfully, there was always a risk in terms of how audiences would react to that vision. Dark humor, which requires a delicate balance between the excesses of the comic and the cruel, is often difficult to pull off, and I had no idea how audiences, or I, would react. In order for the play to work on the stage, its outrageous, grotesque humor—a sort of gallows humor that laughs in the face of horror—must come through. Otherwise, the play is too painful, too ugly, to tolerate. Yet as soon as I heard the audience laughing at the play's opening outrage, I knew it was going to work. It was not exactly an uncomfortable laughter, but a strange laughter of both disbelief and relief. The production's atmosphere of exaggeration and comic book caricature was able to get across a sense of heightened, absurd cruelty that filled the space until it had no place to go and had no choice but to burst into laughter, a laughter of absurdity and exaggeration that my students, who generally respond very well to this play, have simply called "too crazy."

It was during the early 1990s, when I was at Rutgers University working on my doctoral dissertation on Williams, that I first became interested in the shifts I saw taking place in Williams' work from the 1960s, the brutal critical reception of his later work, and the lack of understanding exhibited by the critical establishment. My dissertation, *"Freer Forms" or "Rambling Discourses"? The Later Plays of Tennessee Williams and the Dynamics of Critical Reception*, was completed in 1995. After some significant revision, the manuscript was published as *The Politics of Reputation: The Critical Reception of Tennessee Williams' Later Plays* in 1999 by Associated University Presses, and was the first book devoted to Williams' later plays. Although I didn't know it at the time, I was about to participate in the reassessment of Williams' late work that had begun to emerge in scholarship, publishing, and theater production.

My book explored Williams' later plays in terms of their critical reception in the United States. It analyzed the reactions of both the popular and academic press to Williams' work after 1961, and argued that the expectations and biases of critics prevented them from accepting Williams' departure from the earlier, more traditional dramatic forms that were presented on Broadway, to the minimalist explorations of character, language, and action that challenged realistic presentation altogether. Documenting the establishment and decline of Williams' reputation in order to examine the assumptions and ideological investments of the critics who had categorized Williams only on the basis of his early dramaturgy, *Politics* went on to compare Williams' later reception with the reception of playwrights whom Williams admired and who were celebrated for their rejections of domestic and psychological realism, such as Samuel Beckett, Harold Pinter, and Edward Albee. While Williams' later achievements were often uneven, some of his best later plays combine an exploitation of the linguistic and dramatic irony that had become part of the accepted theatrical experience by the 1960s and '70s, with the poetic nuances that distinguished his work during the 1940s and '50s.

The Politics of Reputation was published on a tide of renewed interest in Williams' career, largely enabled by the death of Maria St. Just in February 1994.[4] During her tenure as co-executor of the Rose Williams' Trust, St. Just approved the publication of only three previously unpublished plays, *Tiger Tail*, *The Red Devil Battery Sign*, and *The Notebook of Trigorin*. Devoted to safeguarding Williams' early reputation from the personal and artistic trials of his later years and from his homosexuality, St. Just maintained strict control over his unpublished and unperformed material and only authorized what she found appropriate and thought would be critically successful. She apparently agreed with the negative reactions to Williams' late plays, and generally refused to allow productions, publications, or quotations from the unpublished later work. With her death, this material was open to scholars and directors, and new scholarly criticism, conference panels, journals, and discussions on Williams' work began to increasingly appear, along with new productions of both the early (pre-*Glass Menagerie*) and the late plays that had not previously been available.

Several of Williams' post-1961, late plays, many experimental and a few more traditional, had already been published during Williams' lifetime by New Directions. These titles included *The Gnädiges Fräulein* (1966), *The Mutilated* (1966), *I Can't Imagine Tomorrow* (1966), *The Two-Character Play/Out Cry* (which had been revised from 1967–1976 for several productions), *The Seven Descents of Myrtle* (1968) (revised in 1975 as *Kingdom of Earth*), *In the Bar of a Tokyo Hotel* (1969), *Confessional* (1970), *The Frosted Glass Coffin* (1970), *Small Craft Warnings* (1972), *The Red Devil Battery Sign* (1975), *Vieux Carré* (1977), and *A Lovely Sunday for Creve Coeur* (1978). In 1981 New Directions published volumes 6 and 7 of *The Theatre of Tennessee Williams*, which, in addition the one-acts from *27 Wagons Full of Cotton* (1945) and *Dragon Country* (1970), included five new—more grotesque and slightly sinister— late one-acts: *Demolition Downtown* (1970), *Steps Must Be Gentle* (1980), *Lifeboat Drill* (1979), *Now the Cats with Jeweled Claws* (1981), and *This is the Peaceable Kingdom* (1978).

In the years right after Williams' death, New Directions continued to publish a few of the late plays, particularly ones from the late 1970s and '80s. In early 1983, prior to his death, Williams had already made corrections to the final proof pages of the 1980 full-length play, *Clothes for a Summer Hotel,* that was published that same year, and he already had signed the contract for the volume *Stopped Rocking and Other Screenplays,* published in 1984. *The Collected Stories of Tennessee Williams* was published in 1985, *The Red Devil Battery Sign* (1975) was published in 1988, and *Tiger Tail* (1977), Williams' own stage adaptation of the film *Baby Doll,* was published in 1991. *Something Cloudy, Something Clear* (1981) was scheduled for publication in 1993, but Maria St. Just withheld her approval on the grounds that the material was "too sensitive," (i.e. too gay), so the play was finally published in 1995. And in 1997, another 1981 play, Williams' adaptation of Chekhov's

The Sea Gull—The Notebook of Trigorin—became available. There remained, however, a cache of unpublished later plays (most also in multiple earlier drafts), at the offices of New Directions, as well as in the archives at the Harry Ransom Humanities Research Center at the University of Texas, The Harvard Theatre Collection, The New Orleans Historic Collection, The Department of Special Collections at the University Research Library at the University of California, Los Angeles, Columbia University Library, and among the private papers of Williams' friends, agents, and former secretaries, particularly John Uecker, who was Williams' last secretary and was sharing his two-room suite at the Hotel Elyseé in New York City the day Williams died. These plays were often either ignored or judged to be inferior or inappropriate for publication, and so seemed destined to not see the light of day.

Throughout the 1970s and '80s, both Williams' published and unpublished post-1961 work received some critical attention from academic circles. The scholarship on the late plays at that time was often insightful, but scant. Scholars were beginning to assess their value in the context of developments in theater since the 1960s. Collections and overviews by scholars such as Stephen Stanton, Felicia Hardison Londré, Jac Tharpe, and C. W. E. Bigsby began to address the later plays at some level, and were opening the doors to perceiving them as serious offerings. In 1979, Stanton founded the *Tennessee Williams Newsletter* (Fall 1979–Spring 1981), which then became *The Tennessee Williams Review* (Spring 1981–Spring 1983). While these ventures were short-lived, they were indicative of the growing interest in Williams studies during the 1980s, and led to a series of festivals, conferences, and journals dedicated to his work. In 1986, the Tennessee Williams/New Orleans Literary Festival was launched, and in 1989 Kenneth Holditch founded *The Tennessee Williams Literary Journal*, which remained active until 2003. In 1986, Albert J. Devlin edited a collection of interviews, *Conversations with Tennessee Williams,* that became an organized resource for Williams' interviews throughout his career.

By the 1990s, the unpublished or unproduced later plays were beginning to receive more attention. In addition to the work I was doing in the mid-1990s at Rutgers University and, later, Eastern

Michigan University, critical reassessments of Williams' later plays were being published by Philip C. Kolin at the University of Southern Mississippi and Linda Dorff at the University of Houston. During the 1990s and early 2000s, Kolin published "The Existential Nightmare in Tennessee Williams's *The Chalky White Substance*" in *Notes on Contemporary Literature*, "*Something Cloudy, Something Clear*: Tennessee Williams's Postmodern Memory Play" in the *Journal of Dramatic Theory and Criticism*, "Williams' *The Frosted Glass Coffin*" in *The Explicator*, "*The Remarkable Rooming-House of Mme. Le Monde*: Tennessee Williams's Little Shop of Comic Horrors" in the *Tennessee Williams Annual Review*, and "A Play about Terrible Birds: Tennessee Williams's *The Gnädiges Fraulein* [sic] and Alfred Hitchcock's 'The Birds'" in *South Atlantic Review*.

In 1998, the *Tennessee Williams Annual Review* was founded by Robert Bray, and was quickly becoming an invaluable resource for criticism of Williams' work, both early and late. In the 1999 issue of the *Review*, Dorff published her very insightful essay on Williams' later plays, "Theatricalist Cartoons: Tennessee Williams's Late, 'Outrageous' Plays." She saw these plays as a shift toward "grotesque parody," and cited Williams' 1965 Preface to *Slapstick Tragedy*, where he describes the plays as "vaudeville, burlesque, and slapstick, with a dash of pop art thrown in." Dorff continued her work on the late plays with the publication of "'All very [not!] Pirandello!' Radical Theatrics in the Evolution of *Vieux Carré*" in the 2000 issue of the *Review*, and was also discussing the possible future publication of some of Williams' lesser-known later plays with New Directions, a broad project that she proposed be done in three volumes. She was working on a scholarly book on the late plays and a proposed documentary called *Tennessee Williams' Dragon Country*, when she died suddenly of a heart attack in 2000. Yet even with her work unfinished, the essays she did publish made a significant contribution to how Williams' later reputation was being (re)constructed.

It was also during the 1990s that scholars were increasingly reassessing the Williams canon through a variety of new theoretical lenses. David Savran's book *Communists, Cowboys, and Queers: The Politics of Masculinity in the Work of Arthur Miller and Tennessee*

Williams (1992) was groundbreaking in its reading of Williams' work in the context of gay politics and postmodern theory. Throughout the 1990s, John Clum, Nicholas de Jongh, Robert Vorlicky, and Steven Bruhm were all taking a new look at the politics of sexuality in Williams' oeuvre. In 1995, Dorff had organized a panel on the late plays at the ATHE conference in San Francisco, which included David Savran, Robert Vorlicky, Steven Bruhm, Allean Hale, and Lyle Leverich, who had just completed volume one of Williams' official biography, *Tom: The Unknown Tennessee Williams*. By the mid- and late 1990s, George Crandell, Robert Martin, and Matthew C. Roudané were producing collections that illuminated Williams' late work in complex ways, and Ruby Cohn's essays, "Late Tennessee Williams" in Martin's volume, and "Tennessee Williams: the last two decades" in Roudané's, were making important contributions to the scholarship of the late plays. While Kolin, Dorff, and I were all independently working on exploring Williams' late canon and reevaluating his later reputation, Allean Hale, Dan Isaac, David Roessel, and Nick Moschovakis were working with New Directions to bring to light much of Williams' early work that had not been previously published. New Directions began to publish several of his previously unavailable early full-length plays during the late 1990s and early 2000s, as well as new collections of his letters, poetry, and essays in response to the renewed interest in his work. What are often referred to as Williams' full-length "apprentice plays," written during the late 1930s and early 1940s before *The Glass Menagerie* made him a success, became available for the first time: *Not About Nightingales* (1938; pub. 1998), *Spring Storm* (1938; pub. 1999), *Stairs to the Roof* (1941; pub. 2000) *Fugitive Kind* (1937; pub. 2001), and *Candles to the Sun* (1937; pub. 2004). In the early '90s, Peggy Fox had given a copy of *Not About Nightingales* to Maria St. Just, who in turn shared the manuscript with Vanessa Redgrave, who wanted to see it produced. Redgrave's theater company, Moving Theatre (founded in 1993 with Corin Redgrave and Kilka Markham), eventually co-produced the play in association with the Alley Theatre of Houston, Texas, and the Royal National Theatre in London in March 1998. It was directed by Trevor Nunn and moved to Broadway at the Circle in the Square Theatre in January 1999.

Three of these "apprentice plays" were edited and introduced by Allean Hale, who has been a formidable contributor to the scholarship of both Williams' early and late plays, and two by Dan Isaac, who had also been writing about Williams' work for several years. In 1991, Hale had introduced scholars to a previously unpublished play, revealing "The Secret Script of Tennessee Williams" in *Southern Review*. She discussed a manuscript that had been tucked away in the UCLA archives, one that Williams sold to UCLA in 1970. The manuscript, *The Day on Which a Man Dies (an occidental* Noh *play)*, was the result of Williams' meeting with the Japanese writer Yukio Mishima in 1957, and Williams' subsequent travels to Japan to explore Kabuki, Gutai, and Noh theater in 1959. The play is dated in Williams' handwriting as finished in 1960. And in the 2003 and 2005 issues of the *Tennessee Williams Annual Review*, respectively, Hale published "Confronting the Late Plays of Tennessee Williams," which was an overview of the negative reception Williams' plays received from the popular press and the scholarly work that had been done to date on these plays, and "Tennessee Williams's *Three Plays for the Lyric Theatre*," where she discussed Williams' trio of late "lyric" plays that he submitted to New Directions in 1980, two of which remained unpublished at the time.

By the early 2000s, a growing interest in Williams' late plays was well-established in the world of Williams scholarship. Three seminal volumes of essays that addressed the later work, Ralph Voss's *Magical Muse: Millennial Essays on Tennessee Williams*, Philip Kolin's *The Undiscovered Country: The Later Plays of Tennessee Williams,* and Robert Gross's *Tennessee Williams: A Casebook*, appeared in 2002. The Tennessee Williams Scholars Conference, which annually presents new work by Williams scholars in conjunction with the Tennessee Williams/New Orleans Literary Festival, organized a panel titled "Looking at the Late Plays of Tennessee Williams," also in 2002. I appeared on the panel with Robert Bray (who runs the Scholars Conference), Allean Hale, Ruby Cohn, Philip Kolin, Brenda Murphy, and Thomas Keith. It was at this conference where I met Keith for the first time and discovered our shared interest in the potential of the late plays. The following year, a panel titled "The Unpublished Tennessee Williams" at the Scholars Conference continued the conversation on the later work, featuring Allean Hale, Thomas Keith, Philip Kolin, Nicholas Moschovakis, and Robert Bray.

In 2005, David Roessel and Nicholas Moschovakis, who had together edited a new volume, *The Collected Poems of Tennessee Williams*, for New Directions in 2002, solidified the renewed interest in Williams' work when they drew attention to several previously unpublished, primarily early, one-acts they had discovered in the Williams archives. They went on to edit and introduce a volume of thirteen of these plays, published under the title of *Mister Paradise and Other One-Act Plays*. Major productions of a number of these new plays were being launched before the publication of *Mister Paradise*. Roessel and Moschovakis had brought *The Palooka*, one of the early plays that would be included in the volume, to the attention of Michael Wilson, who presented it as part of a program of Williams' one-acts titled *8 By Tenn,* a double bill at Hartford Stage in 2003. Another play that was included in the production, *The One Exception* (which would eventually be published in *The Traveling Companion and Other Plays*), was a late one-act that had been edited for the first time by Bray in the *Tennessee Williams Annual Review* 3 in 2000. In April 2004, Michael Kahn worked with Roessel and Moschovakis to direct an evening of five one-acts, four of them from the new volume, in an evening titled *Five By Tenn* at the Kennedy Center in Washington, and later at the Manhattan Theater Club in New York. Both productions were reviewed in *The New York Times*. The *Times* and *American Theatre Magazine* were two of the more significant publications that were covering the new Williams productions throughout the 2000s.

Williams projects were flourishing during this time, as scholars, publishers, theater producers, and the press were resurrecting Williams' reputation and, it seems, working to restore his status as "America's Greatest Playwright." In 2000, *The Selected Letters of Tennessee Williams, Volume I: 1920–1945* was published by New Directions, edited by Albert J. Devlin and Nancy Tischler, followed by *Volume II: 1945–1957* in 2004. In 2006, New Directions reissued Williams' *Memoirs* (1975) with a new introduction by John Waters; and in 2007, Yale University Press published Williams' journals under the title *Notebooks,* edited by Margaret Bradham Thornton. The Library of America produced a two-volume collection, *Tennessee Williams: Plays 1937–1955* and *Tennessee Williams: Plays 1957–1980*, in 2000, edited by Mel Gussow and Kenneth Holditch. Most recently, in 2009, *New Selected Essays: Where I Live*, a collection of essays by Williams, was published by New Directions, edited, with an afterword, by John S. Bak, and with the Foreword by John Lahr.

While working on *The Traveling Companion and Other Plays*, I spent several years reading various drafts of the plays, and Keith and I began to work on the project in 2005, selecting twelve to edit for publication. The volume finally included *The Chalky White Substance* (1980), *The Day on Which a Man Dies (an Occidental Noh play)* (1960), *A Cavalier for Milady* (c. 1976), *The Pronoun 'I' (a short work for the lyric theatre)* (c. 1975), *The Remarkable Rooming-House of Mme. Le Monde* (1982), *Kirche, Küche, Kinder (An Outrage for the Stage)* (1979), *Green Eyes, or No Sight Would Be Worth Seeing* (1970), *The Parade, or Approaching the End of a Summer* (1962; revisions 1978), *The One Exception* (1983), *Sunburst* (c. 1980), *Will Mr. Merriwether Return from Memphis?* (1969), and *The Traveling Companion* (1981). Most of the plays in the volume are one-acts, with the exception of *Kirche, Küche, Kinder* and *Will Mr. Merriwether Return from Memphis?* Keith was also working as the scholarly editor on the previously unpublished final full-length, *A House Not Meant to Stand* (1982) that was also published in 2008, with the Introduction by Keith and the Foreword by director and producer, Gregory Mosher.

Some of the plays in *The Traveling Companion* volume, such as *Kirche, Küche, Kinder* (under the title *Kirche, Kutchen, und Kinder*) and *Will Mr. Merriwether Return from Memphis?* received initial performances in small theaters (the Bouwerie Lane Theatre in New York City and the Tennessee Williams Fine Arts Center in Key West, Florida, respectively), but a definitive edition had never before been published. Others, *The Traveling Companion, The One Exception*, and *The Remarkable Rooming House of Mme. Le Monde*, were published in a magazine, a literary journal, and a limited edition. Most of them, however, existed in multiple draft form and had never been performed or published, received minor

productions, or were just recently being produced in conjunction
with the publication of *The Traveling Companion and Other Plays*.

David Kaplan, along with Jef Hall-Flavin and Patrick Falco, has
been responsible for producing and/or directing world premieres of
several of the later plays from *The Traveling Companion and Other
Plays* at the annual Provincetown Tennessee Williams Festival. *The
Parade, The Pronoun 'I', The Remarkable Rooming-House of Mme.
Le Monde, Green Eyes,* and *Sunburst* are some of the plays the
Festival has recently premiered. And while the White Barn Theatre
in Westport, Connecticut, produced a variant draft of *The Day on
Which a Man Dies* in 2001, Kaplan was the first to direct and present
the 1960 version in Chicago in February 2008.

In 1996, *The Chalky White Substance* and *The Traveling
Companion* premiered in New York City with the Running Sun
Theatre Company on a double-bill titled *Tennessee Williams'
Guignol,* directed by John Uecker. Grand Guignol is a type of drama
that emphasizes the horrifying or macabre—the gruesome, the
sinister, the dark side of human nature. This genre of short plays
depicting violence, horror, and sadism was popular in 20th-century
French cabarets, and takes its name from le Théâtre du Grand-
Guignol, which flourished in the Pigalle section of Paris from 1897–
1962. The genre was introduced in England in 1908, but remained
essentially a French form. Guignol was a traditional Lyonnaise
puppet character similar to "Punch" of the English "Punch and
Judy" puppet shows, and became the archetype for puppet theater
in France. Graphic murders, rape, insanity, and the baser human
instincts were frequent subjects of Grand Guignol, and many of
Williams' later plays embrace this dark sensibility. In fact, a page
typed by Williams and dated August 1982 (six months before his
death), located in the archives of the Harvard Theatre Collection,
announces his plan for an evening of "Williams' *Guignol.*" He
suggests three evenings in repertoire: I. *Sunburst* and *Chalky White
Substance*; II. *Night Waking: Strange Room* and *The Remarkable
Rooming-House of Mme. Le Monde*; and III. *A Monument for Ercole.*
In a note at the top of the page, Williams writes that, "While these
works have been written with as much attention to style as I always
use, I must admit their intention is to shock and so I have called

them my *Guignol*." Clearly, Williams knew exactly what he was doing when he offered the world these plays.

While a few of Williams' late plays such as *This Is (An Entertainment), Masks Outrageous and Austere*, or *The Everlasting Ticket* remain in various drafts unpublished, and some short plays exist only in fragments, most of the complete, unpublished manuscripts have become available. Three late one-acts will be available in April of 2011—*Kingdom of Earth* (1967, a one-act version), *I Never Get Dressed Till After Dark on Sundays* (1973), and *Some Problems for the Moose Lodge* (1980)—in a new collection, *The Magic Tower and Other One Act Plays*, published by New Directions, edited by Thomas Keith, and with a foreword by Terrence McNally. While I have not sought to provide a comprehensive bibliography of the work that has been published by and about Williams since his death, and my references therefore remain necessarily incomplete, I have attempted to offer a sense of the (re)construction of his reputation, particularly his later reputation, as a journey during the last twenty-five years or so. Williams scholarship remains active and salient, as his work continues to be interpreted in fresh contexts, and new productions of his late plays appear every year. Kaplan and the Provincetown Tennessee Williams Theater Festival continue to present world premieres of the newly published or soon to be published Tennessee Williams, while Cyndy Marion's White Horse Theater Company, with its New York productions of *In the Bar of a Tokyo Hotel* and *Clothes for a Summer Hotel*, continues to offer new interpretations of his work.

In her 1963 book written with Lucy Freeman, *Remember Me to Tom*, Williams' mother Edwina writes that during the early 1940s her son had been convinced that after World War II was over, the world would be ready for new plays, since "the future accepts more readily what the present rejects."[5] By the time Edwina's book was published, Williams' prediction could be applied once again, anticipating, or at least hoping, that the vision of his post-1961 plays would be understood and appreciated one day. In a 1977 interview with Barbaralee Diamonstein on *About the Arts,* John Guare discussed how American playwrights were being destroyed by the commercial interests of theater producers, and were not being given the chance to experiment and grow. When asked for an example, Guare cited Tennessee Williams:

> In our own lifetime, Tennessee Williams, who is our greatest playwright, who, after he stopped turning out what they thought were commercially feasible plays, was just dismissed. And his later plays one day will be discovered and appreciated and used and they'll learn how [these plays should] be performed. They're extraordinary pieces of work. But...producers stopped being interested in his work after it stopped being *Cat on a Hot Tin Roof* and...*Streetcar Named Desire*. It was him moving into new fields.[6]

Guare was ahead of his time in recognizing the value of Williams' late work, and in acknowledging that the "new fields" Williams was moving into were exciting and worthy of attention. The resurrection of Williams' later reputation during the last fifteen years in particular has apparently proved him right. In his later years, Williams went beyond the struggle, hope, and tragedy of his early plays, engaging a kind of laughter that bursts forth through pain to the freedom of exaggeration and excess—the camp, the grotesque, the irreverent— always moving forward in his celebration of what he often referred to as "the strange, the crazed, the queer."[7]

" If Tennessee's works are

not about that grasping, denial,

and dispensation of power,
"
what are they about?

TENNESSEE WILLIAMS IS NEVER APOLITICAL

Amiri Baraka

The idea that Tennessee Williams' work was apolitical is one of those canards meant to make great artists neutral in the world according to a willfully shallow measure that seeks to disconnect all art from the world—especially great art—so the rulers can go on with their anciently normal practice of exploiting and oppressing the majority of people. To say that Tennessee Williams' work is apolitical is to be ignorant of what politics is—or to lie. It's much like the hopeless art curator at the Museum of Modern Art who claimed in his memorial to the great Afro-American painter Jacob Lawrence was not political, that those chronicles of Toussaint L'Ouverture, Nat Turner, Harriet Tubman, and John Brown were just blocks of color in contrived space. This is to make formalism a dismal scam. The same is true of Williams, that critics who would hold such ridiculous ideas believe that politics refers only to membership in a political party or proselytizing toward specific platform planks of reform or reaction.

Politics, first of all, is about the gaining and maintaining the use of power. If Tennessee's works are not about that grasping, denial, and dispensation of power, what are they about? Human life itself, or life itself in its most general concatenations, is about some relationship to power. The very fact that one of the most open struggles in our society is whether you even have sufficient power

282 TENN AT ONE HUNDRED

to be what you are—or not to be—without suffering at the hands of those with more power. Certainly if you are black, or a woman, or gay, or poor, it should be obvious that you have to struggle to simply be who you are. The civil rights movement, or the gay rights movement and the struggle against women's oppression, or the anti-imperialist struggles, give open voice and paradigm to that.

When Tennessee said that only Brecht used the stage for politics, that he himself was concerned with humanity, certainly his tongue was lodged way up high in his cheek. Humanity, to become humanity, or civilized rather than barbaric, is a continuing struggle. You can't become civilized, you can't become humanity, without a struggle. What Williams seems to me is exactly that. The many victims that Williams writes about are usually those dehumanized by persons or institutions claiming to be more human. In other words, just like in *Animal Farm*, some people in this society are more human than others. Particularly the South of the United States, and in some regards the South of the whole world, is especially naked as a dehumanized being.

I cannot think of a single Williams play that is not about the struggle for power. Blanche DuBois versus Stanley Kowalski is obviously enough, in *Streetcar*, the power to control, the power to define, and here with the quirky reversal of the outsider as insider versus the insider. The gender does make Blanche an outsider in one sense, but her claim to aristocracy would make her an ultimate insider. The recurring presence of repressive institutions used to overpower these victims, usually as the allies of powerful figures: the asylum Blanche apparently is taken to, or Violet Venable, as she rises into her madness in *Suddenly Last Summer*, one of my all time favorites.

The twist here—of *Suddenly*, from *Streetcar*—and one wonders with what face Tennessee has effected the reversal: Miss Catherine acquitted of madness by Doctor Sugar is seemingly spared the nut house that the evil mother Violet has put her in in hopes of digging the knife into her skull in order to censor her memory of how her son Sebastian died—Sebastian with all the arrows!—to make her stop saying "those vile things."

Suddenly is one of the most overtly political plays Williams wrote, at the same time it is a work that uses metaphor to speak of world politics. Catherine's whole rush of brutal memory—that Cukrowicz (the Polish word for sugar) rushes to its dénouement—describing Sebastian as whiter than usual, wearing white clothes under a white sky, everything in there is white. The mad litany indicts the omni-whiteness of everything that's part of the oppression of the Head of the Wolf, Cabeza de Lobo, where Sebastian is murdered and his flesh, as she screams, devoured.

The cannibalism that's featured in the book *One Arm*, in one of Williams' short stories, "Desire and the Black Masseur," a man whose black masseur escalates his presumed therapy until he has broken the protagonist/victim's bones, then eats his flesh. In both cases, it is the powerless who reverse the normal oppression—the normal oppressed to oppressor roles—found in imperialistic and racist societies—that in both works the white man is consumed by victims of his passion and greed. In *Suddenly*, the victim, Sebastian, in turn victimizes the young men who he uses, one supposes sexually, but also there is the implication that it is food which they are making gestures for, when they mime putting food in their mouths or on their tongues: Sebastian, in other words, as sexual organ or food.

They finally start calling him names and chase him up the endless street, about which, of course, in the film Miss Catherine, says, "Where was he going? To nowhere. It led to nowhere."

The metaphor in its most narrow interpretation is certainly sexual, but it is about the power of the young men who have been attracted by Sebastian placing Catherine up on a public beach in a bathing suit that makes her look naked. The young men begin to beat tin cans and pots. As Catherine says, they used them as cymbals. They used them as symbols—cymbals, symbols. Williams makes certain we know that the metaphor, even to the murder or the cannibalism, is symbolic. Certainly the Latin-like Cabeza de Lobo, the head of the wolf, resembles the south of the border sites of U.S. imperialism and savage exploitation.

Sweet Bird of Youth, of course, is even more openly political, both as the struggle for power and electoral politics. The boss, or the big daddy, like an image directly from Williams' life, the oppressive big shot, the male figure, dominates his daughter and violently separates her from her would-be lover, but even more brutally has the boy—Chance his name is, Chance!—captured and castrated.

That castration image goes throughout Williams' plays: the castrated image as a punishment for attempting to usurp the power hoarded by the power figure institution. It is punishment for the condition of the powerless. It confirms or is imposed to make certain victims are powerless: castrated. The Boss, in *Sweet Bird of Youth*, is also the father, a slave-owner-like politician who has also castrated and tortured black men to demonstrate his unfettered power, as an example to those blacks and poor whites, Chance, who would despoil the purity of white Southern maidenhood. We could say he never had a chance. The fading movie star who uses Chance as a sexual object and sometimes chauffeur on the promise of opening his career doors for him as an actor, leaves Chance without a chance as well.

The Big Daddy of *Cat on a Hot Tin Roof* is likewise a controller and castrator, if not physically, in all the other ways possible. His son Brick is faced with the choice of becoming by declaration and by sexual action perhaps another Big Daddy. In the film role of Maggie the Cat, Elizabeth Taylor—who played Catherine in the film of *Suddenly*—is tortured by sexual relationships that are impossible or obstructed. None of these male figures she would love can be "real men." Williams' depiction of sexual relationships, even when there are no actual sexual relations, are always tortured and perverse. This is also like Engels' description of sexual love in the distorted landscape of capitalism: it is not possible.

A play so sharply political one wonders how any intelligent observer can deny its political impact: *Orpheus Descending*, where another Southern racist theme with another Big Daddy or Boss, or power figure, controlling land, institutions, commanding people, castrates and burns his victims: those with less power. The central murders of the pregnant wife, and her lover—the young man in the snake skin jacket who has impregnated her, a guitar player like Elvis Presley—are also the central metaphors, the woman, the artist's new life, all destroyed by another southern power theme. Again and again in Tennessee's works we see this confrontation of power versus the powerless. The fact is that the poetic power of Tennessee's work does not lessen its political statement, it enhances it.

Tennessee was, before he had written any plays, a poet. It is the poetry that raises the intensity of the dialogue creating that ideal that Mao Tse Tung spoke of in the Yenan Forum on Arts and Letters in 1941: "We want an art that is artistically powerful, and politically revolutionary." That Williams used his life in extended paradigm—its pain and its vision—also makes me quote another thing from Mao: "Art is the ideological reflection of the world in the mind of the artist."

Originally given as a talk at the Provincetown Tennessee Williams Theater Festival on September 28, 2007.

" He loved humanity

like King Kong loved

" his little blonde.

THE GORGEOUS UNSTOPPABLE

John Patrick Shanley

Every artist is born in jail and Tennessee Williams' jail was called St. Louis. If you're the creative type, the first thing you do when you're born in jail is to decorate your cell. The next thing you do is plan your breakout. Every major artist is full to bursting, looking for the mud and paint and music needed to execute an escape from the initial circumstances of his life. Some call this escape transcendence. When Tennessee decorated his cell, the play was entitled *The Glass Menagerie*. When he staged his breakout, the play was *Streetcar*. Tennessee Williams found the clay and fire and seafood of his soul's escape in New Orleans. This is the scene of his beautiful crime. Here we are. Why are we here? We are here to remember Tennessee, the inmate who got away.

Who was this man?

Tennessee Williams is like walls of paintings in decadent mansions of insane relatives to whom we are closely related. He is forgotten bitter perfumes and prostitution, dead fiancés and mad tea parties, wounded birds singing in the dark, and the moral force of God grabbing you by the jacket. He is here in New Orleans because he chose New Orleans, and he has more right to be here dead than most of us do who are alive.

What a playwright. What a ghost! I don't know about you all, but I'm going to be careful what I say because certainly he's here. He had poetry. He had size. He had structure. He had grand themes. He was crazy. He wrote bad plays. He was rude. He was genteel. He wrote some of the greatest plays of the twentieth century or any century. He was washed up. He was regional. He was horny and stoned and soulful and fragile and on fire, a fire that could not go on and yet it did go on. Whenever I'm discouraged, I think of Tennessee Williams. He was a gorgeous unstoppable beast.

He had a pain in him like a gigantic family at war. Titanic mothers, giant fathers, wounded tentative sisters, young sons crippled and brave. No one of them without hope. No one of them sole holder of any truth. Understanding and compassion rise up out of his work like a heroic soldier that will not leave the wounded or even the dead behind. Williams carries all forward in his muscular, loving arms. He was a natural-born hero, and the certainty I feel that he is here in his beloved New Orleans makes me suffer. It makes me suffer because when he's around, I feel my own cowardice. I feel my every scar, my every wound, my own history of cruelty, given and got. His compassion includes me as I really am. He reminds me of the pain I have caused and the pain I don't admit.

I once sat in a restaurant in the seventies, and I was very poor and struggling and a playwright, and a casting director bought me a hamburger. He pointed out to me that Tennessee Williams was a few tables away. He asked if I wanted to meet him. I said no. I looked across that space like it was the broken-off edge of the world. It was like asking if I wanted to meet the whirlwind. I couldn't meet Tennessee Williams any more than I could shake hands with Amerigo Vespucci or the French and Indian War.

Tennessee Williams wasn't a person to me. I know that's wrong. I know he was a person. I know there were people who knew him and called him Tom. Some of those people are here right now. But I could no more call that man Tom than I could call Charles Dickens, Charley Boy. It's not gonna happen. To me, Tennessee Williams was the ocean. He was a geologic movement. He turned America into something else.

America was a young country that thought of itself in simple terms. Mr. Williams looked straight through that and saw Big Daddy, and Stanley and Blanche, and Amanda Wingfield, and guys named Chance and Brick and Kilroy. He saw Orpheus with a guitar, mythological landscapes on the Camino Real. He made Elizabeth Taylor confess that bad people had eaten her boyfriend. He revealed our personal terror, our small-town crushing loneliness, our ruthless cruelty, our greed, and our stupidity and sudden beauty. He changed our idea of beauty.

Beauty is unexpectedly everywhere in his work all at once. His desperate and fine characters erupt like Gauguin flowers out of that wanton lurid jungle imagination, out of that sweaty, almost ovulating scenery. The rank fertility of his work stinks of waste and death and Southern cooking, of subtle aromas and rotting books of poetry stained with illicit sexual fluids and watery blood. The danger! The danger! He was like a bear licking sugar off you. If you laughed, he might tear your head off.

The more powerful the electricity, the more extreme its positive and negative poles. Williams' extremities were most famously embodied by Stanley Kowalski and Blanche Dubois: a rampage of masculinity that will survive and a feminine delicacy that may not. *Streetcar* is full of panting flesh and indifferent brutality, transparent pretense and ruthless hunger, but at the end of the day what it's really about is survival. Williams the man was a miracle of survival. When I was a young playwright in that restaurant and he was thirty feet away, there was no point in going any closer.

If you want to see Mount Fuji, stand back!

There he was, eating a salad or something. He was out of fashion. He was still the most produced playwright in the world, but movie stars had stopped clamoring to play his parts. The productions were smaller and fewer. He was less popular. He'd drunk a lot, taken a lot of pills, freely admitted that he didn't remember the sixties at all. But he had continued to write through thick and thin, in the face of an ever diminishing critical and popular response.

He looked pretty happy. He looked chipper. I wonder how many of us would look so well, so unencumbered, after such a ride. We all know why he survived, and why, even in death, he is here right now dominating this room. His Love. He loved humanity like King Kong loved his little blonde. I feel the danger of his big-beast hedonistic greedy love like the carnal humidity that comes up out of a lion's gullet. He loved humanity so much that he's still standing somewhere just over our heads smelling us like a chicken dinner.

He did die though. He died. He's dead. They put him in the ground to keep the crows off him. And that frightens me. Because if he can die, if Tennessee Williams can die, then what chance do the rest of us stand?

When he died, a great tree went down. That's how life goes, doesn't it? Then time goes by and people look back and notice this massive unequalled achievement, this single circle of sun in the canopy of trees of such a diameter! Who was this man? How did he do what he did? The wind blows and we feel something in our abdomens. Somebody big went by. And he's gone. Or is he? I think he's still rising up out of us like a summer steam. I think he's part of who we are and we should remember that and be proud and tell our kids. We have greatness in us, and part of its name is Tennessee Williams.

We are here to remember this man. It's a worthy thing to do. When I claim membership in the human race, he is one of the reasons I am not ashamed.

Originally given as a talk on the occasion of Williams' induction into the Poet's Corner at The Cathedral Church of St. John the Divine, New York City, November 5, 2009, and at the Tennessee Williams/New Orleans Literary Festival, March 25, 2010.

CREDITS AND PERMISSIONS

"Fragile Drama Holds Theater in Tight Spell." Chicago Tribune. Reprinted by permission via PARS International Corp.

NOTES

TENNESSEE WILLIAMS' ST. LOUIS BLUES

1. "St. Louis Outnumbers New York City as Movie House Center." *Greater St. Louis* August 1924: 28.

POETS-PLAYWRIGHT'S MODEST BEGINNINGS

1. Lyle Leverich. *Tom: The Unknown Tennessee Williams.* New York: Crown Publishers, 1995, 107.
2. Leverich. *Tom*, 126.
3. Leverich. *Tom*, 153–154.
4. Tennessee Williams. *The Notebooks of Tennessee Williams.* Ed. Margaret Bradham Thornton. New Haven: Yale UP, 2006, 61, 63.
5. Tennessee Williams. *Memoirs.* New York: New Directions Publishing, 2006, 122.
6. Tennessee Williams. *Fugitive Kind.* New York: New Directions Publishing, 2001, xii–xiii.
7. Leverich. *Tom*, 168.
8. Williams. *The Notebooks*, 165.

THE YEAR 1939: BECOMING TENNESSEE WILLIAMS

1. Tennessee Williams. *Conversations with Tennessee Williams.* Ed. Albert J. Devlin. Jackson: UP of Mississippi, 1986.
2. Tennessee Williams. *The Selected Letters of Tennessee Williams, Volume I: 1920–1945.* Ed. Albert J. Devlin and Nancy M. Tischler. New York: New Directions, 2000.
3. Williams, *Letters I*, 163.
4. Humanities Research Center, University of Texas at Austin.
5. Tennessee Williams. *The Notebooks of Tennessee Williams.* Ed. Margaret Bradham Thornton. New Haven: Yale UP, 2007.
6. Raymond Williams. *Modern Tragedy.* Stanford, Calif.: Stanford UP, 1966, 108.
7. Williams, *Notebooks*, 14, Jan. 1939.
8. Lyle Leverich. *Tom: The Unknown Tennessee Williams.* New York: Crown Publishers, 1995, 482–83.
9. Williams, *Notebooks*, 29, Jan. 1939.
10. Williams, *Notebooks*, 21, Nov. 1936; September 15, 1937.
11. Williams, *Notebooks*, ca. 20, June 1937.
12. Williams, *Notebooks*, 16, Sept. 1937.
13. Jim Parrott. "Tennessee Travels to Taos." *Tennessee Williams Literary Journal* 1 (1989): 13.
14. Monroe, Harriet. *A Poet's Life: Seventy Years in a Changing World.* New York: Macmillan, 1938, 321.
15. Edgar Lee Masters. *Vachel Lindsay: A Poet in America.* New York: Charles Scribner's Sons, 1935, 290.
16. Monroe, *A Poet's Life*, 337.
17. Monroe, *A Poet's Life*, 333.
18. Williams, *Letters I*, 150–51.
19. Williams, *Letters I*, 171.

20. Masters, *Vachel Lindsay*, 271.

21. Williams, *Letters I*, 176.

22. Masters, *Vachel Lindsay*, 335.

23. Tennessee Williams. *Springfield, Illinois* (n.d.). Typescript. Austin, Texas: Harry Ransom Humanities Research Center, University of Texas at Austin.

24. Ruggles, Eleanor. *The West-Going Heart: A Life of Vachel Lindsay*. New York: W. W. Norton, 1959.

25. Williams, *Letters I*, 168.

26. Williams, *Letters I*, 173.

27. Williams, *Letters I*, 173.

28. James Cortese. *Richard Halliburton's Royal Road*. Memphis, Tennessee.: White Rose Press, 1989, 52.

29. Jonathan Root. *Halliburton: The Magnificent Myth*. New York: Coward-McCann, 1965, 57.

30. Root, *Halliburton*, 109, 8.

31. Tennessee Williams. *The Glass Menagerie* (1945). In *The Theatre of Tennessee Williams* Vol. 1. New York: New Directions, 1971, scene 6.

32. Williams, *Notebooks*, 14, June 1939.

33. Root, *Halliburton*, 154.

34. Tennessee Williams. "The Angel in the Alcove" (1948). *Collected Stories*. New York: New Directions, 1985, 123.

35. Williams, *Letters I*, 202.

36. Williams, *Notebooks*, 17, Sept. 1939.

37. Williams, *Notebooks*, 19, Dec. 1939.

38. Williams, *Notebooks*, 21, Dec. 1939.

39. Tennessee Williams. "A Writer's Quest for Parnassus" (1950). *Where I Live: Selected Essays*. Ed. Christine Day and Bob Woods. New York: New Directions, 1978, 28.

40. HRC, letter to the Dakins, 28, Oct. 1933.

41. Ruggles, *West-Going Heart*, 353.

42. Ruggles, *West-Going Heart*, 411–12.

43. Root, *Halliburton*, 152.

44. Tennessee Williams. "Suitable Entrances to Springfield or Heaven" (n.d.). Typescript. Newark, Delaware.: U of Delaware Library.

45. Tennessee Williams. "Something Wild" (1949). *Where I Live: Selected Essays*. Ed. by Christine Day and Bob Woods. New York: New Directions, 1978.

46. Williams, *Notebooks*, 25, May 1939.

47. Williams, *Letters I*, 274.

BATTLE IN BOSTON: TENNESSEE WILLIAMS FIRST PROFESSIONAL PRODUCTION

1. Theresa Helburn. *A Wayward Quest: The Autobiography of Theresa Helburn*. Boston: Little, Brown, 1960, 99.

2. In addition to *Heartbreak House*, the Guild's productions of Shaw in the 1920s included *Back to Methuselah* (1922), *The Devil's Disciple* (1923), *Saint Joan* (1923), *Caesar and Cleopatra* (1925), *Arms and the Man* (1925), *Androcles and the Lion* (1925), *Pygmalion* (1926), *The Doctor's Dilemma* (1927), and *Major Barbara* (1928).

3. Lawrence Langner. *The Magic Curtain: The Story of a Life in Two Fields, Theatre and Invention*. New York: Dutton, 1951, 142.

4. Examples include O'Neill's *Mourning Becomes Electra* (1932), *Ah, Wilderness!* (1933), and *The Iceman Cometh* (1946); Behrman's *Biography* (1932), *Rain From Heaven*, and *End of Summer* (1936); Barry's *The Philadelphia Story* (1939) and *Without Love* (1942); Anderson's *Elizabeth the Queen* (1930), *Both Your Houses* (1932), and *Mary of Scotland* (1933); Sherwood's *Reunion in Vienna* (1931), *Idiot's Delight* (1936), and *There Shall Be No Night* (1939); Saroyan's *The Time of*

Your Life (1939) and *Love's Old Sweet Song* (1939); Riggs' *Green Grow the Lilacs* (1931); Powell's *Jigsaw* (1934); Hecht's *To Quito and Back* (1937); and Treadwell's *Hope for a Harvest* (1941).

5. Tennessee Williams to Audrey Wood. Jan. 1940. Tennessee Williams Collection, Harry Ransom Humanities Research Center, University of Texas at Austin.

6. Tennessee Williams to Audrey Wood. March 1940. Tennessee Williams Collection.

7. Tennessee Williams to Audrey Wood. 30 Nov. 1939. Tennessee Williams Collection.

8. Langner. *Magic Curtain*, 331.

9. For a description of the script's evolution from earliest drafts to final form, see Robert Bray "*Battle of Angels* and *Orpheus Descending*" in *Tennessee Williams: A Guide to Research and Performance*, ed. Philip C. Kolin. Westport, Connecticut: Greenwood Press, 1998, 22–23.

10. Tennessee Williams. *Battle of Angels* in *Plays 1937–1955*. New York: Library of America, 2000, 220.

11. Ibid., 258.

12. Ibid., 251.

13. Ibid., 198, 232.

14. Ibid., 252, 254.

15. Ibid., 251.

16. Cecil Brown. "Interview with Tennessee Williams" (1974), in *Conversations with Tennessee Williams*, ed. Albert J. Devlin. Jackson: UP of Mississippi, 1986, 254.

17. Tennessee Williams. "The History of a Play (With Parentheses)," in *Plays 1937–1955*. New York: Library of America, 2000, 281.

18. Williams, *Battle of Angels* (published version), 196.

19. Ibid., 264.

20. Ibid., 242.

21. Ibid., 268.

22. Tennessee Williams, *Battle of Angels* (Nov. 1939 version), Tennessee Williams Collection, 3:2:39.

23. Ibid., 3:2:44; 3:2:46.

24. Ibid., 3:2:48.

25. Edwina Dakin Williams. *Remember Me to Tom*. With Lucy Freeman. New York: G. P. Putman's Sons, 1963, 119.

26. John Gassner. "Report on Discussion of Tennessee Williams's *Battle of Angels*. 9 April 1940. Theatre Guild Correspondence, Yale Collection of American Literature, Beinecke Rare Book and Manuscript Library, Yale University.

27. Ibid.

28. Tennessee Williams, "Notes for Revisions on Battle of Angels by Tennessee Williams." Theatre Guild Correspondence.

29. Tennessee Williams to John Gassner. 11 April 1940. Theatre Guild Correspondence.

30. Tennessee Williams to Rosina and Walter Dakin. 14 May 1940. Box 1, folder 7, Dakin Williams Collection, Tennessee Williams Papers, Rare Book and Manuscript Library, Columbia University, New York.

31. Tennessee Williams to Edwina Williams. May 1940. Box 1, folder 3, Dakin Williams Collection, Tennessee Williams Papers..

32. Tennessee Williams to Audrey Wood. 5 July 1940. Tennessee Williams Collection.

33. Myra is renamed "Lady" in *Orpheus Descending*.

34. Quoted in Tennessee Williams to Bertha Case. Summer 1940. Tennessee Williams Collection.

35. The Theatre Guild to Tennessee Williams. 9 Oct. 1940. Theatre Guild Correspondence.

36. Lyle Leverich. *Tom: The Unknown Tennessee Williams*. New York: Crown, 1995, 385.

37. Tennessee Williams to Theresa Helburn. 11 Oct. 1940. Theatre Guild Correspondence.

38. See handwritten notes in *Battle of Angels* Press Book. Theatre Guild Collection, Yale Collection of American Literature, Beinecke Rare Book and Manuscript Library, Yale University, New Haven.

39. Williams, "History of a Play," 281.

40. Tennessee Williams to the Williams family. Nov. 1940. Box 1, folder 4, Dakin Williams Collection, Tennessee Williams Papers.

41. Langner, *Magic Curtain,* 332; Tennessee Williams to Edwina and Cornelius Williams. 3 Jan. 1941. Box 1, Tennessee Williams Papers.

42. *New York Times* clipping, 18 Dec. 1940, *Battle of Angels* Press Book, Theatre Guild Collection.

43. Williams, *Battle of Angels* (1940 promptbook), 2:43.

44. Ibid., 2:42.

45. Ibid., 2:73.

46. Ibid., 2:75.

47. Williams, "History of a Play," 283.

48. Ibid., 285.

49. See, for example, "Plays Here," *Boston Globe.* 31 Dec. 1940; Alexander Williams, "Miriam Hopkins Opens in Theater Guild's New Drama of South, *Battle of Angels,*" *Boston Herald.* 31 Dec. 1940; Joyce Dana, "*Battle of Angels* Opens on Wilbur's Stage," *Boston Record.* 31 Dec. 1940. All reviews are in the *Battle of Angels* Press Book, Theatre Guild Collection.

50. "Miriam Hopkins Returns." *Boston Transcript.* 31 Dec. 1940. *Battle of Angels* Press Book, Theatre Guild Collection.; "Plays Here."

51. George Jean Nathan. "First Nights & Passing Judgments." *Esquire* April 1943, 153.

52. "Massachusetts Sees *Lady in the Dark* and *Battle of Angels.*" *New York Times* 5 Jan. 1941. *Battle of Angels* Press Book, Theatre Guild Collection.

53. Elinor Hughes. "Second Thoughts on Hart, Williams Plays." *Boston Herald* 5 Jan. 1941. *Battle of Angels* Press Book, Theatre Guild Collection.

54. Quoted in Leverich, *Tom,* 396.

55. Williams, "History of a Play," 280.

56. Margaret Webster. "Censorable Lines." Theatre Guild Correspondence.

57. George Ross. "So This Is Broadway." *New York World-Telegram* 31 Dec. 1940. *Battle of Angels* Press Book, Theatre Guild Collection.

58. Leonard Wheildon. "Battle Called Misunderstanding." *Boston Transcript* 7 Jan. 1940. *Battle of Angels* Press Book, Theatre Guild Collection.

59. Tennessee Williams, *Battle of Angels* (1940 promptbook), Theatre Guild Collection, 2:35.

60. Wheildon, "Battle Called Misunderstanding."

61. Ibid.

62. "Make Play Clean or Close, Angels Told." *Boston Record* 7 Jan. 1941. *Battle of Angels* Press Book, Theatre Guild Collection. "Clean Up or Shut *Angels.*" *Boston News* 6 Jan. 1941. Theatre Guild Correspondence.

63. Margaret Webster. *Don't Put Your Daughter on the Stage.* New York: Knopf, 1972, 72.

64. "Make Play Clean or Close."

65. "Clean Up or Shut *Angels.*"

66. John Haggott to Theresa Helburn. Telegram, 7 January 1941. Theatre Guild Correspondence.

67. Webster, *Don't Put Your Daughter on the Stage,* 72.

68. "Play Must Have Lines Taken Out." *Boston Post* 7 Jan. 1941. *Battle of Angels* Press Book, Theatre Guild Collection.

69. "Changes Ordered in Stage Play, *Battle of Angels.*" *Boston Globe* 7 Jan. 1941. *Battle of Angels* Press Book, Theatre Guild Collection.

70. Wheildon, "Battle Called Misunderstanding."

71. Webster, *Don't Put Your Daughter on the Stage,* 72.

72. Joseph Heidt to Washington, D.C., newspapers. Telegram, 2 January, 1941 Theatre Guild Correspondence.

73. Williams, "History of a Play," 280.

74. Webster, *Don't Put Your Daughter on the Stage,* 69.

75. Leverich, *Tom,* 392.

76. Webster, *Don't Put Your Daughter on the Stage*, 69.

77. Lawrence Langner and Theresa Helburn to Boston Subscribers. 16 Jan. 1941. Theatre Guild Correspondence. "The Theater Guild Writes Letter to Its Subscribers." *Boston Herald* 26 Jan. 1941. *Battle of Angels Press Book*, Theatre Guild Collection.

78. Lawrence Langner to Tennessee Williams. 8 July 1941 and 6 June 1945. Theatre Guild Correspondence.

79. After the Theatre Guild rejected his revised *Battle of Angels*, Williams discussed a possible production with Erwin Piscator at the New School's experimental Dramatic Workshop in late 1941 and early 1942. As he was considering ideas for revisions, Williams stopped short of what was probably the politically minded Piscator's suggestion to have the African American Conjure Man use the store-turned-"museum" from the prologue and epilogue "for sociological instruction," and he eventually abandoned the project. (See Tennessee Williams, "Notes on New Ideas," Tennessee Williams Collection.)

80. By 1948, Lawrence Langner was ready to stage *Battle of Angels* at Westport "in any form that Tennessee wants it produced," but even this offer fell on deaf ears. (See Langner to Audrey Wood, 3 Nov. 1948, Audrey Wood Papers, Harry Ransom Humanities Research Center, University of Texas at Austin.)

81. Williams, "History of a Play," 278; quoted in Robert Van Gelder, "Playwright with 'A Good Conceit': Of Tennessee Williams and His Outlook on the Stage," 22 April 1945, Audrey Wood Papers.

82. The Theatre Guild produced radio versions of *Summer and Smoke* (1949) and *The Glass Menagerie* (1951 and 1953). Langner produced *27 Wagons Full of Cotton* at the Westport Country Playhouse in 1956, and the Theatre Guild staged *Portrait of a Madonna* on Broadway in 1959.

RESCUING THE GLASS MANAGERIE

1. *Time*. "Exit of the Executioner." 3 Sept. 1965.

2. *Time*. 28, Sept. 1942.

3. Tennessee Williams. "A Reply to Mr. Nathan." *New Selected Essays: Where I Live*. Ed. John S. Bak. New York: New Directions, 2009, 193.

4. *Chicago Herald-American*. 15 April 1945.

5. George Jean Nathan. *Passing Judgments for the Theater*. New York: Alfred A. Knopf, 1935.

6. George Jean Nathan. "Dempsey as an Actor." *American Mercury* Nov. 1928.

7. Brooks Atkinson, who held the position, had retired temporarily to become a war correspondent in China.

A NIGHT TO GO DOWN IN HISTORY

"Tenn are you really happy?" *Life* 16 Feb. 1948.

"I could scarcely read Brooks Atkinson." Irene Mayer Selznick. *A Private View*. New York: Alfred A. Knopf, 1983, 313.

"What I couldn't have foreseen." Selznick, *A Private View*, 312.

"...made Gadge a king." Richard Schickel. *Elia Kazan: A Biography*. New York: HarperCollins, 2005, 21-22.

AUDREY WOOD AND TENNESSEE WILLIAMS

1. Tennessee Williams. "A Playwright Named Tennessee," in *Conversations with Tennessee Williams*. Ed. Albert J. Devlin. Jackson: UP of Mississippi, 1986, 28–29.

2. Tennessee Williams. *Suitable Entrances to Springfield or Heaven: A Play in Homage to Vachel Lindsay*. N.d. TS. U of Delaware Library, Newark, Delaware.

3. *Represented by Audrey Wood*. Audrey Wood with Max Wilk. Garden City, New York:

Doubleday, 200.

WORST PLAY BY THE BEST PLAYWRIGHT

1. My thanks to Brian Parker for his generosity in sharing some of his research for this chapter.

2. J. P. Shanley. "*Camino Real* Ends its Run Saturday." *New York Times* 4 May 1953: 2+.

3. *New York Theatre Critics' Reviews*, 14 (1953): 330–32.

4. Wolcott Gibbs. "Erewhon." *The New Yorker* 28 March 1953: 68–69.

5. Edith Sitwell. Letter. *The New York Times* 5 April 1953: sec 2:3.

6. Richard Maney. "The Last Rites of Closing Nights." *The New York Times Sunday Magazine* 23 May 1954: 78.

7. in Brian Parker. "Documentary Sources for *Camino Real*." *Tennessee Williams Annual Review* (1998): 46.

8. Tennessee Williams. "Ten Blocks on the Camino Real." *American Blues*. New York: Dramatists Play Service, 1948, 43.

9. See, for example, Parker and Jan Balakian. "*Camino Real*: Williams's Allegory About the Fifties." *The Cambridge Companion to Tennessee Williams*. Ed. Matthew C. Roudané. Cambridge: Cambridge UP, 1997.

10. Tennessee Williams. *The Selected Letters of Tennessee Williams, Volume II: 1945-1957*. Eds. Albert J. Devlin and Nancy M. Tischler. New York: New Directions, 2004, 419.

11. Williams, *Letters II,* 438.

12. Williams, *Letters II*.

13. Quoted in Williams, *Letters II,* 443.

14. Elia Kazan. Letter to Tennessee Williams. 17 Nov. 1952. MS. Harry Ransom Humanities Research Center, University of Texas at Austin.

15. Elia Kazan. *A Life*. New York: Alfred A. Knopf, 1988, 497.

16. Henry Hewes. "Tennessee Williams—Last of Our Solid Gold Bohemians." *Saturday Review* 28 March 1953: 25–26.

17. Kazan letter to Williams.

18. Quoted in Williams, *Letters II,* 462.

19. Tennessee Williams. *Notebooks*. Ed. Margaret Bradham Thornton.New Haven: Yale UP, 2006, 557.

20. Tennessee Williams. *Five O'Clock Angel: Letters of Tennessee Williams to Maria St. Just 1948-1952*. New York: Alfred A. Knopf, 1990, 67.

21. Brenda Murphy. *Tennessee Williams and Elia Kazan: A Collaboration in the Theatre*. Cambridge: Cambridge UP, 1996, 84.

22. Murphy, *Tennessee Williams and Elia Kazan,* 94.

23. "Williams Play Leaves Audience in Confused Mood." *New Haven Register* 24 Feb. 1953.

24. Bone. "Camino Real." *Variety* 25 Feb. 1953: 56.

25. Henry T. Murdock. "'Camino Real' at Forrest, Latter Day Tour of Dante." *Philadelphia Inquirer* 3 March 1953.

26. R. E. P. Sensenderfer. "It's Anybody's Guess What Tennessee Williams Is Saying in New Play—But It's Exciting Theater." *Philadelphia Bulletin* 5 March 1953: np.

27. Linton Martin. "'Camino Real' Is Powerful As a Surrealistic Fantasy." *Philadelphia Inquirer*, nd.

28. Martin, "Camino Real."

29. Donald Spoto. *The Kindness of Strangers: The Life of Tennessee Williams*. New York: Ballantine, 1986, 207.

30. Tennessee Williams. "Playwright Seeks a Creation of a World Whose Existence is Out of Time." *New York Times* 15 March 1953: 2: 1.

31. Williams, "Playwright Seeks Creation".

32. Kazan, *A Life,* 497.

33. Kazan, *A Life,* 497–8.

34. John McClain. "Williams Play Baffling to Some." *New York Journal-American* 20 March 1953.

35. John Chapman. "Symbols Clash in *Camino Real.*" New York *Daily News* 20 March 1953.

36. Robert Coleman. "*Camino Real* Will Please Some, Anger Others." New York *Daily Mirror* 20 March 1953.

37. William Hawkins. "*Camino Real* is Pure Emotion." *New York World-Telegram* 20 March 1953.

38. Brooks Atkinson. "Tennessee Williams Writes a Cosmic Fantasy Entitled 'Camino Real.'" *New York Times* 20 March 1953, sec. 2: 26.

39. Walter Kerr. "Camino Real." *New York Herald Tribune* 20 March 1953: 12.

40. Walter Kerr, "Camino Real."

41. "New Play." *Newsweek* 30 March 1953: 63.

42. "New Play in Manhattan." *Time* 30 March 1953: 46.

43. Eric Bentley. *What is Theatre?* New York: Limelight, 1984, 75, 77–8.

44. Harold Clurman. *Lies Like Truth.* New York: Macmillan, 1958, 84–5.

45. Clurman, *Lies Like Truth,* 86.

46. Walter Kerr. "The Crucible." *New York Herald Tribune* 23 January 1953.

47. Clurman, *Lies Like Truth,* 86.

THE MAKING AND SELLING OF BABY DOLL

1. Murray Schumach. *The Face on the Cutting Room Floor: The Story of Movie and Television Censorship.* New York: William Morrow, 1964, 96.

2. Quoted. in Elia Kazan. *Elia Kazan: A Life.* New York: Alfred Knopf, 1988, 96.

3. Quoted. in Kazan, *A Life,* 564.

4. National Legion of Decency. "*Baby Doll* News Release," 13 Dec. 1956. *Baby Doll* file. Production Code Administration files. Margaret Herrick Library of the Academy of Motion Picture Arts and Sciences.

5. Production Code Administration. "Report on *Baby Doll,*" December 1956. *Baby Doll* file. Production Code Administration files.

6. Leonard J. Leff and Jerold L. Simmons. *The Dame in the Kimono: Hollywood, Censorship, and the Production Code from the 1920s to the 1960s.* New York: Anchor Books, 1990, 154.

7. "*Baby Doll* News Release," 13 Dec. 1956. *Baby Doll* file. Production Code Administration files.

8. Quoted. in Leff and Simmons, 177.

9. Quoted. in Schumach, 73.

10. Quoted. in Leff and Simmons, 175.

11. Quoted. in Schumach, 74.

12. Leff and Simmons, 175.

13. Schumach, 76.

14. Quoted. in Schumach, 77.

15. Robert Sklar. *Movie-Made America.* New York: Vintage Books, 1976, 175.

16. Leff and Simmons, 52.

17. Schumach, 182.

18. Sam Staggs. *When Blanche Met Brando.* New York: St. Martin's Press, 2005, 254.

19. Quoted. in Leff and Simmons, 182.

20. Kazan, *A Life,* 63.

21. Kazan, *A Life,* 449.

22. Finlay McDermid. Letter to Steve Trilling. March 1952. *Baby Doll* file. Production Code Administration files.

23. Finlay McDermid. Letter to Steve Trilling. July 1952. *Baby Doll* file. Production Code Administration files.

24. Joseph Breen. Letter to Jack Warner. Aug. 1952. *Baby Doll* file. Production Code

Administration files.

25. David Weisbart. Letter to Tennessee Williams. June 1953. *Baby Doll* file. Production Code Administration files.

26. Finlay McDermid. Letter to Steve Trilling. Jan. 1954. *Baby Doll* file. Production Code Administration files.

27. Finlay McDermid. Letter to Steve Trilling. Sept. 1955. *Baby Doll* file. Production Code Administration files.

28. Geoffrey Shurlock. Letter to Jack Warner. Oct. 1955. *Baby Doll* file. Production Code Administration files.

29. Elia Kazan. Letter to Jack Warner. Nov. 1955. *Baby Doll* file. Warner Brothers Studios files. University of Southern California Special Collections.

30. Elia Kazan. Letter to Jack Warner. Nov. 1955. *Baby Doll* file. Warner Brothers Studios files.

31. Erik Barnouw. *Tube of Plenty: The Evolution of American Television*, 2nd revised ed. New York: Oxford UP, 1990, 193.

32. Quoted. in Nina C. Leibman. *Living Room Lectures: The Fifties in Film and Television*. Austin: U of Texas P, 1995, 95.

33. Quoted. in Leibman, 78.

34. McDermid. Letter to Elia Kazan, May 1955. *Baby Doll* file. Production Code Administration files.

35. Jack Vizzard. Letter to Jack Warner. July 1956. *Baby Doll* file. Warner Brothers Studios files.

36. Sidney Schreiber. "MPAA Document on *Baby Doll*." March 1957. *Baby Doll* file. Warner Brothers Studios files.

37. Production Code Administration. "Report on *Baby Doll*," Dec. 1956. *Baby Doll* file. Production Code Administration files.

38. Letter to Jack Warner, Nov. 1955. *Baby Doll* file. Warner Brothers Studios files.

39. Warner Brothers' censorship report, Dec. 1956. Warner Brothers Studio files.

40. Ibid.

41. "The Most Spectacular 24-Sheet Posting in Warner History!" Dec. 1956. *Baby Doll* file. Warner Brothers Studios files.

42. "Your '*Baby Doll*': A Big Ad-Pub Campaign." Dec. 1956. *Baby Doll* file. Warner Brothers Studios files.

43. "Your '*Baby Doll*': A Big Ad-Pub Campaign," Dec. 1956. *Baby Doll* file. Warner Brothers Studios files.

44. Anonymous. "Review of *Baby Doll*." *Le Monde* 22 Dec. 1956: 16.

45. Edwin Schallert. "Review of *Baby Doll*." *Los Angeles Times* 27 Dec. 1956: E3.

46. Philip K. Scheuer. "Review of *Baby Doll*." *Los Angeles Times* 25 Nov. 1956): E7.

47. George H. Jackson. "Review of *Baby Doll*." *Los Angeles Herald Express* (Dec. 27, 1956): E5.

48. Thomas Reddy. "Review of *Baby Doll*." *Los Angeles Examiner* 27 Dec. 1956): E1.

49. Lowell Redelings. "Review of *Baby Doll*." *Citizen News* 27 Dec. 1956: 22.

50. Clive Hirschorn. *The Warner Brothers Story*. New York: Crown, 1979, 326.

51. Kazan, 564.

52. Kazan, 180.

53. Kazan. "*Baby Doll* Director's Contract," Oct. 1955. *Baby Doll* file. Warner Brothers Studios files.

54. Kazan, 180.

55. Kazan, 564.

56. Leff and Simmons, 181

57. Frank Miller. *Censored Hollywood: Sex, Sin and Violence on the Screen*. Atlanta: Turner Publishing, 1994, 180.

58. Leff and Simmons, 232.

59. Anonymous. "Review of *Baby Doll*." *Los Angeles Times* 24 Dec. 1956: E4.

60. Ibid.

61. Production Code Administration "Report."

62. Anonymous. "Review of *Baby Doll.*" *New York Times* 3 Feb. 1957: A12.

63. Miller, 179.

64. Miller, 179.

65. Anonymous. "*Baby Doll* Update." *Los Angeles Times* 7 Jan. 1957: C13.

66. Production Code Administration. "Report on *Baby Doll,*" December 1956. *Baby Doll* file. Production Code Administration files.

67. Neal Gabler. *An Empire of Their Own: How the Jews Invented Hollywood*. New York: Anchor Books, 1989.

68. Thomas Dougherty. "The Acceptable Bigotry." *Los Angeles Times* 12 Oct. 1999: B9. PCA files.

69. Ibid.

70. Leff and Simmons, 256.

71. Sklar, 296.

72. Ibid.

73. Ibid.

BENDING THE CODE: FILMING THE ROSE TATTOO

1. Tennessee Williams. To Audrey Wood. 19 September 1953. *The Selected Letters of Tennessee Williams, Vol II: 1945–1957*. Ed. Albert J. Devlin and Nancy M. Tischler. New York: New Directions, 2004, 498–499.

2. Hal B. Wallis and Charles Higham. *Star-maker: The Autobiography of Hal Wallis*, New York: Macmillan, 1980, 134.

3. This is not to say, of course, that Italian neorealist films always avoid erotic sensationalism. One of the most enduring images of that cinema is the shot of a very busty Silvana Mangano, dressed in skin-tight shorts, soaked to the skin as she works the paddies in *Bitter Rice* (Giuseppe de Santis, 1949).

4. Williams, *Letters II*, 342.

5. Wallis and Higham, *Autobiography*, 139.

6. Ibid., 140.

7. Quoted in Brian Parker. "Multiple Endings for The Rose Tattoo." *The Tennessee Williams Annual Review* (1951): 53.

8. Tennessee Williams. Letter to Wallis. 14 June 1954. Harry Ransom Humanities Research Center, University of Texas at Austin.

9. Joseph Breen. Letter to Hal B. Wallis. 12 May 1952. Production Code Administration files. Margaret Herrick Library of the Academy of Motion Picture Arts and Sciences.

10. Paul Nathan. Forwarded memo to Vizzard. 15 May 1952. PCA/Herrick. After he left the PCA, Vizzard wrote a somewhat sensational account of his experiences, *See No Evil: Life inside a Hollywood Censor*, in which he makes clear that he did not share the cultural conservatism of Breen and his other colleagues. Vizzard observes: "In a climate of permissiveness, like the present, there is no body of respected opinion that forms a consensus on the side of controls. Instead, one hears slogans on all sides that are very popular with the electorate, but which are the fruit of a kind of anti-intellectualism that is against the hard think, and the honest think." At the same time, he admits, "We are steeped in self-gratifications almost beyond belief," which makes "the maintenance of a middle ground…as difficult as trying to pick up a puddle of mercury between the tips of the fingers." To put it simply, Breen did not see any reason to stake out "a middle ground" of this kind.

11. Williams' arguments over the script cited here and below are from his "Notes on the Filming of Rose Tattoo." PCA/Herrick.

12. In fact, those within the industry were well apprised of the potential difficulties involved in "sex comedies" even before the contentious filming of *The Moon is Blue*, which was eventually released without a certificate because Preminger refused to modify to the censors' satisfaction the essential feature of the property: its so very genteel spoofing of middle-class mores, including the

somewhat hypocritical fixation on official virginity in an age that condoned unchaperoned dating and what was then known as "petting." Even though Herbert's play has a moral theme (the brassy heroine, who keeps her virtue, receives a marriage proposal from her erstwhile seducer, while the "wolf" figure, played largely for comic relief, is brought to see the error of his ways), Hollywood producers were at first reluctant to bid on the property. Warner Brothers, and Paramount both passed on the offer from Preminger and Herbert, who then were forced to form their own production company in order to make the film. For further details of the resulting controversy, which shook the PCA badly because the film did very well despite the absence of a certificate, see Skinner, *Cross and Cinema*, 112–116. The Legion, perhaps expressing solidarity with the PCA, gave *The Moon is Blue* a "C" rating, despite the raters of the Catholic Theatre Movement (a soon-to-pass-into-history Broadway version of the Legion) having awarded it a "B."

13. Breen to Wallis, 6 May 1952. PCA/Herrick.

14. Ibid.

15. All above quotations are from Breen to Wallis, 5 May 1953 PCA/Herrick.

16. Breen to Wallis et al. 13 April 1954. PCA/Herrick.

17. Breen to Kanter et al. 20 April 1954. PCA/Herrick.

18. This important document was provided to the authors by Mr. Richard Taylor, who received it from Stella Adams, one of Williams' cousins. It is printed in an online issue of the *Tennessee Williams Annual Review* 2003. <http://www.tennesseewilliamsstudies.org>.

19. Many letters from Williams to Kazan explore the boundaries that exist and must sometimes be crossed between collaborators. For example, on November 23, 1954, he wrote Kazan, addressing "a clash…between our views," and insisting, "that's what makes us probably the best working combo in the theatre! We have to give a little, both ways, and arrive at the golden mean. I am usually for something less explicit. You are usually for something more explicit. The reason may be that nobody knows quite as well as the writer the things that are buried in his script. On the other hand, the writer is often unable to tell when these things do not communicate to anyone but himself." (WUCA).

20. Williams, *Letters II*, 517–518.

21. Ibid., 538.

22. Wallis and Higham, *Autobiography*, 144.

23. Williams, *Letters II*, 590.

TENNESSEE WILLIAMS AND THE SWEDISH ACADEMY

1. For a detailed analysis of Williams' stay in Sweden as well as a discussion of how the critics reviewed the theme of homosexuality in *Cat on a Hot Tin Roof*, see my article "Torn between the 'Swedish Sin' and 'homosexual freemasonry': Tennessee Williams, sexual morals and the closet in 1950s Sweden." *The Tennessee Williams Annual Review* 11 (2010): 19–39.

2. Dotson Rader. "The Art of Theatre V: Tennessee Williams." *The Paris Review* 81 (1981). Rpt. in *Conversations with Tennessee Williams*. Ed. Albert J. Devlin. Jackson: UP of Mississippi, 1986, 357.

3. At the time of writing, the records up until 1959 are accessible to researchers, given they are granted permission by the Permanent Secretary of the Academy. In this context, I would like to express my gratitude to Peter Englund, the Swedish Academy's Permanent Secretary, and Madeleine Broberg from The Nobel Library of the Swedish Academy.

4. Napier Wilt. "Letter of nomination to the Swedish Academy." 23 Jan. 1958.

5. Ebbe Linde. "Tennessee Williams." Typewritten report to the Swedish Academy, 1958, 2. Further page references to this document are given in the text. All Swedish quotes have been translated by the author.

6. The Swedish premiere of *The Glass Menagerie* took place on 8 Feb. 1946 at the Royal Dramatic Theater in Stockholm and was directed by Stig Torsslow.

7. Between September 1955 and November 1956, five different productions of *Cat* were mounted in Sweden. The next play to be staged was *Suddenly Last Summer* in February 1959, which means that when Linde was writing his report, not a single Williams play was running.

8. "Evaluation of the Nobel Committee of the Swedish Academy." Stockholm, Sep. 1958; signed by Anders Örling.

9. The official homepage of the Swedish Academy. Web. 19 Apr. 2010. <http://www.svenskaakademien.se/web/Laureates.aspx>.

10. Quoted. on: The Official Site of the Nobel Prize. Web. 16 Aug. 2010. <http://nobelprize.org/>.

11. Eve Kosofsky Sedgwick. *Epistemology of the Closet*. Berkeley: U of California P, 1990, 23.

12. Gregory Woods. *A History of Gay Literature. The Male Tradition*. New Haven & London: Yale UP, 1998, 196.

13. For an analysis of Williams' aesthetics of the closet, see: David Savran. *Communists, Cowboys, and Queers: The Politics of Masculinity in the Work of Arthur Miller and Tennessee Williams*. Minneapolis: U of Minnesota P, 1992; Michael Paller. *Gentlemen Callers: Tennessee Williams, Homosexuality, and Mid-Twentieth-Century Drama*. New York: Palgrave Macmillan, 2005; John S. Bak. *Homo Americanus: Ernest Hemingway, Tennessee Williams, and Queer Masculinities*. Fairleigh Dickinson UP, 2010.

14. Unlike the short stories, Williams' major plays up to that point and *Mrs. Stone* had been translated into Swedish and were available in book form.

15. Gindt. "Torn between the 'Swedish Sin' and 'homosexual freemasonry'," 28-35.

16. A similar pattern later emerged after the Scandinavian premiere of *Suddenly Last Summer* at Malmö City Theater in February 1959 under the direction of Frank Sundström. Swedish critics wrote openly about the dead poet Sebastian's homosexuality, condemned his decadent lifestyle, but never uttered a word about the social discrimination that homosexuals faced both in the U.S. and in Sweden. See: Dirk Gindt. "Anxious Nation and White Fashion: *Suddenly Last Summer* in the Swedish folkhem." *Nordic Theatre Studies* vol. 21 (2009): 98-112.

17. Jens Rydström. "Från fula gubbar till goda föräldrar: Synen på sexualitet och genus i lagstiftning och debatt 1944-2004." *I den akademiska garderoben*. Ed. Anna-Clara Olsson and Caroline Olsson. Stockholm: Atlas, 2004, 37-65; Göran Söderström. "Keijne- och Haijbyaffärerna." *Homo i Folkhemmet: Homo- och bisexuella i Sverige 1950-2000*. Ed. Martin Andreasson. Göteborg: Anamma, 2000, 92-117.

18. The Belgian Maeterlinck is mostly known for the play *The Blind* (1910), which is one of the defining plays of the symbolist movement.

19. Hauptman is best remembered for his social drama *The Weavers* (1892), which heavily attacked the inhumane working conditions of German weavers in the late nineteenth century.

20. Similar motivations were offered for the choice of two contemporary U.S. novelists, William Faulkner (1949) "for his powerful and artistically unique contribution to the modern American novel" and Ernest Hemingway (1954) "for his mastery of the art of narrative, most recently demonstrated in *The Old Man and the Sea*, and for the influence that he has exerted on contemporary style." All the quoted motivations are retrieved from the official homepage of the Swedish Academy. Web. 19 April. 2010. <http://www.svenskaakademien.se/web/Laureates.aspx>.

21. Savran. *Communists, Cowboys, and Queers*; Anne Fleche. *Mimetic Disillusion: Eugene O'Neill, Tennessee Williams, and U.S. Dramatic Realism*. Tuscaloosa & London: U of Alabama P, 1997; Mary Ann Corrigan. "Realism and Theatricalism in *A Streetcar Named Desire*." *Critical Essays on Tennessee Williams*. Ed. Robert A. Martin. New York: G. K. Hall & Co, 1997, 83-93; Esther M. Jackson. "Tennessee Williams: The Idea of a 'Plastic Form'." *Critical Essays on Tennessee Williams*. Ed. Robert A. Martin. New York: G. K. Hall & Co, 1997, 191-208.

22. Tennessee Williams. "Production Notes." *The Glass Menagerie*, in *The Theatre of Tennessee Williams*, Vol. 1. New York: New Directions, 1971 [1945], 131. For a discussion of Williams' idea of a plastic theater, see: Richard E. Kramer. "'The Sculptural Drama': Tennessee Williams's Plastic Theatre." *The Tennessee Williams Annual Review* 5 (2002): 1-10. Web. 17 Aug. 2010. <http://www.tennesseewilliamsstudies.org/archives/2002/3kramer.pdf>.

23. See for instance: Linda Dorff. "Theatricalist Cartoons: Williams' Late, 'Outrageous' Plays." *The Tennessee Williams Annual Review* 2 (1999): 13-33; Ruby Cohn. "Tennessee Williams: The Last Two Decades." *The Cambridge Companion to Tennessee Williams*. Ed. Matthew C.

304   TENN AT ONE HUNDRED

Roudané. Cambridge: Cambridge UP, 1997, 232–43; Allean Hale. "Confronting the Late Plays of Tennessee Williams." *The Tennessee Williams Annual Review* 6 (2003): 1–10. Web. 17 Aug. 2010. <http://www.tennesseewilliamsstudies.org/archives/2003/5hale.pdf>; Annette J. Saddik. *The Politics of Reputation: The Critical Reception of Tennessee Williams' Later Plays.* Madison, NJ: Fairleigh Dickinson UP, 1999; Philip C. Kolin ed. *The Undiscovered Country: The Later Plays of Tennessee Williams.* New York: Peter Lang Publishing, 2002; Robert Bray ed. "Looking at the Late Plays of Tennessee Williams." *The Tennessee Williams Annual Review* 5 (2002): 1–16. Web. 17 Aug. 2010. <http://www.tennesseewilliamsstudies.org/archives/2002/1panel_lateplays.pdf>.

24. David Savran. "The Canonization of O'Neill." *Modern Drama* 50.4 (2007): 578.

25. Savran. "The Canonization of O'Neill", 574–5.

26. McDé. "100 pjäser i kappsäcken." *Aftonbladet* 12 Dec. 1945.

27. Theater scholar Tom Olsson has critically queried this notion of an "O'Neill tradition", pointing out that Dramaten focused above all on the plays that could be staged in a psychologically realist mode (and were thus compatible with the dominant acting style of the period), whereas it ignored the more experimental plays (which, instead, were produced in continental Europe). Tom J. A. Olsson. *O'Neill och Dramaten: En studie kring arbetet med och mottagandet av fjorton olika O'Neill-uppsättningar på Dramatiska teatern åren 1923–1962.* Stockholm: Akademilitteratur, 1977, diss.

28. Olsson. *O'Neill och Dramaten,* 99–147; Karin Helander. *Teaterns korsväg: Bengt Ekerot och 1950-talet.* Stockholm: Carlssons, 2003, 127–41.

29. During the same period, the only play by Miller to be staged was Alf Sjöberg's production of *A View from the Bridge* in 1958.

30. Sven Åke Heed. *Stadsteatertanken i svensk teater. Ny svensk teaterhistoria* 3: 1900-talets teater. Eds. Tomas Forser & Sven Åke Heed, Hedemora: Gidlund, 2007. 196. See also: Helander. *Teaterns korsväg,* 13-9.

31. Urban Stenström. *Inte en katt i Uppsala.* Svenska Dagbladet 15 Oct. 1955.

32. Carl Björkman. "Segrande katta: Tennessee Williams' göteborgspremiär." *Vecko-Journalen* 37 (1955): 10.

33. Ivar Harrie. "Katt på hett plåttak' storseger för Vasan." *Expressen* 28 Nov. 1956.

34. Per Erik Wahlund. *Sydstatspjäs i Göteborg.* Svenska Dagbladet 3 Sep. 1955.

35. Björkman. *Segrande katta,* 10.

36. S.B-l. "Katt på hett plåttak." *Dagens Nyheter* 3 Sep. 1955.

37. Erwin Leiser. "'Cat' in Uppsala." *Morgon-Tidningen* 15 Oct. 1955.

38. Nils Beyer. "Katt på hett plåttak." *Morgon-Tidningen* 3 Sep. 1955.

39. A. B-nd. "Katten på plåttaket." *Arbetet* 20 Oct. 1956.

40. For further discussion on the so-called third act controversy, see: Brian Parker, "Bringing Back Big Daddy." *The Tennessee Williams Annual Review* 3 (2000): 91–9.

41. Dave Sandstroem. "Nomad på hett plåttak." *Sydsvenska Dagbladet* 19 Oct. 1956.

42. Scholars have long argued that such a judgment seems rather unfair, as Williams at this point in his career was hardly a novice desperate to have his play produced. See for instance: Nancy M. Tischler. *Tennessee Williams: Rebellious Puritan.* New York: Citadel, 1961, 206–11; Brenda Murphy. *Tennessee Williams and Elia Kazan: A Collaboration in the Theatre.* Cambridge: Cambridge UP, 1992, 126–30.

PULP WILLIAMS

1. Tennessee Williams. *Conversations with Tennessee Williams.* Ed. Albert J. Devlin. Jackson: UP of Mississippi, 1986, 54.

2. T. E. Kalem. *Time.* LXXIX.10 1962: 53.

3. Kalem, 53.

4. Steven Heller and Elaine Lustig Cohen. *Born Modern: The Life and Design of Alvin Lustig.* San Francisco: Chronicle Books, 2010, 50.

5. Jerry Roberts. *The Great American Playwrights on the Screen.* New York: Applause

Books, 2003, 537–556.

6. Marshall Lee. *Book Making*. 3rd ed. New York/London: W. W. Norton & Co., 2004, 29.

7. Peter Haining, *The Classic Era of Crime Fiction*. London: Prion Books, 2002, 66, 93, 96, 105, 108, 123, 130, 144, 180, 185, 204.

8. Sam Staggs, *When Blanche Met Brando*. New York: St. Martin's Press, 2005, 245.

9. Richard F. Leavitt. *The World of Tennessee Williams*. New York: G. Putnam & Sons, 1978, 77.

10. Tennessee Williams. *A Streetcar Named Desire*. New York: Signet-New American Library, 1951.

11. Tennessee Williams. *The Rose Tattoo*. New York: Signet-New American Library, 1955.

12. Tennessee Williams. *Baby Doll*. New York: Signet-New American Library, 1956.

13. Tennessee Williams. *Cat on a Hot Tin Roof*. New York: Signet-New American Library, 1958.

14. Devlin, *Conversations*, 304.

15. Tennessee Williams. *Suddenly Last Summer*. New York: Signet-New American Library, 1960.

16. Tennessee Williams. *The Fugitive Kind*. New York: Signet-New American Library, 1960.

17. Tennessee Williams. *Summer and Smoke*. New York: Signet-New American Library, 1961.

18. Tennessee Williams. *Summer and Smoke*. New York: New Directions, 1948.

19. Tennessee Williams. *The Roman Spring of Mrs. Stone*. New York: Signet-New American Library, 1961.

20. Tennessee Williams. *The Night of the Iguana*. New York: Signet-New American Library, 1964.

21. Tennessee Williams. *Sweet Bird of Youth*. New York: Signet-New American Library, 1962.

MR. WILLIAMS IS ADVISED TO STAY SILENT

1. Hugh Wheeler would go on in later years to win acclaim (and three Tony awards) writing books for the musicals *Candide*, *A Little Night Music* and *Sweeney Todd*.

2. *Village Voice* 29 June 1961.

3. *The Reporter* 15 May 1955.

4. *The Reporter* 16 April 1959.

5. Miss Mannes didn't much like *Waiting for Godot* either. Seeing the play in London in 1955 she wrote, "I doubt whether I have seen a worse play. I mention it only as typical of the self-delusion of which certain intellectuals are capable, embracing obscurity, pretense, ugliness and negation as protective coloring for their own confusions."

6. *New York Times Magazine* 12 June 1960.

7. *The New York Times 7* Aug. 1960.

8. *Commonweal* 12 Jan. 1960.

9. Homophobic editorial policy held sway at the *Village Voice* at this time and for a few years to come. "The Great Faggot Rebellion" was how the paper titled its Stonewall coverage in 1969, not yet a time when the word faggot was ironically appropriated by the gay community.

10. *The New York Times* 29 Dec. 1961.

11. Tennessee Williams. *Notebooks*. Ed. Margaret Bradham Thornton. New Haven: Yale UP, 2006, 53. See the entry for August 31, 1936.

12. It would close after sixty-eight performances.

13. *New York Review of Books* 13 June 1985.

14. Freud's ideas about homosexuality were markedly different than the Freudians. See Michael Paller's "The Couch and Tennessee," *Tennessee Williams Annual Review* 3 (2000).

15. Paller, "The Couch," *TWAR*.

16. Tennessee Williams. Interview with C. Robert Jennings. *Playboy* 1973. Reprinted in *Conversations with Tennessee Williams*. Ed. Albert J. Devlin. Jackson: UP of Mississippi, 1986.

17. Doug Arell. "Homophobic Criticism and Its Disguises: The Case of Stanley Kauffmann." *Journal of Dramatic Theory and Criticism* Spring 2002.

18. *Time*, Jan. 21, 1966. Kauffmann's article is dated Jan 23.

19. Caffé Cino paid off the police not to enforce various codes including the Wales Padlock Law.

20. Edward Alwood. *Straight News: Gays, Lesbians, and the News Media*.New York: Columbia UP, 1996.

21. Robert Brustein. Personal interview in Cambridge. 15 September 2010.

22. Ibid.

23. In a 1977 *New York Times* review of *Tennessee Williams' Letters to Donald Windham 1940–1965*, which contains some of Williams' most beautiful letters, including openly erotic ones, there is this unfortunate comment by Brustein: "The love that previously dared not speak its name has now grown hoarse from screaming it." Williams' *Memoirs* published in 1975 was similarly derided by reviewers who were reacting, in part, to the book's candor about gay sex. Even a reader as sympathetic as Allean Hale began her review with the sentence, "Now comes Tennessee Williams' *Memoirs*, and if he has not exactly opened his heart, he has opened his fly."

24. *New York Times*. 8 May 1977.

25. D. H. Lawrence. *Studies in Classic American Literature*. New York: T. Seltzer, 1923.

TOO GROTESQUE AND TOO FUNNY FOR LAUGHTER

1. George du Maurier. *Trilby*. New York: Harper and Brothers Publishers, 1894, 23.

2. Tennessee Williams. *Conversations with Tennessee Williams*. Ed. Albert J. Devlin. Jackson: UP of Mississippi, 1986, 218.

3. Thomas Keith. Introduction. *A House Not Meant to Stand*. By Tennessee Williams. New York: New Directions, 2008, xv.

4. William Prosser, who directed the premiere of *Will Mr. Merriwether Return from Memphis?* in Florida in 1980, completed a manuscript championing Williams' late plays after finding out he was HIV-positive in the mid-1980s. He felt that the later plays had been misunderstood and unfairly dismissed by critics, and wanted to counter their negative reception. According to his life partner, Eric Stenshoel, Prosser found a publisher but St. Just refused to allow quotations from the later work, and Prosser died in 1991 with the book unpublished. After St. Just's death, however, Stenshoel went to work securing permissions for the manuscript, and *The Late Plays of Tennessee Williams* was finally published posthumously in 2009.

5. Edwina Dakin Williams. *Remember Me to Tom*. With Lucy Freeman. New York: G. P. Putman's Sons, 1963, 128.

6. Diamonstein-Spielvogel Archive. Web. <http://library.duke.edu/digitalcollections/dsva/>.

7. Tennessee Williams. *The Collected Poems of Tennessee Williams*. Eds. David Roessel and Nicholas Moschovakis. New York: New Directions, 2002, 150.

SELECTED BIBLIOGRAPHY AND WORKS CITED

Bak, John S. *Homo Americanus: Ernest Hemingway, Tennessee Williams, and Queer Masculinities.* Madison, NJ: Fairleigh Dickinson UP, 2010.

Barnouw, Erik. *Tube of Plenty: The Evolution of American Television*, 2nd revised ed. New York: Oxford UP, 1990.

Bentley, Eric. *What is Theatre?* New York: Limelight Editions, 1984.

Beyer, Nils. "Katt på hett plåttak." *Morgon-Tidningen* 3 Sep. 1955.

Björkman, Carl. "Segrande katta: Tennessee Williams' göteborgspremiär." *Vecko-Journalen* 37 (1955): 10–11.

Bray, Robert ed. "Looking at the Late Plays of Tennessee Williams." *The Tennessee Williams Annual Review* 5 (2002): 1–16. Web. 17 Aug. 2010.<http://www.tennesseewilliamsstudies.org/archives/2002/1panel_lateplays.pdf>.

Breen, Joseph. Letter to Jack Warner. Aug. 1952. MS. *Baby Doll* file. Production Code Administration files. Margaret Herrick Library of the Academy of Motion Picture Arts and Sciences.

Clum, John. *Acting Gay: Male Homosexuality in Modern Drama.* New York: Columbia UP, 1992.

Clurman, Harold. *Lies Like Truth.* New York: Macmillan, 1958.

Cohn, Ruby. "Tennessee Williams: The Last Two Decades." *The Cambridge Companion to Tennessee Williams.* Ed. Matthew C. Roudané. Cambridge: Cambridge UP, 1997. 232-43.

Coleman, Robert. *Daily Mirror* 20 March 1953; John Chapman. *Daily News.*

Corrigan, Mary Ann. "Realism and Theatricalism in *A Streetcar Named Desire.*" *Critical Essays on Tennessee Williams.* Ed. Robert A. Martin. New York: G. K. Hall & Co, 1997. 83–93.

Cortese, James. *Richard Halliburton's Royal Road.* Memphis, Tennessee: White Rose Press, 1989.

Crandell, George W., ed. *The Critical Response to Tennessee Williams.* Westport, CT: Greenwood Press, 1996.

Devlin, Albert J., ed. *Conversations with Tennessee Williams.* Jackson, MS: UP of Mississippi, 1986.

Donald Spoto. *The Kindness of Strangers: The Life of Tennessee Williams.* Boston: Little, Brown, 1985.

Dorff, Linda. "'All very [not!] Pirandello!' Radical Theatrics in the Evolution of *Vieux Carré.*" *Tennessee Williams Annual Review* 3 (2000): 1–23.

_____. "Theatricalist Cartoons: Williams' Late, 'Outrageous' Plays." *The Tennessee Williams Annual Review* 2 (1999): 13–33.

Dotson Rader. *Tennessee: Cry of the Heart.* Garden City: Doubleday, 1986.

Dougherty, Thomas. "The Acceptable Bigotry" *Los Angeles Times* 12 Oct. 1999.

Fleche, Anne. *Mimetic Disillusion: Eugene O'Neill, Tennessee Williams, and U.S. Dramatic Realism.* Tuscaloosa & London: U of Alabama P, 1997.

Gabler, Neal. *An Empire of Their Own: How the Jews Invented Hollywood.* New York: Anchor Books, 1989.

Gindt, Dirk. "Anxious Nation and White Fashion: *Suddenly Last Summer* in the Swedish *Folkhem.*" *Nordic Theatre Studies* 21 (2009): 98–112.

_____. "Torn between the 'Swedish Sin' and 'homosexual freemasonry': Tennessee Williams, sexual morals and the closet in 1950s Sweden." *The Tennessee Williams Annual Review* 11 (2010): 19–39.

Gross, Robert F., ed. *Tennessee Williams: A Casebook.* London: Routledge, 2002.

Hale, Allean. "Confronting the Late Plays of Tennessee Williams." *The Tennessee Williams Annual Review* (2003): 1–10. Web. 17 Aug. 2010.

_____. "The Secret Script of Tennessee Williams." *Southern Review* 27:2 (Spring 1991): 363–75.

_____. "Tennessee Williams's *Three Plays for the Lyric Theatre.*" *Tennessee Williams Annual Review* 7 (2005): 89–103.

Harrie, Ivar. "Katt på hett plåttak' storseger för Vasan." *Expressen* 28 Nov. 1956.

Hawkins. *World-Telegram* 20 March 1953.

Heed, Sven Åke. "Stadsteatertanken i svensk teater." *Ny svensk teaterhistoria 3: 1900-talets teater.* Eds. Tomas Forser & Sven Åke Heed, Hedemora: Gidlund, 2007. 195–235.

Helander, Karin. *Teaterns korsväg: Bengt Ekerot och 1950-talet.* Stockholm: Carlssons, 2003.

Hewes, Henry. "The Last of Our Solid Gold Bohemians." *Saturday Review* 28 March 1953: 25–27.

Hirschorn, Clive. *The Warner Brothers Story.* New York: Crown, 1979.

Jackson, Esther M. "Tennessee Williams: The Idea of a 'Plastic Form." *Critical Essays on Tennessee Williams.* Ed. Robert A. Martin. New York: G. K. Hall & Co, 1997. 191–208.

Jackson, George H. Jackson. "Review of *Baby Doll*." *Los Angeles Herald Express* 27 December 1956): E5.

Kazan, Elia. *Elia Kazan: A Life.* New York: Alfred Knopf, 1988.

Keith, Thomas. Introduction to *A House Not Meant to Stand.* New York: New Directions, 2008.

Kolin, Philip C. "The Existential Nightmare in Tennessee Williams's *The Chalky White Substance.*" *Notes on Contemporary Literature* 23 (January 1993): 8–11.

_____. "A Play about Terrible Birds: Tennessee Williams's *The Gnädiges Fraulein* [sic] and Alfred Hitchcock's *The Birds.*" *South Atlantic Review* 66:1 (Winter 2001): 1–22.

_____. "*The Remarkable Rooming-House of Mme. Le Monde*: Tennessee Williams' Little Shop of Comic Horrors." *Tennessee Williams Annual Review* 4 (2001): 39–48. New York: Peter Lang Publishing, 2002.

_____. "*Something Cloudy, Something Clear*: Tennessee Williams' Postmodern Memory Play" in the *Journal of Dramatic Theory and Criticism* 12 (Spring 1998): 35–56.

_____ ,Ed. *The Undiscovered Country: The Later Plays of Tennessee Williams.* New York: Peter Lang Publishing, 2002.

_____. "Williams' *The Frosted Glass Coffin.*" *The Explicator* 59:1 (2000): 44–46.

Kramer, Richard E. "'The Sculptural Drama': Tennessee Williams's Plastic Theatre." *The Tennessee Williams Annual Review* 5 (2002): 1–10. Web. 17 Aug. 2010. <http://www.tennesseewilliamsstudies.org/archives/2002/3kramer.pdf>.

Leff, Leonard J. and Jerold L. Simmons. *The Dame in the Kimono: Hollywood, Censorship, and the Production Code from the 1920s to the 1960s.* New York: Anchor Books, 1990.

Leibman, Nina C. *Living Room Lectures: The Fifties in Film and Television.* Austin: U of Texas P, 1995.

Leiser, Erwin. "'Cat' in Uppsala." *Morgon-Tidningen* 15 Oct. 1955.

Linde, Ebbe. "Tennessee Williams." Type-written report to the Swedish Academy, 1958.

Londré, Felicia Hardison. *Tennessee Williams.* New York: Frederick Ungar Publishing Co., 1979.

Leverich, Lyle. *Tom: The Unknown Tennessee Williams.* New York: Crown Publishers, 1995.

Maney, Richard. "The Last Rites of Closing Nights." *The New York Times Sunday Magazine* 23 May 1954: 17, 77–78.

Martin, Robert A., ed. *Critical Essays on Tennessee Williams.* New York: Twayne Publishers, 1997.

Masters, Edgar Lee. *Vachel Lindsay: A Poet in America.* New York: Charles Scribner's Sons, 1935.

McDé. "100 pjäser i kappsäcken." *Aftonbladet* 12 Dec. 1945.

McDermid, Finlay. Letter to Steve Trilling. March 1952. *Baby Doll* file. Production Code Administration files. Margaret Herrick Library of the Academy of Motion Picture Arts and Sciences.

Miller, Frank. *Censored Hollywood: Sex, Sin and Violence on the Screen.* Atlanta: Turner Publishing, 1994.

Monroe, Harriet. *A Poet's Life: Seventy Years in a Changing World.* New York: Macmillan, 1938.

Morgon-Tidningen 15 Oct. 1955.

Murphy, Brenda. *Tennessee Williams and Elia Kazan: A Collaboration in the Theatre.* Cambridge: Cambridge UP, 1992.

National Legion of Decency. "*Baby Doll* News Release." 13 Dec. 1956. *Baby Doll* file. Production Code Administration files. Margaret Herrick Library of the Academy of Motion Picture

Arts and Sciences.

New York Theatre Reviews 13 (1953): 384–386.

New York Theatre Reviews 14 (1953): 330-332.

O'Connor, Jacqueline. *Dramatizing Dementia: Madness in the Plays of Tennessee Williams.* Bowling Green, OH: Bowling Green State U Popular P, 1997.

Olsson, Tom J.A. *O'Neill och Dramaten: En studie kring arbetet med och mottagandet av fjorton olika O'Neill-uppsättningar på Dramatiska teatern åren 1923-1962.* Stockholm: Akademilitteratur, 1977, diss.

Paller, Michael. *Gentleman Callers: Tennessee Williams, Homosexuality, and Mid-Twentieth-Century Drama.* New York: Palgrave MacMillan, 2005.

Parker, Brian. "Bringing Back Big Daddy." *The Tennessee Williams Annual Review* 3 (2000): 91–9.

———. "Documentary Sources for *Camino Real.*" *The Tennessee Williams Annual Review* 1998: 41–52.

Parrott, Jim. "Tennessee Travels to Taos." *Tennessee Williams Literary Journal* 1 (1989), 9–13.

Production Code Administration. "Report on *Baby Doll.*" Dec. 1956. *Baby Doll* file. Production Code Administration files.

Prosser, William. *The Late Plays of Tennessee Williams.* Lanham, MD: Scarecrow Press, 2009.

Rader, Dotson. "The Art of Theatre V: Tennessee Williams." *The Paris Review* 81 (1981). Rpt. in *Conversations with Tennessee Williams.* Ed. Albert J. Devlin. Jackson: UP of Mississippi, 1986. 325–60.

Reddy, Thomas. "Review of *Baby Doll.*" *Los Angeles Examiner* 27 Dec. 1956: E1.

Redelings, Lowell. "Review of *Baby Doll.*" *Citizen News* 27 Dec. 1956: 22.

Ronald Hayman. *Tennessee Williams: Everyone Else is an Audience.* New Haven: Yale UP, 1993.

Root, Jonathan. *Halliburton: The Magnificent Myth.* New York: Coward- McCann, 1965.

Roudané, Matthew C., ed. *The Cambridge Companion to Tennessee Williams.* Cambridge: Cambridge UP, 1997.

Ruggles, Eleanor. *The West-Going Heart: A Life of Vachel Lindsay.* New York: W. W. Norton, 1959.

Rydström, Jens. "Från fula gubbar till goda föräldrar: Synen på sexualitet och genus i lagstiftning och debatt 1944-2004." *I den akademiska garderoben.* Ed. Anna-Clara Olsson and Caroline Olsson. Stockholm: Atlas, 2004. 37–65.

S.B-l. "Katt på hett plåttak." *Dagens Nyheter* 3 Sep. 1955.

Saddik, Annette J. "'The Inexpressible Regret of All Her Regrets': Tennessee Williams's Later Plays as Artaudian Theater of Cruelty." In *The Undiscovered Country.* Ed. Philip C. Kolin. New York: Peter Lang Publishing, 2002: 5–24.

———. *The Politics of Reputation: The Critical Reception of Tennessee Williams' Later Plays.* Madison, NJ: Fairleigh Dickinson UP, 1999.

———. "Recovering 'Moral and Sexual Chaos' in Tennessee Williams' *Clothes for a Summer Hotel.*" *North Carolina Literary Review,* 18 (2009): 53–65.

———. "'Something about the Deep South of America and London's East End': Tennessee Williams's Late Plays and In-Yer-Face Theatre." *Valley Voices* 10:1 (Spring 2010): 58–71.

Sandstroem, Dave. "Nomad på hett plåttak." *Sydsvenska Dagbladet* 19 Oct. 1956.

Savran, David. *Communists, Cowboys, and Queers: The Politics of Masculinity in the Work of Arthur Miller and Tennessee Williams.* Minneapolis, MN: U of Minnesota P, 1992.

———. "The Canonization of O'Neill," *Modern Drama* 50.4 (2007): 565-81.

Schallert, Edwin. "Review of *Baby Doll.*" *Los Angeles Times* 27 Dec. 1956: E3.

Scheuer, Philip K. "Review of *Baby Doll.*" *Los Angeles Times* 25 Nov. 1956): E7.

Schreiber, Sidney. "MPAA Document on *Baby Doll.*" March 1957. *Baby Doll* file. Warner Brothers Studios files. University of Southern California Special Collections.

Schumach, Murray. *The Face on the Cutting Room Floor: The Story of Movie and Television Censorship.* New York: William Morrow, 1964.

Sedgwick, Eve Kosofsky. *Epistemology of the Closet.* Berkeley: U of California P, 1990.

Shurlock, Geoffrey. Letter to Jack Warner. Oct. 1955. *Baby Doll* file. Production Code

Administration files.

Sklar, Robert. *Movie-Made America*. New York: Vintage Books, 1976.

Smith, Bruce. *Costly Performances: Tennessee Williams: The Last Stage*. New York: Paragon House, 1990.

Söderström, Göran. "Keijne-och Haijbyaffärerna." *Homo i Folkhemmet: Homo-och bisexuella i Sverige 1950–2000*. Ed. Martin Andreasson. Göteborg: Anamma, 2000. 92-117.

Spoto, Donald. *The Kindness of Strangers: The Life of Tennessee Williams*. New York: Ballantine, 1986.

Staggs, Sam. *When Blanche Met Brando*. New York: St. Martin's Press, 2005.

Stenström, Urban. "Inte en katt i Uppsala." *Svenska Dagbladet* 15 Oct. 1955.

Thompson, Judith J. *Tennessee Williams' Plays: Memory, Myth, and Symbol*. New York: Peter Lang Publishing, 2002.

Tischler, Nancy M. *Tennessee Williams: Rebellious Puritan*. New York: Citadel, 1961.

Vizzard, Jack. Letter to Jack Warner. July 1956. *Baby Doll* file. Warner Brothers Studios files. University of Southern California Special Collections.

Voss, Ralph, ed. *Magical Muse: Millennial Essays on Tennessee Williams*. Tuscaloosa: U of Alabama P, 2002.

Wahlund, Per Erik. "Sydstatspjäs i Göteborg." *Svenska Dagbladet* 3 Sep. 1955.

Walter Kerr, *Herald Tribune*, 23 Jan. 1953.

Warner Brothers Studios. "*Baby Doll* Advertising Memos." Dec. 1956. *Baby Doll* file. Warner Brothers Studios files. University of Southern California Special Collections.

Weisbart, David. Letter to Tennessee Williams. June 1953. *Baby Doll* file. Production Code Administration files. Margaret Herrick Library of the Academy of Motion Picture Arts and Sciences.

Williams, Edwina Dakin. *Remember Me to Tom*. With Lucy Freeman. New York: G. P. Putman's Sons, 1963.

Williams, Raymond. *Modern Tragedy*. Stanford, Calif.: Stanford UP, 1966.

Williams, Tennessee. "The Angel in the Alcove" (1948). *Collected Stories*. New York: New Directions, 1985.

——. "Cairo, Shanghai, Bombay!" (n.d.). Typescript. Harry Ransom Humanities Research Center, University of Texas at Austin.

——. *Candles to the Sun*. Introduction and Ed. Dan Isaac. New York: New Directions, 2004.

——. *The Collected Poems of Tennessee Williams*. Eds. David Rossel and Nicholas Moschovakis. New York: New Directions, 2002.

——. *The Collected Stories of Tennessee Williams*. Introduction by Gore Vidal. New York: New Directions, 1985.

——. *Five O'Clock Angel: Letters of Tennessee Williams to Maria St. Just 1948-1952*. New York: Alfred A. Knopf, 1990.

——. *Fugitive Kind*. Ed. Allean Hale. New York: New Directions, 2001.

——. *A House Not Meant to Stand*. Ed. Thomas Keith. New York: New Directions, 2008.

——. *Mister Paradise and Other One-Act Plays*. Eds. Nicholas Moschovakis and David Roessel. New York: New Directions, 2005.

——. *The Magic Tower and Other One-Act Plays*. Ed. Thomas Keith. New York: New Directions, 2011.

——. *New Selected Essays: Where I Live*. Ed. John S. Bak. New York: New Directions, 2009.

——. *Not About Nightingales*. Ed. Allean Hale. New York: New Directions, 1998.

——. *The Notebook of Trigorin*. Ed. Allean Hale. New York: New Directions, 1997.

——. *Notebooks*. Ed. Margaret Bradham Thornton. New Haven: Yale UP, 2006.

——. "Production Notes." *The Glass Menagerie*, New York: New Directions, 1999 [1945].

——. *The Selected Letters of Tennessee Williams Vol I: 1920-1945*. Eds. Albert J. Devlin and Nancy M. Tischler. New York: New Directions, 2000.

——. *The Selected Letters of Tennessee Williams, Volume II: 1945-1957*. Eds. Albert J. Devlin and

Nancy M. Tischler. New York: New Directions, 2004.

_____. *Something Cloudy, Something Clear*. New York: New Directions, 1995.

_____. *Springfield, Illinois* (n.d.). Typescript. Austin: Harry Ransom Humanities Research Center, University of Texas at Austin.

_____. *Spring Storm*. Ed. Dan Isaac. New York: New Directions, 1999.

_____. "Suitable Entrances to Springfield or Heaven" (n.d.). Typescript. Newark, Delaware, University of Delaware Library.

_____. *Ten Blocks on the Camino Real*, in *American Blues*. New York: Dramatists Play Service, 1948.

_____. *The Theatre of Tennessee Williams, Volumes 1-8*. New York: New Directions, 1971-1992.

_____. *The Traveling Companion and Other Plays*. Ed. Annette J. Saddik. New York: New Directions, 2008.

_____. "Why Did Desdemona Love the Moor?" (August 1939). Typescript. Austin, Texas: Harry Ransom Humanities Research Center, University of Texas at Austin.

Wilt, Napier. "Letter of nomination to the Swedish Academy." Dated 23 Jan. 1958.

Woods, Gregory. *A History of Gay Literature. The Male Tradition*. New Haven & London: Yale UP, 1998.

CONTRIBUTORS

AMIRI BARAKA is the author of over 40 books of essays, poems, drama, and music history and criticism, a poet icon and revolutionary political activist who has recited poetry and lectured on cultural and political issues extensively in the USA, the Caribbean, Africa, and Europe. His play *Dutchman*, written under the name of LeRoi Jones, is considered an American classic. He has won an Obie, the American Academy of Arts & Letters award, and the James Weldon Johnson Medal for contributions to the arts. He is a Fellow of the American Academy of Arts and the former Poet Laureate of New Jersey.

ROBERT BRAY is the author/editor of *Tennessee Williams and His Contemporaries*, over two dozen essays on Williams, and the introductions to the New Directions editions of *Vieux Carre* and The *Glass Menagerie*. With Barton Palmer he is the author of *Hollywood's Tennessee: The Williams Films and Postwar America*. He also founded and edits *The Tennessee Williams Annual Review* and directs the yearly Tennessee Williams Scholars Conference held in New Orleans. He is Professor of English at Middle Tennessee State University in Murfreesboro.

VINCENT BROOK has worked as a film editor and screenwriter. He has written numerous articles, anthology essays, and encyclopedia entries, and has authored or edited the following books: *Something Ain't Kosher Here: The Rise of the 'Jewish' Sitcom* (Rutgers, 2003), *You Should See Yourself: Jewish Identity in Postmodern American Culture* (Rutgers, 2006), and, as editor, *Driven to Darkness: Jewish Émigré Directors and the Rise of Film Noir"* (Rutgers 2009). He lectures at UCLA, USC, California State University Los Angeles, and Pierce College.

CLAUDIA WILSCH CASE teaches theatre history and dramatic literature at Lehman College/City University of New York and has also taught in the Theatre Ph.D. Program at the CUNY Graduate Center. She holds a D.F.A. in Dramaturgy and Dramatic Criticism from Yale University and is completing a book on the Theatre Guild. Her scholarly work has been presented at national and international conferences and has been published in *Theatre Journal*, *Contemporary Theatre Review*, *Performing Arts Resources*, the *Tennessee Williams Annual Review*, *Theater magazine*, *TheatreForum*, and *Theatre Symposium*. She is also a published literary translator and dramaturg.

AL DEVLIN is the editor of *Conversations with Tennessee Williams* (University Press of Mississippi). With Nancy Tischler he edited Volume 1 of *The Selected Letters of Tennessee Williams*, which received the Morton N. Cohen Award "for a distinguished edition of letters"—given biennially by the Modern Language Association. Volume II appeared in 2004. He has written numerous articles on aspects of Williams. Devlin is also the author of *Eudora Welty's Chronicle* (University Press of Mississippi) and edited *Eudora Welty: A Life in Literature* (University Press of Mississippi). He has edited two special Welty numbers for the *Mississippi Quarterly* and received the biennial award of the Eudora Welty Society for "distinguished achievement." His current project is an estate-authorized edition of the correspondence of Elia Kazan. He is Professor of English at the University of Missouri-Columbia.

ALLEAN HALE is a published and produced playwright, and since 1983 has emerged as a leading authority on the work of Tennessee Williams, with dozens of articles on his plays and life. She edited four of Williams's plays for New Directions: *Not About Nightingales*, *The Notebook of Trigorin*, *Fugitive Kind*, and *Stairs to the Roof*. She was editorial assistant to Lyle Leverich, Williams' official biographer on *Tom, the Unknown Tennessee Williams* (1995), and consultant on four television documentaries, including the PBS portrait of Williams for American Masters. She served on the editorial board of the *Tennessee Williams Annual Review* until 2010. Adjunct Assistant Professor of Theatre at the University of Illinois at Urbana-Champaign, she serves as dramaturg on Tennessee Williams productions at the University's Krannert Art Center.

KENNETH HOLDITCH is the author, with Richard Leavitt, of *Tennessee Williams and the South*. With Mel Gussow, Holditch edited the Library of America's two volume, *Tennessee Williams Plays*. In 1989 he founded *The Tennessee Williams Literary Journal*. He helped found, and is on the board of advisors, for all four Tennessee Williams Festivals: New Orleans, Columbus, Clarksdale, and Provincetown. A long-time resident of New Orleans, he created the popular Tennessee Williams tour of that town. This spring Hansen Publications will publish his continuation of Richard Leavitt's photo-biography, *Tennessee Williams: His Life, His Art, His World*, incorporating material from the last decade of Williams' life. Dr. Holditch is a professor emeritus of the University of New Orleans.

DIRK GINDT holds a Ph.D. in Performance Studies and has worked as an Assistant Professor at the Center for Fashion Studies at Stockholm University, where, in autumn 2009, he was awarded a two-year research position as a Postdoctoral Associate. Gindt is co-editor of *Fashion: An Interdisciplinary Reflection* (Stockholm: Raster, 2009). He has published in *Nordic Theatre Studies*, *The Tennessee Williams Annual Review* and is also the editor-in-chief of *lambda nordica* for which he has edited a special issue on masculinities (vol. 13, no. 4/2008) and a double issue on queer fashion (vol. 14, no. 3-4/2009). His current research projects investigate the original Swedish stage productions of Tennessee Williams' plays in the 1940s and 1950s as well as the creative collaborations between fashion designers and performance artists.

DAVID KAPLAN is the author of the book *Tennessee Williams in Provincetown* and various articles about Williams, Eudora Welty, the Japanese artist Ito Jakuchu, and productions of Shakespeare's plays in Central Asia. He is curator and co-founder of the annual Provincetown Tennessee Williams Theater Festival now in its sixth year. He has staged plays by Williams throughout the world: *Suddenly Last Summer* in Russia, performed in the Russian language at the Gorky Theater in Samara, Russia; *The Eccentricities of a Nightingale* performed in Cantonese at the acclaimed Hong Kong Repertory Theater. In America he staged the world premieres of Williams' *The Day on Which a Man Dies* (in Chicago) and *The Dog Enchanted by the Divine View* (in Boston).

THOMAS KEITH wrote the introduction to Williams' last full-length play, *A House Not Meant to Stand*, is the editor of *The Magic Tower & Other One-Act Plays*, has contributed to *The Tennessee Williams Encyclopedia*, *Undiscovered Country: The Later Plays of Tennessee Williams*, *The Tennessee Williams Annual Review*, and is the co-editor of *The Selected Letters of Tennessee Williams and James Laughlin* (forthcoming). Keith serves as an advisor to The Provincetown Tennessee Williams Theater Festival and The Tennessee Williams/New Orleans Literary Festival. As a Burns scholar, Keith has contributed articles and chapters to *The Burns Chronicle*, *Electric Scotland*, *The Drouth*, *Studies in Scottish Literature*, *Robert Burns in America*, *Fickle Man: Burns in the 21st Century*, and *The Oxford Companion to Burns* (forthcoming). He received a Roy Fellowship in Scottish Studies from the University of South Carolina in 2004.

JOHN LAHR is the author of eighteen books including three biographies: *Notes on a Cowardly Lion*, about his father Bert Lahr; *Prick Up Your Ears* about British playwright Joe Orton; and *Dame Edna Everage and the Rise of Western Civilization: Backstage with Barry Humphries*. He has edited the diaries of Joe Orton and Kenneth Tynan. In 2002, Lahr became the first drama critic ever to win a Tony Award for his part in writing actress Elaine Stritch's one–woman show, "Elaine Stritch at Liberty," for which he and Stritch also won the Drama Desk Award for the Best Book to a Musical. He has twice won the George Jean Nathan Award for Dramatic Criticism. He is currently working on a biography of Tennessee Williams. Since 1992 he has been the senior drama critic for *The New Yorker*.

MICHAEL PALLER is the author of *Gentlemen Callers: Tennessee Williams, Homosexuality, and Mid-Twentieth-Century Drama* (Palgrave Macmillan, 2005) and *Tennessee Williams in an Hour* (Smith & Kraus 2010) and has written theater and book reviews for the *Washington Post*, *Village Voice*, *Newsday*, and *Mirabella* magazine. He dramaturged the Russian premiere of Tennessee Williams's *Small Craft Warnings* at the Sovremennik Theater in Moscow, directed by Richard Corley. Paller began his professional career as literary manager at Center Repertory Theatre (Cleveland), then worked as a play reader and script consultant for Manhattan Theatre Club, and has since been a dramaturg for George Street Playhouse, the Berkshire Theatre Festival, Barrington Stage Company, Long Wharf Theatre, Roundabout Theatre Company, and others. He is resident dramaturg and director of humanities at The American Conservatory Theater in San Francisco where he's dramaturged over 40 productions and workshops since 2005 and teaches in its MFA acting program.

BARTON PALMER is the author, editor, or general editor of numerous books on various literary and cinematic subjects, among them *After Hitchcock: Influence, Imitation, and Intertextuality* (co-edited with David Boyd), *Harper Lee's To Kill a Mockingbird: The relationship between text and film*, *Twentieth-Century American Fiction on Screen*, *Hollywood's Dark Cinema: The American Film Noir*, and most recently *Larger than Life: Movie Stars of the 1950s*. He is Calhoun Lemon Professor of Literature at Clemson University in South Carolina and is co-author, along with Robert Bray, of *Hollywood's Tennessee: The Williams Films and Postwar America*.

ANNETTE J. SADDIK is the author of *Contemporary American Drama* (2007) and *The Politics of Reputation: The Critical Reception of Tennessee Williams' Later Plays* (1999), and has edited and introduced a collection of Williams' previously unpublished later plays, *The Traveling Companion and Other Plays* (2008). In addition, she has published essays on Williams as well as David Mamet, Sam Shepard, Antonin Artaud, and Tony Kushner in *Modern Drama, TDR: the journal of performance studies, Études Théâtrales, The South Atlantic Review, The Tennessee Williams Annual Review, The Undiscovered Country: The Later Plays of Tennessee Williams, Bloom's Modern Critical Views: Tennessee Williams* and several encyclopedias of theater history. Dr. Saddik also serves on the editorial boards of the journal *Theatre Topics* and the *Tennessee Williams Annual Review*. She is an Associate Professor in the English Department at New York City College of Technology (CUNY), and also teaches in the Ph.D. Program in Theatre at the CUNY Graduate Center.

JOHN PATRICK SHANLEY is from The Bronx. His plays include *Danny and the Deep Blue Sea, Savage in Limbo, Italian American Reconciliation, Welcome to the Moon, Four Dogs and a Bone, Cellini, Dirty Story, Defiance* and *Pirate*. His theatrical work is performed extensively across the United States and around the world. For his play, *Doubt*, he received both the Tony Award and the Pulitzer Prize. In the arena of screenwriting, he has nine films to his credit, most recently *Doubt*, with Meryl Streep, Philip Seymour Hoffman and Amy Adams, which was nominated for 5 Academy Awards, including Best Adapted Screenplay. The film of *Doubt* was also directed by Mr. Shanley. Other films include *Five Corners* (Special Jury Prize, Barcelona Film Festival), *Alive, Joe versus the Volcano*, which he also directed, and *Live from Baghdad* for HBO (Emmy nomination). For his script of *Moonstruck* he received both the Writers Guild of America Award and an Academy Award for best original screenplay. The Writers Guild of America awarded Mr. Shanley the 2009 Lifetime Achievement In Writing.

WILLIAM JAY SMITH was appointed the nineteenth Poet Laureate Consultant in Poetry to the Library of Congress from 1968 to 1970. He has been a member of the American Academy of Arts and Letters since 1975, and is a former vice-president for literature. Smith, noted for his translations, has won awards from the French Academy, the Swedish Academy, and the Hungarian government. Two of his thirteen collections of poetry were finalists for the National Book Award. He is currently completing a memoir, *My Friend Tom: The Poet-Playwright Tennessee Williams* about his close personal friendship with Tennessee Williams beginning in 1935 when they met in college.

SAM STAGGS is the author of *When Blanche Met Brando: The Scandalous Story of A Streetcar Named Desire, Close-up on Sunset Boulevard: Billy Wilder, Norma Desmond, and the Dark Hollywood Dream, All About All About Eve: The Complete Behind-the-Scenes Story of the Bitchiest Film Ever Made!, Mmii: The Return of Marilyn Monroe*, and *Born to Be Hurt: The Untold Story of Imitation of Life*.

INDEX

128
Pacific Ocean, 13, 37
Page, Geraldine, 177, 179
Paller, Michael, 95, 195
Palmer, R. Barton, 135, 151
The Palooka (Williams), 274
The Parade (Williams), 212, 275-276
Parrott, James, 27, 31-34, 36, 39, 88
Pasternak, Boris, 158
Patchen, Kenneth, 172
Pavan, Marisa, 149
Paz, Octavio, 172
Peg o' My Heart (Manners), 62, 63, 72
Pereira, Hal, 149
A Period of Adjustment (Williams), 177
Pershing Avenue, 16
Peter Pan (Barrie), 70, 189
Peters, Margot, 243
Peterson, Virgilia, 187
Phelps, William Lyon, 30
Philadelphia, 98, 100, 102-103
Phillips, Elizabeth Fenwick, 26
Picnic (Inge),114
Pigalle, Paris, 276
Pike, Bishop James, 131
Pilcher, Bram (*Candles to the Sun*), 22
Pinter, Harold, 254, 268
Pirandello, Luigi, 157, 162, 271
Pittsburgh, Pennsylvania, 75
Playboy, 153, 195
Poe, Edgar Allan, xi, 173, 210
Poe, James, 177
Pollitt, Brick (*Cat on a Hot Tin Roof*), 156
Pollock, Jackson, x
Pompeii, 8
Porgy, 46
Pound, Ezra, 172
Powell, Dawn, 47
Preminger, Otto, 66, 125, 142-143
Presley, Elvis, 210, 284
Prim, Minerva, 19
Princeton, 37
The Pronoun 'I' (Williams), 275-276
Provincetown, Massachusetts, 32, 52, 267,
　276-277, 285
Provincetown Tennessee Williams Theater
　Festival, 277, 285

Pulitzer Prize, 75, 96, 103, 115, 174, 226
Queen, Ellery, 173
Queen of England, 247
Quigley, Martin, 122, 133
Quinn, Anthony, 139
Quintero, José, 103, 116, 183
R.U.R. (Čapek), 46
Rader, Dotson, 216, 223, 234
A Raisin in the Sun (Hansberry), 187
Rampart Street, 97
The Red Devil Battery Sign (Williams), 24,
　233-234, 268-269
Redgrave, Corin, 272
Redgrave, Lynn, 180
Redgrave, Vanessa, 253, 272
The Remarkable Rooming-House of Mme.
　LeMonde (Williams), 261-263, 266, 267,
　271, 275, 276
Remember Me To Tom (Edwina Williams),
　211, 216, 277
Reynolds, Burt, 183
Rice, Elmer, 46
Rich, Frank, 80
Riggs, Lynn, 47
Rimbaud, 172
Road, Gerald, 232
Roberts, Meade, 177
Robinson, Davis, 267
Roessel, David, 272, 274
The Roman Spring of Mrs. Stone (Williams),
　157, 159, 172, 177
Rome, 54, 138, 148, 159
Rosario, 139-140, 146, 149-151
Rose, Serafina Delle (*The Rose Tattoo*), 136
The Rose Arbor Players, 16
The Rose Tattoo (Williams), 73, 89, 96,104
　106, 111, 242, 254
The Rose Tattoo (film), 133, 135, 150, 156,
　164, 172, 174-175
Ross, Anthony, 63-64, 69
Rossellini, Roberto, 138
Roudané, Matthew C., 272
Royal Court, 233
Royal Dramatic Theater, 163, 165
Royal National Theatre, 223, 272
Running Sun Theatre Company, 276
Rutgers University, 267, 270

CPSIA information can be obtained at www.ICGtesting.com
Printed in the USA
BVOW11s0331220914

367795BV00013BA/118/P

9 781601 824240